Bible 4

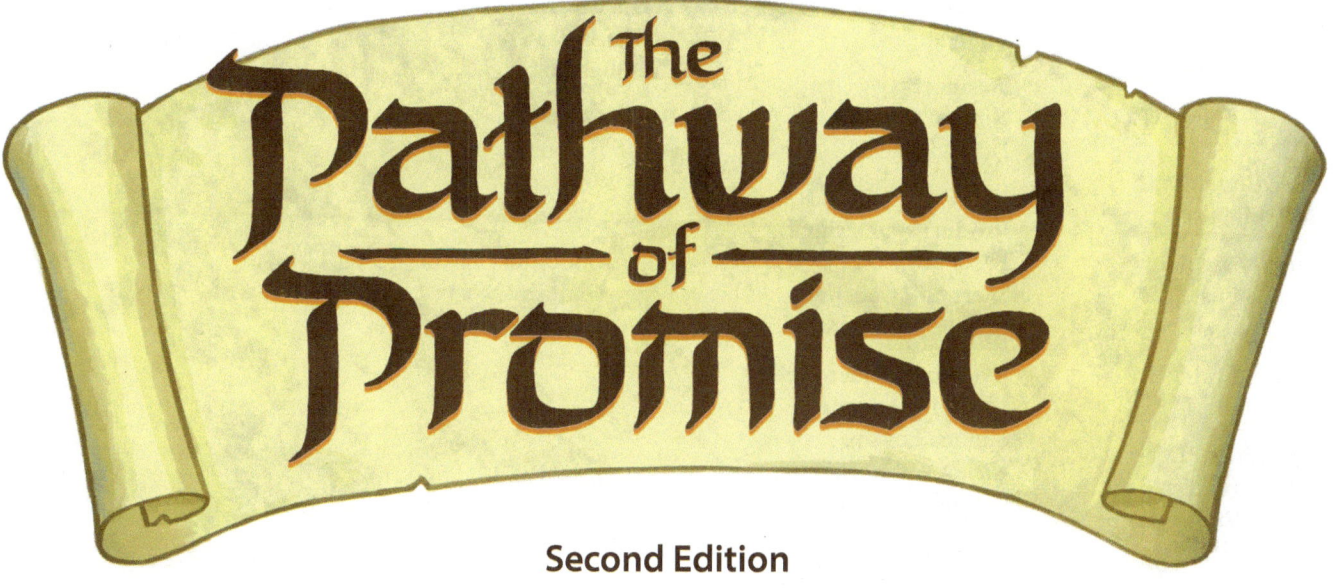

Second Edition

Greenville, South Carolina

Note: The fact that materials produced by other publishers may be referred to in this volume does not constitute an endorsement of the content or theological position of materials produced by such publishers. Any references and ancillary materials are listed as an aid to the student or the teacher and in an attempt to maintain the accepted academic standards of the publishing industry.

Bible 4: The Pathway of Promise Student Edition
Second Edition

Writers
Paul Hornor, MDiv
Daryl Kopp, MA
George Lovely, MA
Sarah Parris

Writer Consultant
L. Michelle Rosier

Biblical Worldview
Brian Collins, PhD
Bryan Smith, PhD

Academic Integrity
Jeff Heath, EdD

Instructional Design
Rachel Santopietro, EdD
Michael Winningham, MA
Lisa Zaspel, MEd

Educational Technology
Larry Hunt, MS

Editors
Nathan Majewski, MA
James Zemke, MA

Cover and Lead Designer
Emily Rush

Designers
Nicole Daniel
Jackson Gaulke
Andrew Roberts

Production Designers
Erika Brunson
Sherry McCollough

Illustrators
Jonathon Grunenwald
David Ryan Lompe
Simona Love
Kelley McMorris
János Orban (Beehive Illustration)
Daniel Rodgers, Advocate-Art Inc.

DesignOps Coordinators
Kaitlyn Quevedo
Lesley Ramesh

Permissions
Maria Andersen
Ruth Bartholomew

Project Coordinators
Allison Brooks
Gary Santiago
Emilee Wendorf

Postproduction Liaison
Peggy Hargis

Photo credits appear on page 277.

The text for this book is set in Adobe Minion Pro, Adobe Myriad Pro, Arial MT, Brother 1816 by TipoType, Calibri by Monotype, Cherry Blossoms by Neil Summerour, Classic Comic by Patrick Griffin, Free 3 of 9 by Matthew Welch, Gelica by Dave Rowland, Gelo by Dalton Maag, Journal by Émigré, Nunito by Vernon Adams, Roboto by Google, Symbol, and Times New Roman PSMT.

All trademarks are the registered and unregistered marks of their respective owners. BJU Press is in no way affiliated with these companies. No rights are granted by BJU Press to use such marks, whether by implication, estoppel, or otherwise.

© 2026 BJU Press
Greenville, South Carolina 29609
First Edition © 2019 BJU Press

Printed in the United States of America
All rights reserved

ISBN 978-1-64626-758-3

15 14 13 12 11 10 9 8 7 6 5 4 3 2 1

Contents

Welcome to *The Pathway of Promise*!	vii
Using Your Book	viii

Chapter 1: Creation and Fall — 3
- The Story of Scripture: Creation, Fall, Redemption 4
- The Creation of All Things 8
- *Fast Facts* about Genesis 8
- *Who were* Adam and Eve? 13
- The Fall of Mankind 16
- Hope for Salvation 19

Chapter 2: Sin's Devastating Consequences — 21
- Cain Murders Abel 22
- From Bad to Worse 24
- *Who was* Noah? 24
- The Worldwide Flood 26
- God's Covenant with Noah 28
- The City of Confusion 30

Chapter 3: God's Covenant with Abraham — 33
- Abraham: Heir of the Promise 34
- *Who was* Abraham? 34
- Lot Walks Away 36
- Chosen though Sinful 38
- Destruction of Sodom and Gomorrah 42
- The Birth of Isaac 43
- *Who was* Isaac? 43
- God's Command to Sacrifice Isaac 44

Chapter 4: The Patriarchs — 47
- Isaac: The Promise Continues 48
- Jacob: God's Gracious Choice 50
- *Who was* Jacob? 50
- A Ladder to Heaven 53
- Jacob Wrestles 54
- Joseph and Judah: Part 1 56
- *Who was* Joseph? 56
- Joseph and Judah: Part 2 60

Chapter 5: God's Covenant with Israel — 65
- God Remembered and Sent a Prophet 66
- *Fast Facts* about Exodus 66
- *Who was* Moses? 67
- Pharaoh's Hard Heart and God's Glory 70
- The Israelites Complain after Deliverance 76

    The Purpose of the Law for Israel......................................77
    The Ten Commandments...79

Chapter 6: Israel Breaks God's Law — 81

    Symbolism of the Tabernacle..82
    Tabernacle Worship Foreshadows Christ................................88
    Fast Facts about Leviticus..88
    The Golden Calf: Moses Intercedes for Israel............................90
    Spying Out the Land...93
    Fast Facts about Numbers...93
    Who was Joshua?..94
    Moses Lifted Up a Serpent in the Wilderness............................96
    The Prophecies of Balaam..97
    Blessings of Obedience and Curses of Disobedience.....................100
    Fast Facts about Deuteronomy.......................................100

Chapter 7: God Keeps His Covenant Promises — 103

    Joshua Leads Israel into Canaan......................................104
    Fast Facts about Joshua..104
    Crossing the Jordan River..107
    The Fall of Jericho...108
    Achan and Ai..110
    The Sun Stood Still..112
    Caleb: A Man of Action..114
    Who was Caleb?...114
    Rest for God's People..116

Chapter 8: Israelites Do What Is Right in Their Own Eyes — 119

    Incomplete Obedience...120
    Fast Facts about Judges..120
    Deborah: A Woman of Courage......................................122
    Who was Deborah?..122
    Who was Jael?..123
    Gideon: A Flawed Deliverer..124
    Who was Gideon?...124
    Abimelech: A Wicked Ruler..129
    Samson: A Worldly Leader...130
    Who was Samson?...130
    Hope in the Darkness...134
    Fast Facts about Ruth..134

Chapter 9: The Kingdom and the King — 139

    Hannah: A Surprising Reversal.......................................140
    Fast Facts about 1 & 2 Samuel......................................140

    Eli: A Failed Priest 142
    Who was Samuel? 142
    Samuel: Calling a Boy 144
    Saul: Israel Demanded a King 146
    Who was Saul? 147
    Saul: Unbelief and Disobedience 149
    David: Anointed to be King 151
    Who was David? 151
    David: Confident in God 153
    David: Path to the Throne 155
    King Saul's Death 156

Chapter 10: God's Covenant with David   159
    David: Elevated to be King 160
    The Davidic Covenant 162
    The Davidic Covenant: Psalm 2 164
    Fast Facts about Psalm 2 164
    Absalom: A Failed Conspiracy 166

Chapter 11: A Kingdom Divided   171
    Solomon Chose Wisdom 172
    Fast Facts About 1 & 2 Kings 172
    Who was Solomon? 172
    The Building of God's House 176
    Solomon Disobeyed God 179
    Jeroboam and the Man of God 181

Chapter 12: Faithful God, Unfaithful People   185
    A Famine in the Land 186
    Who was Elijah? 187
    God against Baal on Mount Carmel 189
    Naboth's Vineyard 192
    Ahab's Death 194
    Elisha and the Shunammite Woman 196
    Who was Elisha? 196
    Naaman and the Dirty River 198
    Jehu the Executioner 200
    The Fall of Samaria and the Northern Kingdom 202

Chapter 13: The Southern Kingdom   205
    Asa Inconsistently Followed the Lord 206
    Fast Facts about 1 & 2 Chronicles 206
    Jehoshaphat: The Faith of a Compromised King 209
    Joash Rejects God 211

The King Who Became Leprous ... 213
  Restoration under Hezekiah ... 214
  The Siege of Jerusalem ... 217
  Fast Facts about Isaiah ... 217
  The Coming King ... 220

Chapter 14: Fall of the Southern Kingdom — 223

  Manasseh: Judah's Most Wicked King ... 224
  Josiah and the Book of the Law ... 226
  Covenant Breaking ... 228
  Fast Facts about Micah ... 228
  Kings and Not-Quite-Kings: Jehoahaz, Jehoiakim, and Jehoiachin ... 230
  Jerusalem: Burned and Plundered ... 232
  Fast Facts about Ezekiel ... 232
  Sent into Exile ... 234
  The Promised New Covenant ... 235
  Fast Facts about Jeremiah ... 235

Chapter 15: Israel in Exile — 239

  Nebuchadnezzar's Humbling ... 240
  Fast Facts about Daniel ... 240
  Who was Daniel? ... 240
  Daniel's Dream ... 243
  The Perfect Shepherd ... 246
  Returning and Rebuilding ... 247
  Fast Facts about Ezra ... 247
  Zechariah: Vision of the High Priest ... 250
  Fast Facts about Zechariah ... 250
  Esther and the Plot to Kill the Jews ... 252
  Fast Facts about Esther ... 252
  Who was Esther? ... 252
  Nehemiah and the Rebuilding of the Walls ... 257
  Fast Facts about Nehemiah ... 257
  Confession and Recommitment ... 259

Chapter 16: Refuge in God Alone — 261

  Malachi's Message ... 262
  Fast Facts about Malachi ... 262
  Christ as Prophet ... 266
  Who Is Jesus? ... 266
  Christ as Priest ... 268
  Christ as King ... 270

Glossary — 273

Welcome to The Pathway of Promise!

Bible 4: The Pathway of Promise will take you from Genesis to Malachi. Along the way, you will learn about the covenants God made with humankind, the presence of God with His people, and the kingdom of God. You will learn about most of the books of the Old Testament, as well as important people that show up in them. You will also have the opportunity to review the 147 Bible Truths.

All of God's promises to people in the Old Testament, including the New Covenant, point to Jesus Christ. This textbook concludes by focusing on Christ as the perfect Prophet, Priest, and King.

Using Your Book

Essential Question
important questions that must be thought about and answered by the end of each lesson

FastFacts about
key information on the books of the Bible being studied in that lesson or chapter

The Creation of All Things

Why is it important for Christians to believe that God made everything good?

In the beginning, God created the heavens and the earth. At first, the earth was formless and empty. It was also dark. But the Spirit of God was active over the deep and dark waters.

FastFacts about
Genesis
Author: Moses
Date: 1425 BC
Theme: Creation, sin, and recreation
Meaning of Genesis: Beginning

Interesting Facts:
- First book of the Bible and the first of the five books of Moses
- Covers 2500 years of history
- Referenced over 100 times in the New Testament

Day 1
When God said, "Let there be light," there was light. God saw His creation of light was good, and He divided it from darkness. He called the light "day" and the darkness He called "night." There was evening and there was morning—one day.

Day 2
God spoke and created the sky. He separated the waters below the sky from the waters in the clouds. There was evening and there was morning. This was the second day of creation.

Hope for Salvation

How can I be saved from my sin?

The man and woman faced death for their sin, just as God had said. But God's judgment on Satan also gave them hope that God would save them. Adam showed this hope in the name he gave the woman: Eve. "Eve" sounded like the word for *living* in their language. Adam knew she would be the mother of all living people to be born after them.

God also made clothes from animal skins for Adam and Eve. This showed that covering the consequences of their sin required death.

God didn't want the sinful couple to eat the fruit from the tree of life. The tree of life symbolized the eternal life that they could have had if they obeyed, so God sent them out of the garden of Eden. Adam and Eve were now away from God's special presence in the place He provided for all their needs. Outside of the garden, they would struggle to till the hard ground to grow food to eat. God placed some cherubim—a type of angel—and a flaming sword that moved in every direction at the entrance to the garden to keep anyone from reaching the tree of life.

? **What will the woman's seed bring?**

Bible Truths

37 What was God's judgment on Satan after Adam and Eve sinned?
God promised to send a human king that would suffer but ultimately destroy Satan.
Genesis 3:15

147 What is your only comfort in life and in death?
My only comfort is that I am not my own, but belong—body and soul, in life and in death—to my faithful Savior, Jesus Christ.
Romans 14:7–9 • 1 Corinthians 3:23
1 Thessalonians 5:23

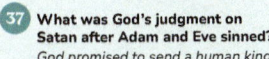

Bible Truths — reviews of Bible Truths that relate to the current lesson

? **During Reading Questions** — helpful questions for reviewing and understanding the information that was read

God also said, "It is not good that the man should be alone." God made a helper for him. He put Adam to sleep and took a rib from Adam's side. From this rib, God made the woman Eve and brought her to the man. This was the first **marriage**. Both man and woman were made in the image of God.

key term — definitions of important words that are likely new to you

key term
marriage
Marriage is a lifelong covenant between one man and one woman. Marriage was directly created, designed, and blessed by God Himself. God used Adam and Eve as the model for what marriage looks like for all people in all places for all time.

Who were Adam and Eve?

- First humans
- First married couple
- God created Adam from the dust of the ground.
- God created Eve from one of Adam's ribs.
- Both made in the image of God
- Adam is the head and representative of all humankind.
- Their sin put the whole of creation under the curse.
- Their sin caused every person to be born a sinner.
- Adam is contrasted with the last Adam, Jesus Christ.

Who was — highlights of the lives of important Bible characters

? **What was not good about Adam's situation in the garden?**

What is marriage?

Bible 4

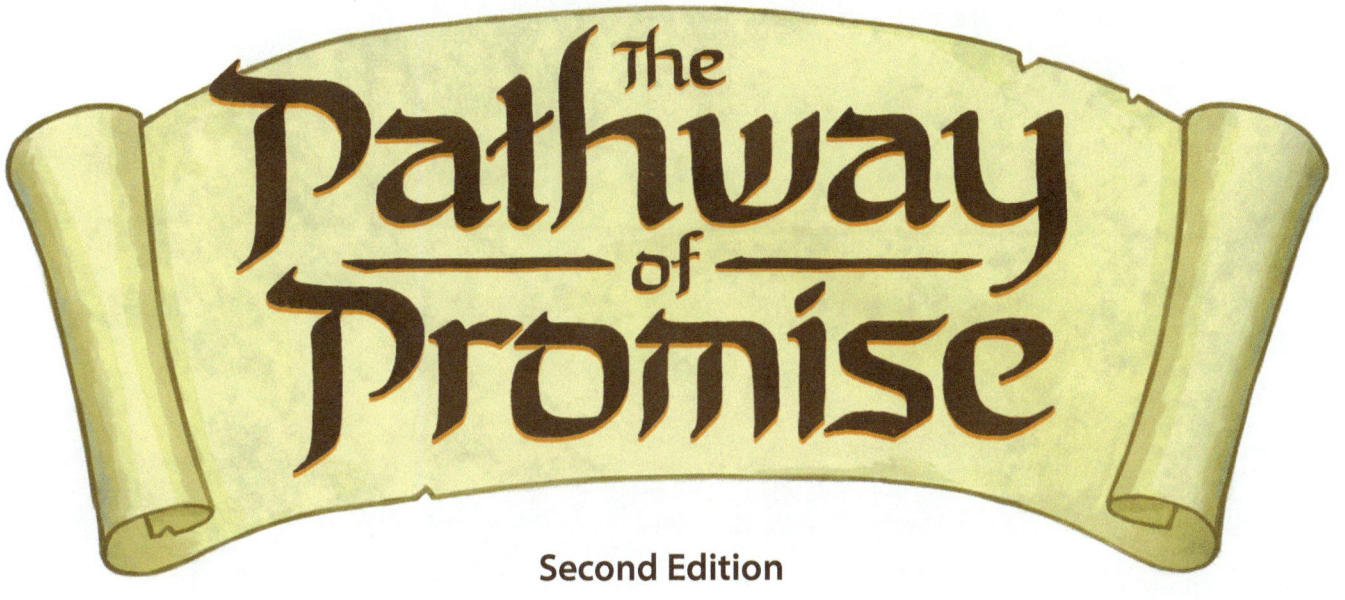

The Pathway of Promise

Second Edition

CHAPTER

Creation and Fall

The Story of Scripture
CREATION, FALL, REDEMPTION

How many stories does the Bible tell?

How many stories are in the Bible? What are some favorite Bible stories? All the stories in the Bible form one big true story. It's an exciting story that begins with creation and ends with new creation. The Bible's one big story has three parts: Creation, Fall, and Redemption. Both the Old Testament and the New Testament are part of this one big story.

Creation

God was not created, but He created everything. Think about that. Everything you see was either created by God or made by humans from what God created. All the trees you see can be traced back to trees created on the third day of creation. All the birds you see can be traced back to birds created on the fifth day of creation. Even all humans can be traced back to the first man and woman—Adam and Eve. God created Adam and Eve in His image on the sixth day of creation. And God didn't only make the things we see. God made the world to work the way it does—even if we can't see or understand why it all works the way it does. Everything God made was good. He said so day after day. When He finished creating everything, God looked at it all and said it was very good.

Fall

But everything is not very good in God's world now. People get sick and die. People hurt others. People steal, cheat, and lie. They stain and damage God's creation. Since God made a perfect world, why is there so much wrong with it now? The Bible answers this question. When God placed Adam and Eve in the garden, they enjoyed a close relationship with Him. They were able to walk and talk with God every day. God gave Adam and Eve a test that allowed them to eat from any tree except one. They had only this one rule to follow. But Adam and Eve rebelled against God. Satan tempted them with the promise that they would be like God and could decide what was right and wrong. Foolishly, they listened to Satan and ate from the tree that God commanded them not to eat from.

Their one sin changed mankind and all of creation. Sin corrupted every part of God's good creation. When Adam and Eve disobeyed God, they immediately became sinners. And all their descendants* are sinners just like them. Now all humans are born wanting to do wrong. Adam and Eve's close relationship with God was broken when they sinned. They were separated from God on the inside before they were separated from God's special presence in the garden. Because of sin, judgment and spiritual **death** have now entered God's perfect world.

Sin also brought physical death on all living things. God's judgment on the world means that everything was corrupted. Thorns now choke out good plants. Animals kill each other to stay alive, and they sometimes even hurt people. People disobey God, want to please themselves, and often even hurt other people.

What is death?

key term

death

Death is the separation of the body from the soul. It is also separation of the person from God.

> **key term**
> **seed**
> Seed is a person born in one's family line. Seed can refer to one specific person (as in Genesis 3:15) or to all of one's offspring. For example, you are the seed of your grandfather and grandmother, and the seed of your parents includes your children and grandchildren.

? What are the three parts of the Bible's one story?

Redemption

Even before God told Adam and Eve about the consequences of their sin, He promised redemption.* God said He would bring about the defeat of Satan through the **seed** of the woman, Eve. Who would this seed be who would defeat Satan and fix God's broken creation? When would He come?

Many years later, God chose Abraham, a seed of Adam and Eve, to be the father of the nation of Israel. God said He would bring blessing to all nations through Abraham's seed. About one thousand years after that, King David, a seed of Abraham, also received a special promise. God promised David that one of his seed would rule over all nations forever. This promised ruler would set everything right that was wrong in the world.

Eventually, about one thousand years after the promise to David, Jesus was born. The New Testament calls Jesus the son of David. It also calls Jesus the son of Abraham because He was the seed of both Abraham and David. Though Jesus was the seed of both these men, He was also the Son of God. Jesus preached that the kingdom of God was near. It was near because the King, Jesus Himself, was there. Jesus is the King who is going to set right all that is wrong in the world. That is bad news for sinners because we are what is wrong with the world. But Jesus died on the cross to redeem sinners. Sinners who trust Jesus and repent from sin become part of Jesus' kingdom. Christ has defeated the power of death. But God's entire creation still groans in pain. Every person experiences sin, misery, and death. The world experiences disasters. These are the consequences of sin. And the consequences of sin that reach us today come from Adam and Eve's sin in the Fall.

Things will change, though. God's Word promises that Jesus will bring about a renewed creation. God will restore every part of His creation. Sin and its consequences will be judged and removed. Those who have died will be resurrected with new bodies. Jesus will return to reign with His people forever. This is the big story of Scripture. The Curse of the Fall will be reversed, God's perfect creation will be restored, and God judges the wicked but rewards the righteous with the hope of glory.

> **?** Who is the seed of the woman who redeems sinners and will remove the Curse from the world?

Bible Truths

2 **What else did God make?**
God made all things.
Genesis 1:1 • John 1:3 • Colossians 1:16

19 **What is the Bible all about?**
The Bible reveals who God is and how He is redeeming His fallen creation through Christ for His own glory.
Genesis 3:15 • Mark 1:15 • I Corinthians 15:1–15 • Revelation 21:1–4

29 **Did Adam and Eve obey God?**
No, Adam and Eve chose to sin against God.
Genesis 3:6

50 **Whom did God send to fulfill His covenant promises and redeem us from sin?**
Jesus Christ is the only Savior, fully God and fully man, whose work reconciles us to the Father.
Matthew 1:21 • John 1:14 • Acts 4:12
Romans 5:10; 9:5 • Galatians 4:4
Colossians 2:9

The Creation of All Things

Why is it important for Christians to believe that God made everything good?

In the beginning, God created the heavens and the earth. At first, the earth was formless and empty. It was also dark. But the Spirit of God was active over the deep and dark waters.

FastFacts about

Genesis

Author: Moses
Date: 1425 BC
Theme: Creation, sin, and recreation
Meaning of *Genesis*: Beginning

Interesting Facts:
- First book of the Bible and the first of the five books of Moses
- Covers 2500 years of history
- Referenced over 100 times in the New Testament

Day 1

When God said, "Let there be light," there was light. God saw His creation of light was good, and He divided it from darkness. He called the light "day" and the darkness He called "night." There was evening and there was morning—one day.

Day 2

God spoke and created the sky. He separated the waters below the sky from the waters in the clouds. There was evening and there was morning. This was the second day of creation.

Day 3

God said, "Let the dry land appear." The dry land was now separate from the waters. He called the dry land "earth" and the waters "seas." Then God commanded the earth to produce plants and trees. He saw that this was good. There was evening and there was morning. This was the third day of creation.

Day 4

God said, "Let there be lights in the sky." God created the sun, moon, and stars. God made the sun the source of light for the day. He made the moon the main source of light for the night. God set the sun and moon to be markers of days, seasons, and years. God saw this was good. There was evening and there was morning. This was the fourth day of creation.

Day 5

God said, "Let the waters swarm with creatures, and let birds fly above the earth." And there were birds and all sorts of sea creatures. God saw this was good. He blessed these creatures so they would fill the waters and the earth. There was evening and there was morning. This was the fifth day of creation.

Day 6

God said, "Let the earth bring forth living creatures after their kinds." All sorts of land animals were created. God saw this was good. Then God said, "Let us make man in our image, after our likeness. Let them rule over all the earth." So God created man and woman in His own image. God saw that everything He made was *very* good. There was evening and there was morning. This was the sixth day of creation.

? How are people different from the rest of God's creation?

Creation or Evolution?

The Bible presents God as the Creator of the universe and all that it contains. Genesis 1–2 tells us that God personally and directly created all things in the span of six normal days. Evolution is the belief that living things exist today because they slowly changed, or evolved, from simple forms of life. An evolutionist is a person who believes this process took a long time. Evolutionists think the earth is billions of years old and came into existence by itself. This event often called the Big Bang. Evolutionists believe that suffering and death have been a part of the world ever since there has been life. They believe that death and suffering play an important part in how life evolved.

There is no God necessary in the theory of evolution. However, some Christians think that God may have used evolution. They think that scientists who teach evolution are right. They look for a way to fit God and evolution together. But they are wrong. The Bible teaches in Genesis 1 that God created all things in one week. Creation did not take billions of years. The order in which God created things is also different from what we might expect. Genesis says God created light before He created the sun and moon.

Most importantly, the Bible teaches that death and suffering are a punishment for sin. Death was not part of God's very good creation. If God created a world full of death and suffering, He would not be a very good God. But evolution works only if there were death and suffering long before humans ever existed. Evolution cannot fit with the Bible's teaching of creation.

? How long did God take to create the world?

> SINCE THE EARTH IS A FEW BILLION YEARS OLD, FOSSILS LIKE THIS FORMED SLOWLY OVER LONG PERIODS OF TIME.

> SINCE THE BIBLE TALKS ABOUT A GLOBAL FLOOD A FEW THOUSAND YEARS AGO, FOSSILS LIKE THIS FORMED BY BEING BURIED RAPIDLY.

What about science? Does science prove evolution? No, Christians who believe the Bible's teaching about creation have the same evidence that evolutionists have. They have the same rocks, fossils, plants, and animals. However, they interpret the evidence differently. It is like creationists and evolutionists look at the evidence through two different pairs of glasses. What kind of glasses does the creationist use to interpret what he sees in the world? The creationist looks through the lens of the Bible. The Bible is God's eyewitness testimony of how He created the world.

The Bible is the lens that corrects our poor vision so we can clearly see God's work of creation. What glasses does the evolutionist use to interpret what he sees in the world? The evolutionist looks at the world though a lens in which God isn't needed. He interprets the world as if there were no God involved. But since God does exist and is the Creator, the evolutionist's glasses distort the way things really are. Evolutionists often come to a wrong understanding of the evidence.

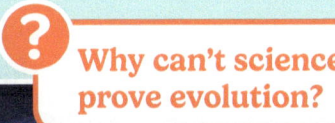

Why can't science prove evolution?

Why should people get married?

The Creation of Man and Woman

God created man and woman in a special way. God formed man from the dust of the ground. Then He breathed the breath of life into his nostrils so man became alive. God placed the man in a garden on a high mountain. A river in the garden watered the ground. This river then divided into four rivers and flowed out into four different parts of the world. God told the man that he was to take care of this garden. He could eat from any of the trees in the garden except one. There were two trees in the center of the garden. One was called the tree of life. The message this tree gave was that mankind could have eternal life if they obeyed God. The second tree was called the tree of the knowledge of good and evil. God told Adam that he was not allowed to eat from this second tree. If he ate from it, he would die.

God also said, "It is not good that the man should be alone." God made a helper for him. He put Adam to sleep and took a rib from Adam's side. From this rib, God made the woman Eve and brought her to the man. This was the first **marriage**. Both man and woman were made in the image of God.

key term
marriage
Marriage is a lifelong covenant between one man and one woman. Marriage was directly created, designed, and blessed by God Himself. God used Adam and Eve as the model for what marriage looks like for all people in all places for all time.

Who were Adam and Eve?

- First humans
- First married couple
- God created Adam from the dust of the ground.
- God created Eve from one of Adam's ribs.
- Both made in the image of God
- Adam is the head and representative of all humankind.
- Their sin put the whole of creation under the curse.
- Their sin caused every person to be born a sinner.
- Adam is contrasted with the last Adam, Jesus Christ.

? What was not good about Adam's situation in the garden?

What is marriage?

How are humans like and unlike God?

The Creation Mandate

God blessed the man and the woman. He commanded that they fill the earth and have dominion over it. Dominion is rule over the earth and all things in it. God made man His representative on the earth. He gave the man and woman the responsibility to fill and rule over His world. He promised them life for obedience. He promised them death for disobedience. Later, this type of agreement would be called a **covenant**.

> **key term**
>
> **covenant**
>
> A covenant is an agreement between two or more people with certain requirements and promises. The Adamic Covenant involved God's promise of life to Adam. He must obey the one command to not eat from the tree of the knowledge of good and evil. But if Adam broke this covenant, God promised death.

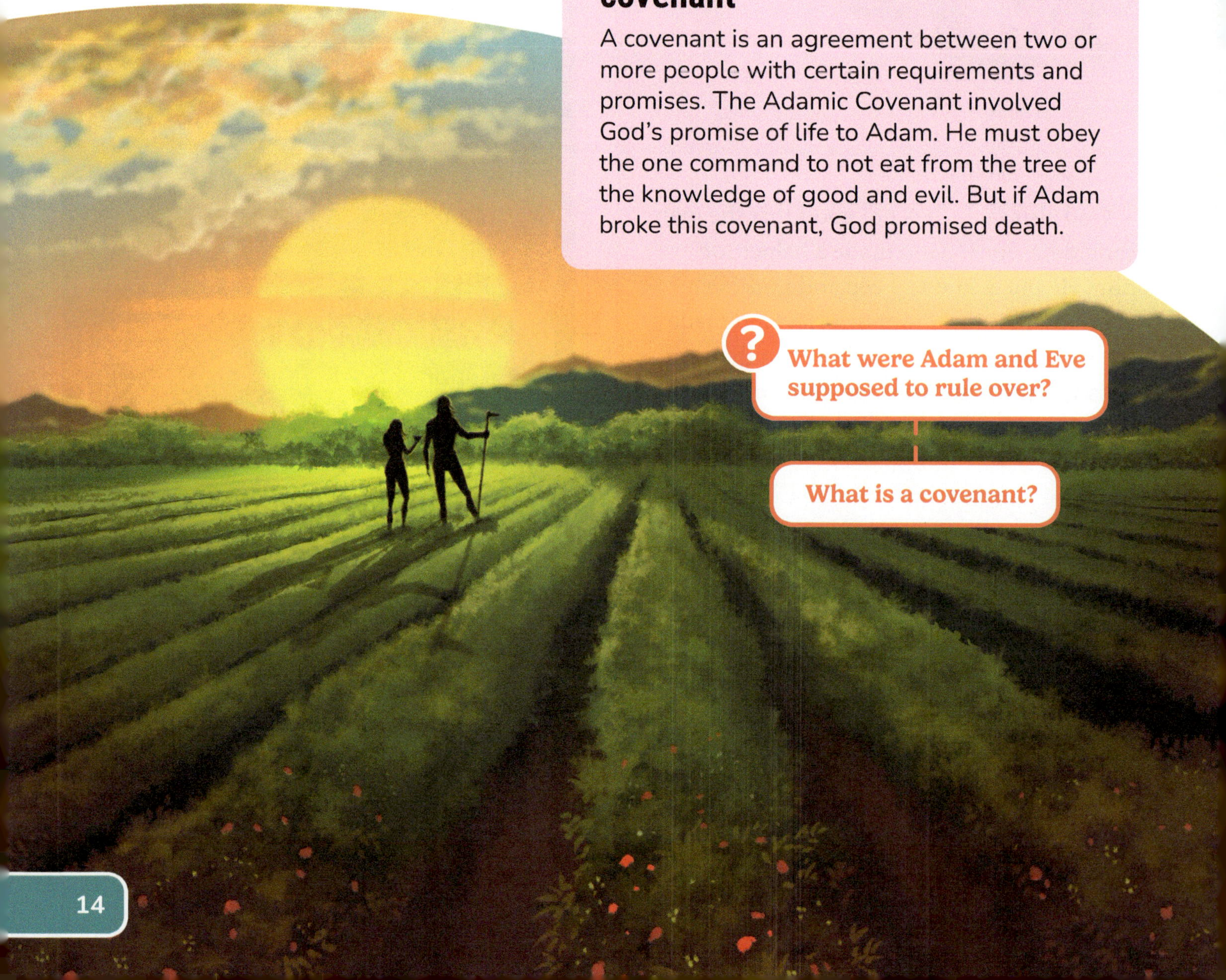

? What were Adam and Eve supposed to rule over?

What is a covenant?

Day 7

God had finished creating all things. Because He was done, God rested from His work of creation on the seventh day. In doing this, God blessed the seventh day and set it apart as a day of rest.

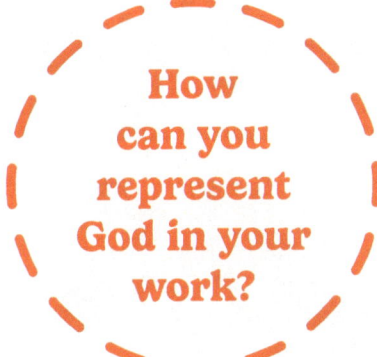

How does the seventh circle represent the seventh day?

Bible Truths

23 **What does it mean for humans to be made in the image of God?**
God created humans with true knowledge, righteousness, and holiness, and He gave them a nature with all the abilities needed to rule over God's world.

Genesis 1:26 • Ephesians 4:24 • Colossians 3:10

24 **Why did God make Adam and Eve in His own image?**
God made them to fill the earth with people and rule over it.

Genesis 1:26–28

25 **What does it mean for humans to have dominion over the earth?**
We are to develop and care for every part of the world for the glory of God and the good of others.

Genesis 1:26–29; 2:5–8, 15; 9:2–3 • Matthew 22:37–39

The Fall of Mankind

Why do I sin?

Sin Brings Death into the World

Of all the animals God created, serpents were the cleverest. Satan used a serpent to tempt the woman to do exactly what God had said not to do. He asked the woman, "Did God say that you could not eat from any tree in the garden?" The woman replied, "God said we could eat from the fruit of the trees. But He said that we could not eat from or touch the fruit from the tree in the middle of the garden. If we do that, we'll die." The serpent assured her, "You will not die. God knows that when you eat from that tree, you will be like Him. You will be able to decide for yourself what is good and what is evil."

The woman looked at the tree. Its fruit looked like good food; it was beautiful to look at. And the serpent said that eating it would make her wise. So she ate some of its fruit. Her husband was with her. She shared that fruit with him, and he ate it. They had disobeyed God's only command. They had broken the Adamic Covenant which God had made with them. Sin invaded God's good creation. Their eyes were opened, but they did not become like God as the serpent had promised.

Instead, they realized that they were not wearing clothes. This was not a problem before they were sinners. But because shame, embarrassment, and fear came with their sin, they sewed together fig leaves to cover their nakedness.

When they heard God walking in the garden, they hid from His presence.

"Where are you?" God asked, even though it was impossible to hide from the all-seeing and all-knowing God.

Adam said, "I heard you, but I was afraid because I was not wearing clothes. So I hid."

"Who told you that you were not wearing clothes? Have you eaten the forbidden fruit?" God asked.

The man said, "The woman you gave me—she gave me the fruit, and I ate."

God asked the woman, "What did you do?"

The woman said, "The serpent tricked me, and I ate."

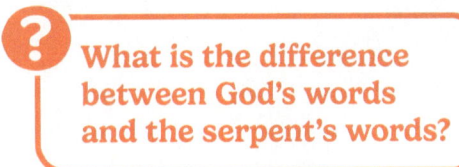

What is the difference between God's words and the serpent's words?

Sin Brings Curses on the World

God told the serpent, "Because you did this, you will be cursed more than the other animals. You will crawl on your belly in the dust." But God's judgment extended beyond the serpent as an animal. God's judgment included Satan who used the serpent. God told Satan, "I will put hatred between you and the woman, and between your seed and her seed. He will strike your head, and you will strike his heel."

Bible Truths

31 **Who tempted Adam and Eve to sin?**
Satan tempted Eve, and she gave the forbidden fruit to Adam.
Genesis 3:1–6 • Revelation 12:9

42 **What do we deserve because of our sin?**
We deserve to be punished by God.
Romans 6:23 • Galatians 3:10

God told the woman, "You will have pain in childbirth, and you will desire to rule over your husband, but he will rule over you."

Finally, God told Adam, "Because you listened to your wife and ate the forbidden fruit, the ground is now cursed. Producing crops for food will now be hard and painful for you."

Adam's sin confirmed God's promise of physical death for disobeying Him. God told the now-sinful couple how their life would end: "You are dust, and you will return to dust."

? **What did sin bring into the world?**

Hope for Salvation

How can I be saved from my sin?

The man and woman faced death for their sin, just as God had said. But God's judgment on Satan also gave them hope that God would save them. Adam showed this hope in the name he gave the woman: Eve. "Eve" sounded like the word for *living* in their language. Adam knew she would be the mother of all living people to be born after them.

God also made clothes from animal skins for Adam and Eve. This showed that covering the consequences of their sin required death.

God didn't want the sinful couple to eat the fruit from the tree of life. The tree of life symbolized the eternal life that they could have had if they obeyed, so God sent them out of the garden of Eden. Adam and Eve were now away from God's special presence in the place He provided for all their needs. Outside of the garden, they would struggle to till the hard ground to grow food to eat. God placed some cherubim—a type of angel—and a flaming sword that moved in every direction at the entrance to the garden to keep anyone from reaching the tree of life.

? **What will the woman's seed bring?**

Bible Truths

37 **What was God's judgment on Satan after Adam and Eve sinned?**
God promised to send a human king that would suffer but ultimately destroy Satan.

Genesis 3:15

147 **What is your only comfort in life and in death?**
My only comfort is that I am not my own, but belong—body and soul, in life and in death—to my faithful Savior, Jesus Christ.

Romans 14:7–9 • 1 Corinthians 3:23
1 Thessalonians 5:23

CHAPTER 2

Sin's Devastating Consequences

Cain Murders Abel

Cain and Abel

Adam and Eve obeyed God's command to be fruitful and multiply. God gave them a son, and they named him Cain. God had promised that a Redeemer would be born. Eve would have been very aware of that promise. She might have thought that Cain, her seed, was that Redeemer when she said, "I have gotten a man with the Lord's help."

Another son, Abel, was also born to Adam and Eve. Abel grew up to be a shepherd, and Cain became a farmer. One day, both sons came to present an offering to God. Cain offered produce from his crops to the Lord. Abel brought the firstborn animals from his flock. He offered the best portions to God. God accepted Abel and his offering but rejected Cain and his offering. As soon as Cain realized that God rejected him and his offering, he became angry at God and at Abel.

God confronted Cain by asking, "Why are you so angry that it shows on your face?" God told Cain that if he did what was right, He would accept him. God also warned Cain by saying, "Sin is crouching at the door. Be careful, Cain; control your sinful desires or they will destroy you."

? What was God's warning to Cain?

The First Murder

Cain rejected God's words and made plans to kill Abel. He had his chance when they were in the field, and there he committed the first murder in history. Once again, God confronted Cain by asking, "Where is your brother Abel?"

Cain replied, "I don't know; am I my brother's keeper?"

God said, "What have you done? I know your brother's blood has been spilled on the ground."

Because of this, God cursed Cain. The ground would no longer yield a worthwhile harvest for him. Cain cried out, "This punishment is too hard for me!"

But God assured Cain that, even though He would send him away from His presence, He would discourage anyone from trying to take his life. God put a mark on Cain and promised that anyone who killed him would be punished seven times worse than Cain was.

? How did Cain respond to God's warning?

The First City's Goods

Cain built a city and named it after one of his sons. Five generations after Cain, a seed of his was born named Lamech. He was the first man in Scripture to have two wives. These wives had sons who began important work for the city. One was a herder of cattle; another was skilled in music. A third son was talented at working with metals. These people were living out the blessing of being fruitful and multiplying and exercising rule over the earth. But this blessing was damaged by their sinfulness. Lamech was a proud and violent man. This is seen in a poem he composed: "I have killed a man for hurting me, a young man for hitting me. Revenge on Cain was times seven, revenge on Lamech will be times seventy-seven." Not only did Lamech admit to killing a young man for hitting him, but he also felt that his life was worth more than Cain's, even though they sinned in the same way.

Seth Replaces Abel

Adam and Eve soon became parents to another son named Seth. Eve praised God for Seth by saying, "God has given me another son to take the place of Abel, whom Cain killed."

Just like Abel, Seth had a good relationship with the Lord. It would be through Seth's descendants, not Cain's, that the promised Redeemer would come.

In Genesis 5, we read a long list of names. After every name are the three words "and he died." Every person mentioned died because they were sinners. Only one person in this list didn't die. Enoch was a sinner who didn't die. He walked with God, and God took him to heaven. This gave hope to people that God would provide a way of salvation. Because of the Fall, we have sin and death for all mankind. But in God, there is life and blessing.

> **?** How did God keep His promise of redemption following Cain's sin?

Bible Truth

39 **What effect did Adam's sin have on mankind's rule over the world?**

The world is now cursed, and mankind no longer seeks the good of others and the glory of God in his rule.

Genesis 3:16–19; 4:17–24

From Bad to Worse

Humankind Is Sinful

The population of the earth grew quickly. At the same time, sinners became more and more ungodly. Hardly anyone cared about following God, and it was getting worse. How bad could it have been? Genesis 6:5 says that "every imagination of the thoughts of [a man's] heart was only evil continually." In other words, *all* people *only* wanted to do evil things. God had told Adam and Eve to fill the earth with people, but people were also filling the earth with violence. God regretted having made humankind. It grieved* Him that He would have to judge them for their horribly sinful ways.

God Is Gracious

God could have destroyed all sinful people at any time He pleased. Instead, God said that He would wait 120 years before He poured out His judgment. But even when judgment came, God wouldn't wipe out every human on earth.

? How bad was humanity's sinfulness before the Flood?

How sinful am I?

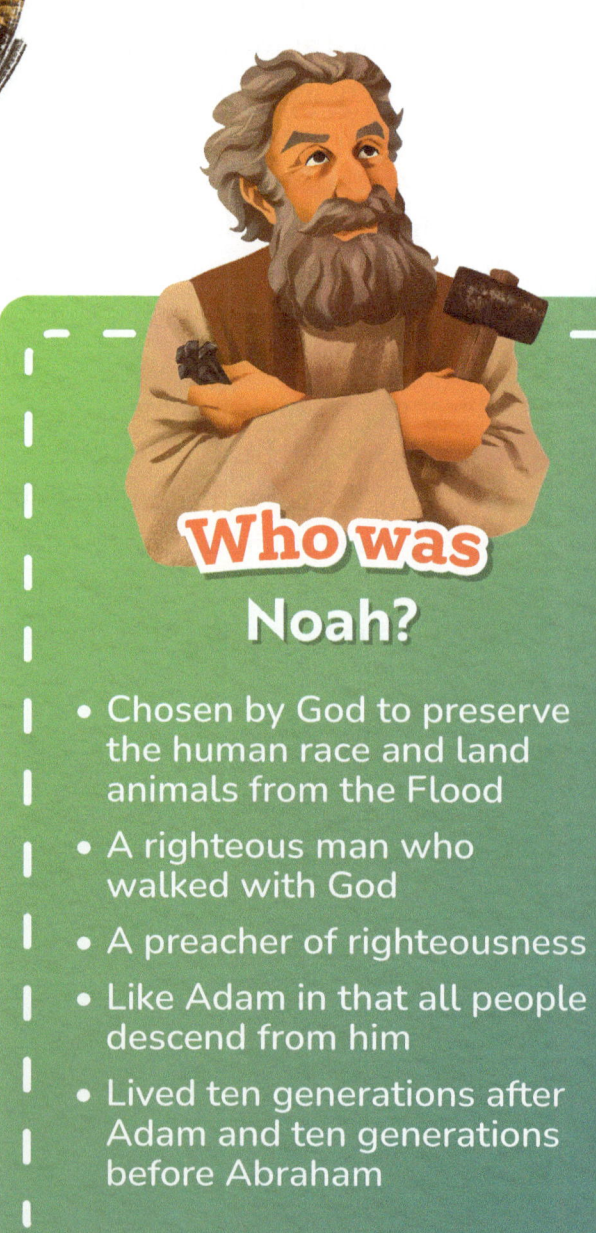

Who was Noah?

- Chosen by God to preserve the human race and land animals from the Flood
- A righteous man who walked with God
- A preacher of righteousness
- Like Adam in that all people descend from him
- Lived ten generations after Adam and ten generations before Abraham

Noah was a sinner too, but God showed him **grace**. As a result, Noah walked with God. God told Noah He was going to destroy every living thing on earth. But God also graciously told Noah that He would save him, his family, and at least a pair of each kind of animal. God was going to use Noah and his three sons to build a massive boat called an ark.

Noah Prepared the Ark

God gave Noah the plans for the big boat. It would be very large. God told Noah to build the ark 300 cubits long, 50 cubits wide, and 30 cubits tall. In today's measurements the ark would have measured as much as 510 feet long, 85 feet wide, and 50 feet tall. God said to make three floors, a window on the upper level, and a door on the side of the boat.

The ark needed to shelter Noah's family, two of every kind of animal, food, and supplies.

> **?** In what two ways did God deal with sinful humanity?

key term
grace
Grace is God's kindness to us that we don't deserve and can't earn. Even though Noah and his family didn't deserve grace, God showed them grace instead of judgment.

Bible Truths

40 **What effect did Adam's sin have on the image of God in all mankind?**
Mankind lost true knowledge, righteousness, and holiness; his abilities to rule over God's world are now used corruptly.

Genesis 4:17–24 • Ephesians 4:24
Colossians 3:10

66 **What is grace?**
Grace is God's kindness to us when we deserve punishment.

Deuteronomy 7:6–9 • Romans 3:23–24
Ephesians 2:7–9

The Worldwide Flood

How can God be just and gracious at the same time?

As the time of judgment drew near, God sent the animals to Noah. Noah was to take at least a pair, one male and one female, of every kind of animal on board. And Noah was to take seven of each of the clean animals on board. After Noah's family and all the animals entered the ark, God shut the door. Noah was six hundred years old when he entered the ark.

It rained forty days and forty nights. These weren't just rainy days. It wasn't just a bad thunderstorm. It rained nonstop for forty days and forty nights. The rain from the sky wasn't enough to cover the earth by itself. Where did the rest of the water come from? A large amount of water was stored underground. God let all that water from the ground flow up while He poured down all the water from the sky. There was so much water that even the highest mountain peaks were covered by about twenty-five feet of water. God's judgment by water made sure that no land animal or person survived.

Now the earth was covered in water, just like on the first day of creation. All the land, plants, land animals, and people outside the ark were destroyed. God had unmade His creation. The sin that corrupted the earth required that God send this global judgment.

Noah Leaves the Ark

Looking out over the water, Noah might have felt all alone. But God remembered Noah. The water stayed on the earth for 150 days. But after that time, the ark came to rest on the top of a mountain. Noah waited several months for the water to drain away. Then Noah released a raven to see if there was dry land other than the tops of the mountains. The raven never came back. Then Noah sent out a dove. The dove couldn't find a place to rest, so it returned to Noah. After a week, Noah sent out the dove again, and it returned with an olive leaf. A week later, he sent the dove out again, and this time it didn't return. Noah knew that this was a sign that it would soon be time to leave the ark. Finally, the earth was dry enough for Noah, his family, and all the animals to leave the ark. By this time, everyone had been on the ark for about a year.

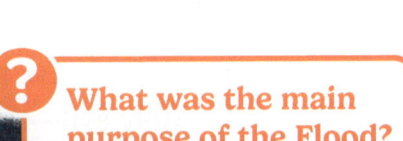

? What was the main purpose of the Flood?

Bible Truth

42 **What do we deserve because of our sin?**

We deserve to be punished by God.

Romans 6:23 • Galatians 3:10

God's Covenant with Noah

How does God show He is trustworthy?

The first thing Noah did after leaving the ark was build an altar and offer a sacrifice* to God. Noah sacrificed some of every clean animal and clean bird that he took on the ark. God was pleased with Noah's burnt offerings.

God knew that the human heart had been evil since the Fall. Washing the earth clean with a flood did not solve the problem of sin. This meant that people would again fill the earth with sin and violence. God would be just to continue to judge the earth like He did with the Flood. Instead, God entered into a covenant with Noah and with every living thing on the earth. This is called the Noahic Covenant. God promised that He would not wipe out every living thing with a flood again. God promised that the seasons would continue until the final judgment. Seasonal patterns would allow people to grow food and meet all their basic needs. The world would continue while God's plan of redemption moved forward.

When everyone came out of the ark, God told Noah and his sons the same thing He had told Adam and Eve. God commanded them to be fruitful and to multiply and fill the earth. And now, Noah and his descendants were told that they could use animals for food. God gave mankind the use of animals for food just as He gave Adam plants for food in the Garden of Eden. What does man have dominion over? Everything. What can man use for food? Everything.

God gave them the prohibition* not to eat any animal with its blood still in it. Then God gave the reason why murder is so horribly evil—to shed someone's blood in murder is to take the life of someone made in the image of God. And so, God also gave the right punishment for murderers—their own lives for the lives they took. God commanded Noah and all people to bring about life and prosper in God's recreated world.

? What did God want Noah's family and the animals to do after the Flood?

The Sign of God's Covenant with Noah

God established a covenant with Noah, his family, and every living thing. God promised never to kill all living things with water ever again. And He gave Noah, his family, and all people everywhere a sign that He would keep His promise. This sign is a rainbow. God comforts all people by bringing out a rainbow when He makes the clouds rain on the earth. God sees each rainbow, and each time, God remembers and keeps His covenant. God will not repeat what He did with the Flood.

? What did God promise in the Noahic Covenant?

Bible Truth

44 **What did God promise in the Noahic Covenant?**
God promised not to judge the whole earth until He had accomplished His plan of redemption.

Genesis 8:20–9:17

The City of Confusion

What happens when people oppose God's good design of His world?

One Tower

After the Flood, all the people on the earth spoke the same language and used the same words. As many of these people moved from the east, they said to each other, "Let's stop here and make bricks to build a city. Let's build a tower that reaches into the heavens, and let's make a name for ourselves so we don't get scattered across the earth." They were rejecting God's command to fill the earth.

God came down to see the city and tower they had built. God said, "All the people on earth are still one group of people who all speak the same language. They have only just begun to work together in rebellion against me. Everything they set out to do, they will do."

Many Languages

God declared, "Let's go down and confuse the language of the people so they can't understand each other." So that is just what God did—He caused all the people to speak new languages. The work on the tower stopped because the people couldn't talk to each other. People packed up and moved away from the city. The city with its unfinished tower was named Babel, which means "confusion." This confusion is how God scattered people to different parts of the earth.

Bible Truth

25 **What does it mean for humans to have dominion over the earth?**
We are to develop and care for every part of the world for the glory of God and the good of others.

Genesis 1:26–29; 2:5–8, 15; 9:2–3
Matthew 22:37–39

❓ How did the people of Babel want to make a name for themselves?

What command of God did the people of Babel reject?

CHAPTER 3

God's Covenant with Abraham

Abraham
HEIR OF THE PROMISE

Moving to a New Land

After God scattered people from the tower of Babel for trying to make a name for themselves, God decided to make a name for one of Noah's descendants, Abram.

Abram lived in Ur, in Mesopotamia. He left Ur because God said, "Move away from your relatives to the land I will show you. I'm going to make you into a great nation. I will make your name great. I will bless you, and you will be a blessing. I will bless those who bless you, and I will curse those who curse you. I will bless all the families of the earth through you."

Abram was seventy-five years old when he left his homeland to follow God's instructions. He, his wife Sarai, and his nephew Lot set out to see where God would lead them.

Once Abram and his household were in Canaan, God appeared to Abram and told him, "I will give this land to your descendants." Abram built an altar there and called on the name of the Lord.

> Why is faith necessary in order to be right with God?

Who was Abraham?

- Chosen by God as the father of the Hebrew nation
- Received the covenant of land, seed, and blessing promised by God
- Father of Isaac and grandfather of Jacob
- His faith in God was counted to him as righteousness.

Abram's faith was tested when there was a severe famine in Canaan. Abram and his household traveled south to Egypt to avoid the famine. But as they neared Egypt, Abram started worrying for his life. He was afraid somebody would kill him to marry his beautiful wife, Sarai. So Abram told Sarai to tell a lie. "Tell everybody that you are my sister. That way, if anyone wants to take you to be his wife, he will not kill me to marry you." As Abram feared, Pharaoh, the king of Egypt, wanted to marry Abram's "sister." Pharaoh gave Abram many animals as gifts. But God sent great plagues to Pharaoh's household because Pharaoh took Abram's wife to be one of his wives. When Pharaoh learned about Abram's lie, he told Abram to take his wife and all his possessions and leave.

> **Bible Truth**
>
> **45** **What did God promise in the Abrahamic Covenant?**
>
> *God promised to give Abraham a land and a seed and to make him a blessing to all people.*
>
> Genesis 12:1–3, 7; 15:1–21; 17:1–14

? What was God going to make from Abram's seed?

Lot Walks Away

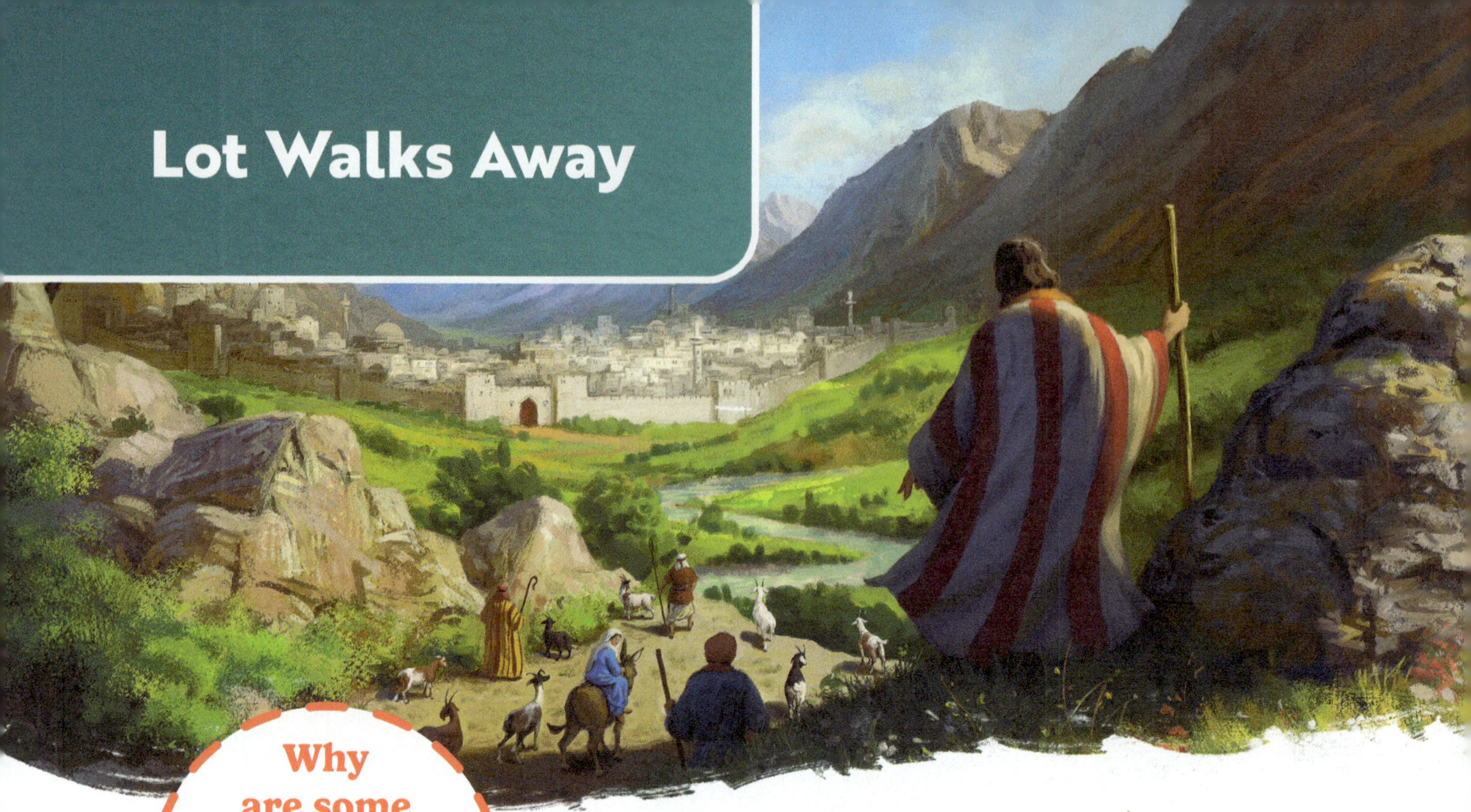

Why are some things that look good actually bad?

Abram was very rich. He led his household out of Egypt and returned to Canaan. Once again, Abram called on the name of the Lord where he had built an altar. Abram's nephew, Lot, was part of Abram's household. Lot also had many animals and possessions, and Abram's shepherds and Lot's shepherds often argued. Abram wanted peace, so he told Lot, "We are family. There shouldn't be these problems between our shepherds. Look at the land and choose where you want to go. Then I will go in the opposite direction." Lot chose the best pastures in the direction of Sodom because they looked like the garden of Eden. But the people of Sodom were very wicked. Eventually, Lot decided to move out of the pastures and into Sodom itself.

After Lot left for Sodom, God appeared to Abram and told him, "Look in every direction. All the land you see, I give to you." God also said, "I'm going to make the number of your descendants as numerous as the dust of the earth." Abram's seed would be too many to count. Abram built an altar to the Lord as an act of worship.

? What was wrong with Lot's decision to take the land closest to Sodom?

The Abrahamic Covenant

As Abram grew older, he was concerned that he did not yet have a son. But God told Abram, "I will give you a son. Look up into the sky. Your seed will be as many as the stars." Even though Abram had no children, he believed God's word that his seed would be many. And God counted Abram's faith to him as righteousness. Abram received righteousness from God, and it was considered as his own based solely on his faith in God. God also promised that that land would belong to Abram's people. The borders would stretch all the way from the river of Egypt to the Euphrates River.

God then made a covenant with Abram. In this covenant, God committed Himself to keep these promises to Abram and his seed. When people made covenants back then, they followed a special ceremony. They sacrificed animals, cut them in two, and walked together through the cut pieces. They were saying to each other, "May I die like these animals if I don't keep my promises." But Abram did not walk between the pieces. God put Abram to sleep. God's presence was seen as a smoking fire pot and a flaming torch. God alone passed through the animal pieces. God was saying that He would bring about the promises no matter what.

Chosen though Sinful

Why does God bless people?

It had been ten years since God called Abram to Canaan, and Abram and Sarai still had no son. Sarai grew impatient. She told Abram to have a child with her servant, Hagar. Abram listened to his wife's advice and did what she said. When Hagar was expecting a child and Sarai wasn't, Sarai became jealous. Sarai mistreated Hagar so much that Hagar ran away. The Angel of the Lord went to Hagar and said, "Return to Sarai. I will make your seed be so great in number that they cannot be counted." The Angel of the Lord heard Hagar's suffering and saw her need. The Angel of the Lord said to Hagar, "You will name your son Ishmael because the Lord has heard your trouble. But he will have many enemies and even be at odds with his extended family."

❓ **In what situation did God still show grace to Abram, even when Abram acted sinfully?**

Father Abraham

Twenty-four years after God told Abram to leave his home, God came to Abram again. By now, Abram was ninety-nine years old. God said, "I will confirm my covenant with you. Your new name will be Abraham because you will be a father to many nations and kings. I make my eternal covenant with you and your seed, and I will be their God. I will give to you and your seed the land of Canaan for an everlasting possession." God saved the most important promise for last when He said, "I will be their God."

God gave Abraham a sign for this covenant. Every male child in his household would be marked with a sign called circumcision. A male who was not circumcised would be cut off from the covenant people and from the covenant promises.

God also changed Sarai's name to Sarah. He promised that Sarah would give birth to the promised son. Abraham asked if Ishmael could be the promised son, but God said no. Sarah would have a son, and his name would be Isaac.

What was the sign of God's covenant with Abraham?

God Visits Abraham and Sarah

Three men appeared to Abraham one day as he was sitting by the door of his tent. One was an appearance of the Lord Himself; the other two were angels. When Abraham saw them approaching, he ran and bowed before them. Abraham said, "Please wash your feet and rest in the shade of this tree." Then he ran to Sarah and said, "Quickly, make some bread." Next, he told a servant to make a special meal for his guests. He brought them the food and stood close by while they ate.

The Lord told Abraham, "I will return in a year, and Sarah will have a son."

Sarah was listening from inside the tent. When she heard that, she laughed to herself because she was too old to have a baby. God asked Abraham, "Why did Sarah laugh? Is anything too hard for the Lord? I will return, and by then Sarah will have a son." After hearing this, Sarah lied that she hadn't laughed, but God told her He knew that she had.

? Why did Sarah laugh when she overheard that she would give birth to a baby boy?

Intercession for Sodom

The Lord told Abraham that He would destroy the very sinful cities of Sodom and Gomorrah. Sodom was where Lot now lived. Abraham asked God, "Will you destroy the righteous people along with the wicked? What if there are fifty righteous people in the city? Will you, the Judge of all the earth, not do what is right?"

God answered, "I will not destroy the city if there are fifty righteous people."

Then Abraham asked, "What if there are forty-five righteous people?"

God replied, "I will not destroy it if there are forty-five righteous people."

Abraham pleaded for the sake of forty, then thirty, then twenty, and then finally for ten righteous people.

And God said, "I will not destroy the city if I find even ten righteous people."

Destruction of Sodom and Gomorrah

What are the consequences of running after sin?

key term
mercy
Mercy is holding back deserved judgment. Being merciful is not punishing someone for having done something that deserves punishment.

God is merciful any time He saves or blesses someone. Every time God saves or blesses someone, He is saving and blessing a sinner who deserves punishment.

Two angels disguised as men visited Lot in Sodom. They came to rescue Lot and his family from God's coming destruction. The men of Sodom noticed that Lot brought two men into his house. They wanted to harm these two visitors, but Lot begged them not to. The angels protected Lot's daughters and Lot himself from the wicked men by blinding them. Then the angels told Lot to get his entire family out of the city immediately before they destroyed it. Lot warned his sons-in-law about God's coming judgment, but they thought he was joking. As the sun rose, the angels continued to urge Lot to leave. Lot was taking too much time, so the angels grabbed Lot, his wife, and his daughters by the hand and took them out of the city. God's **mercy** spared their lives.

The angels gave an important order before leaving to destroy the city. "Escape to the hills and do not look back!" But looking back is exactly what Lot's wife did. As a result, she died just like the wicked people of Sodom and the surrounding cities. But Lot and his daughters found safety in Zoar and eventually in a cave. They escaped the destruction of Sodom and Gomorrah because God spared them and because they obeyed the angel's commands.

? In what ways did God show mercy to Lot and his family?

Bible Truth

143 **What will happen to the wicked in the day of judgment?**
The wicked will be raised and thrown, body and soul, into the lake of fire.

Daniel 12:2 • Revelation 20:11–15

The Birth of Isaac

Why do I think that some things are too hard for God?

God said that Sarah would give birth to a son in exactly a year. God did what He had promised. Sarah gave birth to a son when Abraham was one hundred years old. Abraham named this long-awaited and promised son Isaac. Sarah had laughed in disbelief when God said she would have a son. But now Sarah was so full of joy that she said, "What God has done makes me laugh, and all who hear of Isaac's birth will laugh with me. Who would have thought that I would raise a child with Abraham in his old age?" It was through Sarah's faith in God's promise that she had strength to have a baby in her old age. After all that Sarah experienced, she acknowledged that God is faithful because He does what He promises.

? What can we learn through the birth of Isaac?

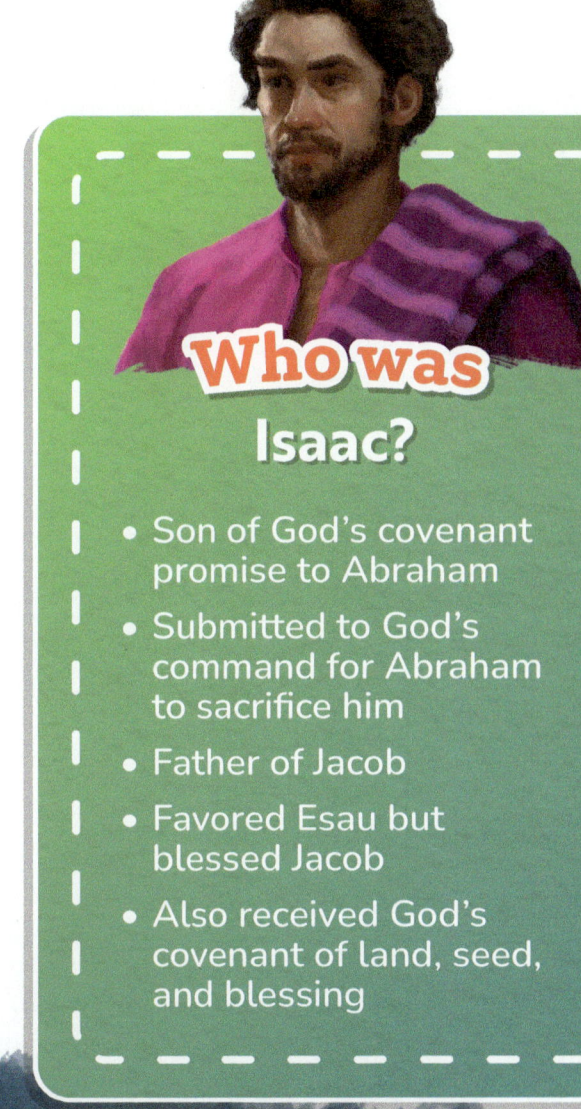

Who was Isaac?

- Son of God's covenant promise to Abraham
- Submitted to God's command for Abraham to sacrifice him
- Father of Jacob
- Favored Esau but blessed Jacob
- Also received God's covenant of land, seed, and blessing

43

God's Command to Sacrifice Isaac

Does God permit human sacrifice?

Isaac grew to be a young man. Hagar and Ishmael were no longer living with Abraham. At this time God tested Abraham's faith. God told Abraham, "Take your only son, Isaac, whom you love so very much. Go to the mountains and sacrifice him as a burnt offering."

Abraham woke up early the next morning. He, Isaac, and two workers gathered everything needed for the sacrifice and started their trip. On the third day, Abraham looked in the distance and saw the place God had told him about. He told his two workers, "You stay here. My son and I will go worship God and come back."

The father and his only son began walking to the place of sacrifice. Abraham had Isaac carry the wood on his back, while he carried the fire and the knife. As they walked, Isaac asked, "I see the fire and the wood for the sacrifice. But where is the lamb that we're going to sacrifice?"

Abraham answered, "God Himself will provide the lamb, my son."

When they reached the mountain that God wanted them to sacrifice on, Abraham built the altar and laid the wood in place. He then tied Isaac up and put him on top of the wood. Then Abraham took the knife in his hand to sacrifice his son.

In that very moment, the Angel of the Lord called out, "Abraham, Abraham!"

Abraham replied, "Here I am."

The Angel of the Lord said, "Do not harm him in any way. Now I know that you fear God, since you have not kept your only son from me." Abraham had demonstrated his faith by his actions. Abraham then saw a ram caught in some bushes by its horns. He offered it as the burnt offering instead of Isaac.

God then confirmed His covenant promises to Abraham again. Because Abraham demonstrated his faith, God promised that his seed would be as numerous as the stars in the sky and the sand on the seashore. And Abraham would also have a Seed who would conquer His enemies. In that Seed, all nations of the earth would be blessed. Abraham and Isaac returned home together.

? What does Abraham's faith that God will provide a sacrifice point to?

Bible Truth

59 **What is the atonement?**
The atonement is Christ's satisfying divine justice by His sufferings and death in the place of sinners.

Romans 3:23–26; 5:8–11
1 Peter 3:18

CHAPTER 4

The Patriarchs

Isaac
THE PROMISE CONTINUES

Why does God keep His promises to us?

When Isaac was forty years old, Abraham arranged for Isaac to be married to a beautiful woman named Rebekah. Isaac prayed for Rebekah because she was not able to have children. God heard his prayers, and soon she was expecting twins. But she was concerned because the twins struggled with each other inside her. The Lord said to Rebekah, "Two nations are in your womb. One will be stronger than the other, and the older will serve the younger." Esau was born first, but Jacob was born right behind him, grasping his brother's heel. Esau grew up to be a hunter and was his father's favorite son. Jacob helped his mother take care of things at home and was her favorite.

One day Esau returned from a hunt and was exhausted. Jacob was cooking a stew, so Esau approached him and said, "Let me eat some of that red stew, because I feel like I am about to faint."

Jacob replied, "Sell me your birthright right now."

Esau said, "Since I am about to die from exhaustion, what use is a birthright to me?"

Jacob made Esau swear that he would give him his birthright. Then Esau ate the bread and stew Jacob had prepared and went on his way. Esau despised his birthright.

Isaac Receives God's Covenant Promises

A famine struck the land where Isaac was living. Isaac had plans to go down to Egypt like his father Abraham had done, but God appeared to him and said, "Do not go down to Egypt. Rather, go live in the land that I will tell you about. I will bless you and give you all these lands and fulfill the promises I made to your father Abraham. I will make your seed like the stars of heaven. I will give all these lands to your seed, and I will bless all the nations through your seed."

? What did God promise to Isaac?

Isaac and Abimelech

Isaac dwelled in Gerar, a city of the Philistines. The king of this land was Abimelech.

Isaac feared for his life because his wife was so attractive. He thought that the Philistine people would kill him to take his wife. He told everyone that Rebekah was his sister. But Abimelech noticed through a window that Isaac and Rebekah were laughing together like a married couple would. The king scolded Isaac for lying about her being his sister.

Isaac settled in Gerar with his family for a while. He planted crops and raised cattle. God blessed him and he became very rich. Isaac then lived in Beersheba, where Abraham had also lived. It was in Beersheba that God appeared to Isaac again and said, "I am the God of Abraham your father. Do not be afraid; I am with you. I will bless you and multiply your descendants for my servant Abraham's sake." In response, Isaac built an altar to God and called upon the name of the Lord.

Bible Truth

45 **What did God promise in the Abrahamic Covenant?**
God promised to give Abraham a land and a seed and to make him a blessing to all people.

Genesis 12:1–3, 7; 15:1–21; 17:1–14

Jacob
GOD'S GRACIOUS CHOICE

Why is grace not something I can earn or something I deserve?

Who was Jacob?

- Grandson of Abraham
- Younger twin brother of Esau
- Name changed by God to Israel
- Father of the twelve tribes of Israel
- Also received God's covenant of land, seed, and blessing
- Died in Egypt but was buried in the cave of Machpelah in Canaan

Jacob Tricks Isaac

When Isaac was an old man, he lost his ability to see. He knew he wasn't going to live much longer. Isaac asked his firstborn, his favorite son Esau, to hunt and kill an animal and prepare him his favorite meal. Isaac wanted to enjoy one last meal, bless Esau, and die. Isaac planned this special occasion, even though God had revealed that the older son would serve the younger. Rebekah overheard their conversation and made a plan for Jacob to get his father's blessing.

Rebekah prepared a delicious meal for Jacob to take to Isaac before Esau returned. Because Esau was hairy, Jacob strapped animal fur around his hands and around his neck to make them feel how Esau felt. Rebekah even had Jacob wear some of his brother's clothes so he would smell like Esau. Then Jacob took the meal of bread and two young goats to Isaac.

"My father," Jacob said.

Isaac replied, "Who are you?"

"I am Esau, your firstborn," Jacob lied. "Please eat and enjoy so you can bless me."

Isaac wondered if it was really Esau, so he asked Jacob, "How did you find the animal so quickly?"

Jacob replied, "Because the Lord your God made me successful."

Isaac still wasn't convinced, so he asked Jacob to come nearer. Isaac felt his hands and said, "The voice is Jacob's, but the hands are Esau's. Are you really my son Esau?"

Jacob said, "I am."

Isaac then feasted on the food. When he was finished, he asked Jacob to come near to him. When Jacob drew near to Isaac, Isaac was now entirely convinced that Jacob was Esau. Isaac proclaimed, "My son smells like the field that the Lord has blessed!" Isaac then asked God to make Jacob successfully produce food and drink from the land. Isaac also asked God to raise up Jacob so other people groups and nations might serve him and bow down to him. He said, "Rule over your brothers, and may your mother's sons bow down to you." Isaac restated God's blessing to Abraham by saying, "Cursed be everyone who curses you, and blessed be everyone who blesses you."

The Blessing Is God's to Give

Just after Jacob had received Isaac's blessing and left, Esau went to his father and said, "Come, Father. Eat the food I have prepared and bless me!"

Isaac was confused. "Who are you?" he asked.

"I am Esau, your firstborn."

Isaac was shaken. He said, "Then who brought me food? I ate his food and blessed him, and the blessing will be his." Isaac realized that he had been tricked into giving the blessing to Jacob.

Esau begged his father, "Don't you have at least one blessing left for me?"

Isaac said, "I have made Jacob the head of this family, so he will inherit my wealth. You will serve your younger brother." Esau pleaded once more with his father for a blessing and wept. Isaac said, "You will serve your brother through your sword. But eventually, you will break away from serving him."

Esau was so incredibly angry at Jacob that he planned to kill him. Rebekah learned of Esau's plans and told Jacob to run away to Haran, where he could stay with her brother Laban.

? **What purpose did the trickery of Jacob and Rebekah serve?**

A Ladder to Heaven

Jacob Receives Promises from God

As Jacob traveled, he spent the night in a place called Luz. There, he had an amazing dream. He saw something like a ladder or stairway reaching from the earth to heaven. Angels were going up and down it. The Lord stood above it and said to Jacob, "I am the Lord God of your father Abraham and your father Isaac. I will give this land to you and your seed. Your seed will be as numerous as dust, and they will fill this land in all directions. In you and your seed, all the families of the earth will be blessed. Remember, I am with you, and I will be with you until I bring you back to this land."

Jacob Vows to Serve the Lord

Jacob woke up from his dream and said, "The Lord was here, and I didn't know it." Jacob was afraid and said, "This is the house of God and the gate of heaven." Jacob called that place Bethel, which means "House of God." He took the stone he had used as a pillow, set it up as a pillar, and poured oil on it. Jacob vowed to follow the God of his father and grandfather if God provided for his material needs. If God would keep the promises He made, Jacob promised to give God back a tenth of everything He gave to him. Jacob put God to the test. He said he was willing to respond with faith and obedience if God showed Himself to be faithful.

Why can we not get to God on our own?

? How do you know that God took the first step in keeping the covenant to Jacob that He made with Abraham and his seed?

Jacob Wrestles

Why can I not wrestle God for a blessing?

Jacob Marries Leah and Rachel

Jacob arrived in Haran and began to work for his uncle, Laban. After a month, Laban asked Jacob how he would like to be paid for his work. Laban had two daughters, Leah and Rachel. Leah was the older sister and was plain in appearance. Rachel was the younger one and beautiful. Jacob told Laban that he would work for him for seven years if he could marry Rachel. Laban agreed to this arrangement.

After seven years, Jacob reminded Laban that it was time to let him marry Rachel. Laban agreed, but he secretly arranged for Jacob to marry Leah instead. The morning after the wedding festivities, Jacob discovered he had married the wrong sister. Laban tricked Jacob, just like Jacob had tricked Isaac. Jacob was very upset, but Laban gave him an excuse. He said that, in Haran, the younger sister cannot marry before the older sister.

Laban said Jacob could also marry Rachel after the one-week honeymoon with Leah. But he added that Jacob must work for him another seven years for Rachel.

God blessed Jacob, and his family grew to eleven sons and a daughter. His flocks of sheep and goats and his herds of cattle also grew rapidly. Over the years, Jacob became a rich man. But working for Laban was becoming more difficult. Laban changed Jacob's wages ten times, and Laban's shepherds were lying about Jacob. It was at this time that God said to Jacob, "Go back to your family's land. I will be with you." After twenty years of working for Laban, Jacob gathered his family and belongings together. He knew they needed to slip away quietly, so they left at night. It was time to go home to Isaac and Rebekah.

? Who was responsible for Jacob's wealth?

Jacob Wrestles with God

As Jacob got nearer to his home, he was told that his brother Esau was coming with four hundred men. What would Esau do to them? Jacob sent gifts of animals and servants. Maybe this gift would cause Esau to feel better about Jacob. That night, while Jacob was walking alone, a man appeared and began to wrestle with him. They wrestled until dawn. Then the man simply touched Jacob's hip socket and put it out of place. Then the man said, "Let me go. It's almost morning." Jacob realized this was someone special.

He replied, "I will not let you go unless you bless me."

The man asked for Jacob's name. Then the man said, "Your name will now be called Israel because you have struggled with God and men and won."

Jacob asked for the man's name, but the man only said, "Why do you ask me my name?" After the man blessed Jacob, Jacob realized what had happened. He called that place Peniel and said, "I have seen God face to face, but I survived." Jacob hobbled away from that wrestling match with a limp leg, a new name, and a changed heart.

 Who was the man Jacob wrestled with?

Joseph and Judah
PART 1

How do I respond when people mistreat me?

Who was Joseph?

- Jacob's favorite son and eldest son of his favorite wife
- Was promoted to be ruler over Egypt, second only to Pharaoh
- Used by God to keep all of Egypt and his whole family alive during a harsh famine
- His land in the Promised Land would be split between his sons, Ephraim and Manasseh.
- Commanded his descendants to take his bones out of Egypt and bury them in the Promised Land when God delivered them

Joseph Tells His Dreams

Jacob and his family now lived in Canaan. Jacob showed favoritism to Rachel's oldest son, Joseph, by giving him a special coat of many colors. Joseph's brothers hated him because Jacob loved him so much. One night, Joseph had a special dream. He dreamed that he and his brothers were harvesting grain. His own sheaf of grain stood, but his brothers' sheaves bowed to Joseph's sheaf. He told this to his brothers, and they hated him even more for this dream. Joseph then had a second dream where the sun, moon, and eleven stars bowed to him. After Joseph told his family this dream, Jacob himself was upset and said, "Do you really think your mother, your brothers, and I will bow down to you?"

Sometime later, Jacob sent Joseph to check on his brothers, who were tending the flocks many miles away. When his brothers saw him coming, they said, "Here comes the dreamer. Let's kill him, throw him in a pit, and tell our father that a wild animal killed him."

But Reuben, the oldest brother, convinced them not to harm Joseph. So instead, they grabbed Joseph, ripped his coat of many colors off him, and threw him into a pit. Reuben was secretly planning to return Joseph to his father. But while Reuben was away, some slave traders were passing by. Judah said, "What would we get if we kill our brother? Let's sell Joseph to the slave traders instead of shedding our own brother's blood." They sold Joseph as a slave, and he was taken down to Egypt.

When Reuben returned and saw what had been done, he was distressed. He said, "The boy is gone; what am I going to do now?" To hide their horrible sin, Joseph's brothers ripped up the colorful coat and covered it in goat's blood. They took the coat to Jacob, and he was convinced that Joseph had been killed by a wild animal. He mourned for Joseph for a long time and would not be comforted.

? Which of Joseph's brothers didn't want to kill him?

Joseph Interprets Dreams

Once in Egypt, Joseph was sold to the captain of Pharaoh's guard, a man named Potiphar. Joseph served his master faithfully and was trusted more than all the other slaves. Despite his loyalty, Potiphar's wife told a terrible lie about Joseph. Joseph was faithful to God and innocent in his actions. Even so, he was sent to prison. Just as God was with Joseph when he was taken to Potiphar's house, God was with Joseph when he was sent to prison. God showed Joseph His faithful love and allowed Joseph to be favored by the prison guard. Just like Joseph had ruled over Potiphar's household, he was now allowed to be in charge of the other prisoners in prison with him.

Eventually, Pharaoh's baker and cupbearer were sent to prison. One night, each of them had a dream. Joseph noticed the next morning that they looked troubled. He asked them, "What's making you so sad?" They replied that they had dreamed, but there wasn't anyone there to tell them what the dreams meant. Joseph replied, "Don't the interpretations of dreams belong to God?" After listening to their dreams, Joseph said the cupbearer would be restored to his position in three days, but the baker would be hanged in three days. Joseph said to the cupbearer, "Please remember me and tell Pharaoh about me so I can be taken out of prison."

Joseph Is Exalted

However, once the cupbearer was restored, he forgot all about Joseph back in prison.

After two years, God sent Pharaoh a dream. In the dream, seven fat cows came out of the Nile River and were eaten by seven thin starving cows, who also came out of the Nile River. Also in the dream, seven full heads of grain were devoured by seven empty heads of grain. No one could tell Pharaoh the meaning of his dream. Then the cupbearer remembered Joseph and mentioned him to Pharaoh. Joseph was called before Pharaoh, who asked him to interpret the dream. Joseph told him that this ability was not his. It was God who would reveal the meaning of the dreams through Joseph. After hearing the dream, Joseph told Pharaoh that there would be seven years of abundant harvest. But then seven years of famine would come. Joseph counseled Pharaoh to save food during the seven years of plenty. Pharaoh told his people that everyone should listen to and obey Joseph. As a sign of authority, Pharaoh gave Joseph his ring and put him in charge of the entire land of Egypt.

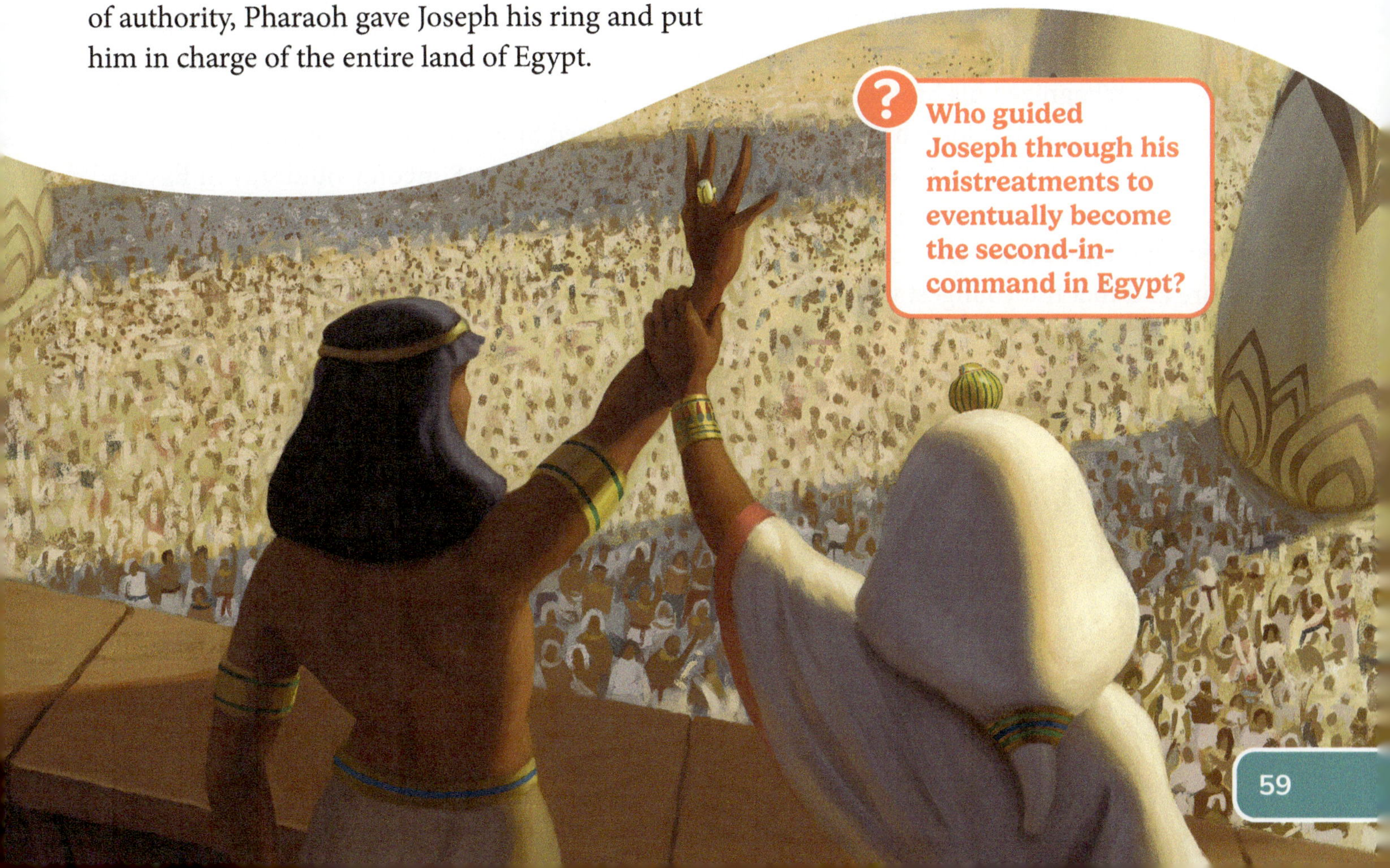

? Who guided Joseph through his mistreatments to eventually become the second-in-command in Egypt?

Joseph and Judah
PART 2

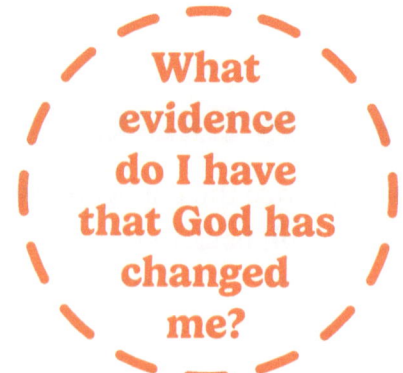

What evidence do I have that God has changed me?

Joseph's Brothers Go to Egypt

The famine affected the entire region, even beyond Egypt. Joseph's father and brothers in Canaan suffered as well. When they heard of the stored food in Egypt, Jacob sent his ten sons to Egypt to buy grain. Jacob kept Benjamin, Joseph's full brother, home. He didn't want any harm to come to him.

When the brothers came to Egypt, they had to meet with Joseph to buy grain. When they approached Joseph, they bowed before him with their faces to the ground. They didn't recognize him because he dressed and talked like an Egyptian. Joseph, however, recognized his brothers. Instead of selling them grain, Joseph accused them of being spies. The brothers explained that they were twelve sons of one man. They even mentioned that one brother was no more and that the youngest was at home. Joseph stuck to his accusation that they were spies and threw them into prison. He said they would not get out until the youngest brother came to Egypt.

But three days later, Joseph allowed nine of the brothers to return home with grain and instructed them not to return without their youngest brother. The brothers immediately felt guilty for having dealt so wrongly with Joseph many years before. Reuben said to his brothers, "Didn't I tell you not to sin against the boy? But you didn't listen. Now we have to pay for his blood." When Reuben said this, Joseph was standing nearby and could hear everything they were saying. He immediately went out and wept. He took one of the brothers named Simeon and tied him up in front of the others. Simeon would stay in Egypt while his brothers took food to their families and returned with the youngest brother.

Joseph's Brothers Return Home

Before Joseph's brothers left Egypt with their sacks of grain, Joseph had secretly commanded that their money be returned to them. When they stopped that night, they discovered their money was in their grain sacks. This made them fearful because Joseph had already accused them of being spies. This also made them look like thieves. They said, "What has God done to us?" The brothers told Jacob all that happened to them. He couldn't believe what was happening to him. He said, "You have taken my children from me. First Joseph, now Simeon, and you want to take Benjamin away from me as well."

But eventually, the grain ran low. Jacob told his sons to return to Egypt to buy more food. Judah reminded his father that Joseph had said he would not sell them more grain unless they brought Benjamin with them. Judah promised to bring Benjamin back safely and to bear the blame forever if anything happened to him. Jacob finally became desperate enough to allow Benjamin to go to Egypt with his brothers.

Joseph Reveals His Identity to His Brothers

When the brothers arrived in Egypt with Benjamin, Joseph requested a meal be prepared for them right away. The brothers were concerned that this may be a trap. They thought Joseph would accuse them of stealing the money they had found in their sacks. Joseph's servant assured them that God was working on their behalf and that there wasn't any misunderstanding—Joseph wanted the money to be given back. Joseph had Simeon taken out of prison. When Joseph arrived for the meal, all the brothers bowed to him and offered him the gifts from home that Jacob had sent. As the brothers sat at their places, they were amazed to see that they were seated by age, and Benjamin received five times more food than anyone else.

Finally, Joseph sent them on their way with plenty of grain in their sacks. He again returned their money to them in their sacks. But he had his own silver cup put in Benjamin's sack. As the eleven brothers traveled home, Joseph's messenger caught up to them, stopped them, and accused them of stealing the cup from Joseph's house. The brothers knew they had not done such a thing. To their horror, Joseph's messenger found the silver cup in Benjamin's sack. All the brothers tore their clothes in grief and despair. They were sure this was punishment for selling Joseph so many years before.

They all went back to Joseph and fell on the ground as they bowed before him. Judah told Joseph everything that had happened since their first trip to buy grain in Egypt. He made it clear that this situation had been extremely stressful for Jacob. Jacob was incredibly worried about Benjamin. Judah said, "My father is old, and his life is attached to the life of his son. If I return to him without Benjamin, he will die. I promised my father I would bring him back or bear the blame forever. Take me as your slave instead."

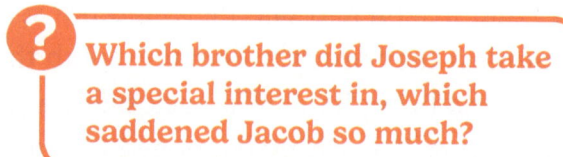

Which brother did Joseph take a special interest in, which saddened Jacob so much?

After hearing these words, Joseph could not hold back any longer. He said, "Clear the room." Everyone left except his brothers. But as Joseph wept for joy, everyone in Pharaoh's house could hear him. Joseph called for his brothers to come closer, then he shocked them with what he said next. "I am Joseph your brother!" They didn't know what to say because they did not understand what this meant for them. He said, "Do not worry! God sent me ahead to preserve the lives of our family. There are still five more years of famine to come. Go back home and get my father and bring him here. Here, we will provide for you and your families." Joseph cried as he hugged each of them, starting with Benjamin.

When Jacob learned that Joseph was alive, his spirit grew very strong. Jacob was so happy to see all the provisions his sons had brought back from Egypt, including the wagons to help him move there. He said, "My son Joseph is still alive. I will go see him before I die."

> **?** Why did God allow such trouble in the life of Joseph?

CHAPTER 5

God's Covenant with Israel

God Remembered and Sent a Prophet

Why can God be trusted to keep His promises?

FastFacts about

Exodus

Author: Moses
Date: 1425 BC
Theme: God faithfully fulfills His promises and graciously reveals Himself as God to His people. He is powerful, unlike false gods.
Meaning of *Exodus*: a road out

Interesting Facts:
- Second of the books of Moses
- Records the revelation of God's covenant name, the deliverance of Israel from Egypt, and the giving of the Ten Commandments

Pharaoh's Threats and God's Protection

Years passed after Jacob and his family moved to Egypt. The offspring of Jacob multiplied and became very large in number. They were now the people of Israel, or the Israelites. A new Pharaoh who did not know Joseph became king of Egypt. By this time, Israel filled the land. Pharaoh said, "We need to keep the Israelite nation from becoming larger. They may join our enemies, defeat us in battle, and run away." He decided to make them slaves. But the harder he made them work, the more baby Israelites were born. So Pharaoh told the Hebrew nurses to kill all the Israelite baby boys when they were born. However, the nurses feared God and let the baby boys live. Because Pharaoh's plan didn't work, he commanded his people to throw all the newborn Hebrew sons into the Nile River.

Moses Is Born and Grows Up

During this time, an Israelite woman gave birth to a boy. She hid her son, but after three months, he could no longer be hidden in her house. She made a waterproof basket, put her son in it, and placed it among the reeds near the riverbank. The baby's sister, Miriam, stayed nearby to watch what would happen to him. Pharaoh's daughter and her maids came to the river to bathe. She saw the basket among the reeds and sent a maid to get it. When Pharaoh's daughter looked in the basket, she said, "This is an Israelite baby." The baby cried pitifully, and she had compassion on him.

Miriam approached Pharaoh's daughter and asked, "Should I find an Israelite woman to take care of him for you?" Miriam brought her mother to Pharaoh's daughter. Moses' mother was paid to take care of the baby until he was older. Because he was taken out of the water, she named him Moses.

? How did Moses escape being killed as a newborn baby?

Who was Moses?

- The man God used to deliver His people from slavery in Egypt
- The mediator between God and the people of Israel
- The prophet who revealed God's laws and commands to Israel
- Had a uniquely close and personal relationship to God
- From the tribe of Levi
- His brother, Aaron, was the first high priest.
- Only viewed the Promised Land from a mountain but wasn't allowed to enter it

Moses grew up as the son of Pharaoh's daughter. But Moses hadn't forgotten he was an Israelite. One day when he was grown up, he saw an Egyptian beating an Israelite. Moses killed the Egyptian and buried his body in the sand. He thought no one saw what he did. But his fellow Hebrews were aware of what he did. When Pharaoh heard about it, he wanted Moses to be killed. Moses ran away to the land of Midian. At a well there, he defended some women who were being bullied while trying to water their flock. Their father heard of Moses' good deed and invited him to stay. Moses married one of the daughters, named Zipporah, and settled in Midian.

Israel Groans

The Pharaoh who wanted to kill Moses died. The new Pharaoh of Egypt kept the suffering Israelites as slaves. God heard the Israelites' cries. He remembered His covenant with Abraham, Isaac, and Jacob. In that covenant, God promised to bring Israel out of slavery and back to the land He had promised to Abraham.

Moses had now lived in Midian for forty years. He spent his days shepherding the flocks of his father-in-law, Jethro. One day, he saw a bush that was on fire. But the bush was not being burned by the fire. Moses moved closer to look at it. God called to him from out of the bush. "Moses, Moses. Do not come closer. This is holy ground; take off your shoes. I am the God of your father, the God of Abraham, the God of Isaac, and the God of Jacob." Moses was afraid to look at God, so he hid his face. God told Moses, "I see and hear My people's hardships, sorrows, and cries. I will rescue them and give them a land flowing with milk and honey. I will send you to Pharaoh, and you will lead My people out of Egypt. They will serve Me on this mountain."

Moses said to God, "If I go to the Israelites and tell them that I have met with the God of their fathers, they will ask me the name of this God. What should I tell them?"

God replied,

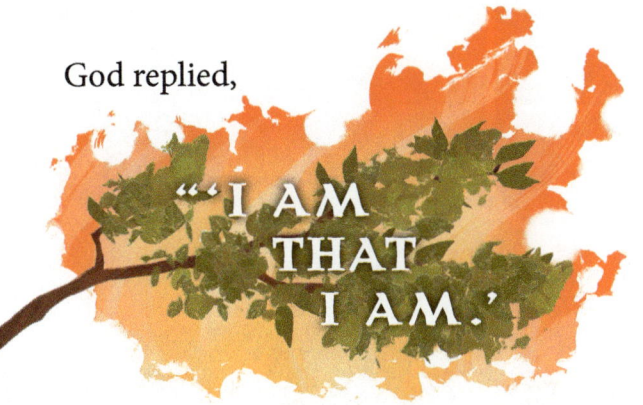

"'I AM THAT I AM.'

Tell Israel that 'I AM' has sent you. This is My name forever, and all generations of people should remember Me by this name. This is what My name 'Lord' means. Say to the king of Egypt, 'The Lord God of the Hebrews has met with us. Let us leave for three days to sacrifice to the Lord our God.' Pharaoh will refuse, and I will strike Egypt with all My wonders. When Pharaoh does finally free Israel, they will take the wealth of Egypt with them."

 **What is God's name?**

Bible Truths

90 What is the third commandment?
The third commandment is "Thou shalt not take the name of the Lord thy God in vain; for the Lord will not hold him guiltless that taketh his name in vain."
Exodus 20:7

91 What does the third commandment teach us?
The third commandment teaches us to reverence God's name, Word, and works.
Psalm 138:1–2 • Matthew 6:9
Revelation 15:3–4 • Genesis 1:26
Ephesians 4:24 • Colossians 3:10

Moses Returns to Egypt

Moses still did not want to return to Egypt. "They will not believe me or do what I say," he told God. "They won't believe that you talked with me."

God performed two signs to overcome Moses' fear and lack of faith. These signs would also help the Israelites believe Moses' message. First, Moses' rod became a snake. But when he obeyed God's command to pick it up by its tail, it became his rod again.

Next, God told Moses to tuck his hand into his robe. When he pulled it out, it was diseased. God had him do this again, and this time the disease disappeared. God said, "If after these two signs the people still don't believe, take water from the river, and it will turn into blood when you pour it out onto the dry ground."

Moses' next excuse for not obeying was that he had difficulty speaking clearly. God rebuked him. "I made man's mouth. Now, go. I will help you speak." But God was angry with Moses' doubting. God told him that his brother back in Egypt, Aaron, would help him.

Moses and his family started the journey to Egypt. God had Aaron meet Moses on the way to Egypt. Moses informed Aaron of everything God had told him. When they arrived in Egypt, Moses and Aaron called together the elders of Israel. They believed the words of God and the signs Moses showed them.

What was Israel's first response to God's words and Moses' signs?

Pharaoh's Hard Heart and God's Glory

How does the Lord show Himself to be the only true God?

When the Israelites heard about God's coming deliverance, they bowed their heads and worshiped Him. Moses and Aaron went straight to Pharaoh and told him that the God of the Hebrews wanted His people to go out into the wilderness and worship Him. Pharaoh refused. He asked, "Who is the Lord, that I should obey His voice to let Israel go? I know not the Lord, neither will I let Israel go." Pharaoh then told the taskmasters to make the Israelites work harder. The Israelites cried out as a result. Moses complained to God because the situation got worse, not better.

God told Moses to say to the people, "I will cause Pharaoh to drive Israel out of Egypt. I gave the patriarchs my covenant promise. I promised Israel the land of Canaan. I said, 'You will be my people, and I will be your God.' I will keep my promises. I will deliver you powerfully from the hardships you face from the Egyptians. Then you will know that I am the Lord your God." But the people didn't listen to Moses because they were worried Pharaoh would punish them again. God told Moses, "Go talk with Pharaoh so he frees my people."

But Moses was also discouraged. He said, "If the Israelites don't listen to me, will the king of Egypt do what I say?"

? What did Pharaoh ask about God?

The First Nine Plagues

"You and your brother will be my representatives before Pharaoh," God told Moses. "Tell Pharaoh what I say. I will harden his heart and will do more signs and wonders in the land. But Pharaoh will not listen to you, and my hand will be against Egypt. I will use powerful judgments to free my people. The Egyptians will know that I am the Lord."

God's judgments against Pharaoh came as a series of ten plagues. At the beginning of each plague, Moses would demand that Pharaoh let the Lord's people go. When Pharaoh would refuse, the plague would come upon Egypt. As the plagues would become worse, Pharaoh would beg Moses to pray to the Lord to take the plague away, and he would promise to let the people go. Moses would do so, but Pharaoh's heart would be hard, and he would not keep his word to free Israel.

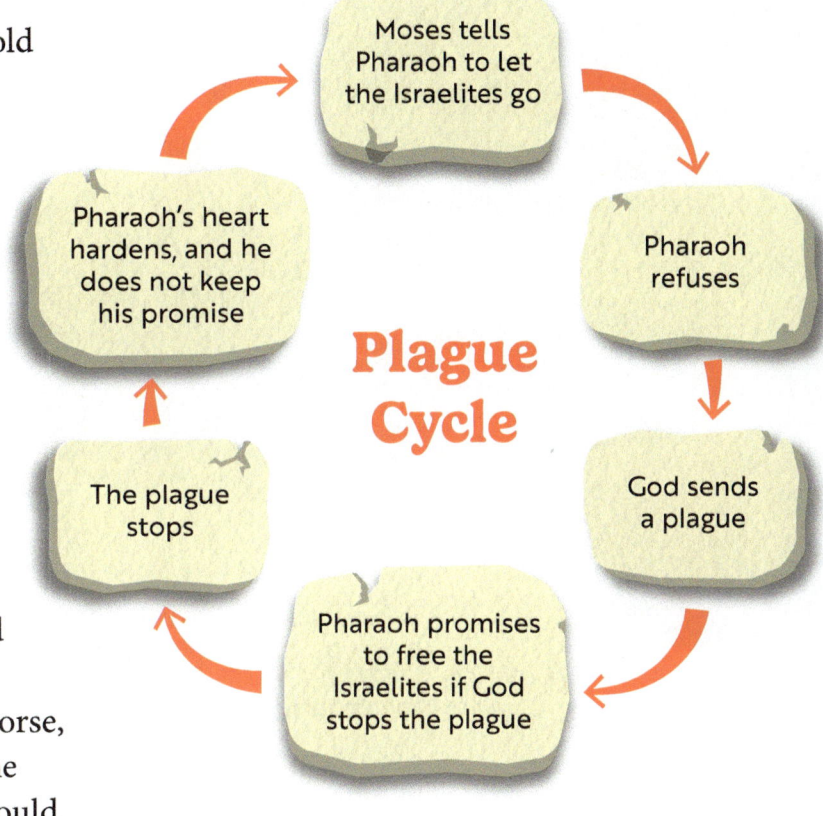

Plague Cycle
- Moses tells Pharaoh to let the Israelites go
- Pharaoh refuses
- God sends a plague
- Pharaoh promises to free the Israelites if God stops the plague
- The plague stops
- Pharaoh's heart hardens, and he does not keep his promise

For the first plague, God turned the Nile River and all the water that could be easily found in Egypt into blood. All the fish in the Nile River died. To find any clean water to drink, people had to dig wells. However, Pharaoh's heart was hard and he would not listen to Moses and Aaron, as the Lord had said.

In the second plague, God filled Egypt with frogs. They were everywhere, even in people's beds and in their food. Pharaoh told Moses, "Ask God to take away the frogs, then I will let Israel go worship the Lord." Moses did just that, but Pharaoh hardened his heart, as the Lord had said, and he did not free the people of Israel.

God sent the third plague, which was lice. The very dust of the ground became lice. They infected every person and animal in Egypt. Yet Pharaoh's heart was still hard, as the Lord had said.

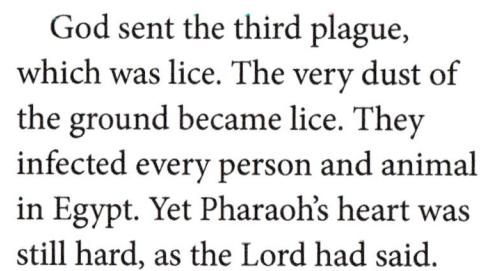

Next, as the fourth plague, God sent thick, terrible swarms of flies. This time, the plague came only to the Egyptians. The section in Egypt where the Israelites lived did not receive this plague. Pharaoh begged for the plague to be taken away. But as soon as the flies were gone, he hardened his heart and didn't let the Israelites leave, as the Lord had said.

The fifth plague was a disease that killed only the Egyptians' large farm animals. Still, Pharaoh's heart was hard, just as the Lord had said.

For the sixth plague, God put painful boils on the Egyptians and their animals. The Lord hardened Pharaoh's heart and he didn't listen to Moses, as the Lord had said.

For the seventh plague, God sent the worst hailstorm Egypt had ever seen. The hail was mixed with fire and fell only in the land of the Egyptians. The trees were destroyed, as were the crops that were growing. Any person or animal caught outside was killed by the hail. Pharaoh finally repented, so Moses stretched out his hands to the Lord and the storm stopped. But when Pharaoh saw that the hailstorm had stopped, he sinned and hardened his heart.

The eighth plague was locusts. God covered Egypt with so many locusts that the ground couldn't be seen. They ate up the crops that had grown after the hailstorm. This time, Pharaoh said that he had sinned against God. But as soon as God removed the locust, God hardened Pharaoh's heart, and he would not let the Israelites go.

The ninth plague was pitch-black darkness. This darkness remained in Egypt for three days, but the Israelites had light where they lived. As in the previous plague, Pharaoh tried to bargain with Moses. He told him that they could go worship God, but they had to let their animals stay in Egypt. Moses refused, the Lord hardened Pharaoh's heart, and Pharaoh angrily sent Moses away. Pharaoh threatened to kill Moses if he saw his face again.

? What did God's judgments teach the Egyptians?

The Passover and the Tenth Plague

The tenth and final plague would hurt the Egyptians the most. God would kill all the firstborn children and animals at midnight. From Pharaoh's family to the family of the poorest slave girl, every Egyptian home would suffer a loss of life. This would produce the loudest and saddest weeping ever known in Egypt.

God told the Israelites to remember this night and celebrate it as a special date from this time forward. It was to be known as Passover. God directed every Israelite home to choose a spotless, one-year-old male lamb from its flock. God told them to kill the lamb at sunset and then take the blood of the lamb and apply it to the three doorposts of their front door. They were then to roast the meat and eat it as a meal with unleavened bread and bitter herbs. There wasn't enough time to let the bread rise. They were to eat the meal while all dressed and ready to leave Egypt. After the meal, they were to burn any of the leftovers.

When the Lord passed through Egypt at midnight, He would pass over the houses that had the lamb's blood on the doorposts. In those houses, the firstborn would not be killed. However, there was great horror in the homes where the firstborn died. Death—the death of the firstborn and of cattle—came upon every Egyptian house. Pharaoh sent a message to Moses while it was still night, telling Israel to take all they had and leave immediately.

God led the Israelites out of Egypt toward the Red Sea. Moses took the bones of Joseph with him. This is because, long ago, Joseph had asked his sons to bury his bones in the land God promised to the patriarchs. God was with the people as they left. He led them with a cloud during the day and with a pillar of fire at night.

? Why did God kill the firstborns in Egypt?

? What was the most hurtful plague?

? How did the Israelites avoid the death of the firstborn?

Walking between Walls of Water

After the Israelites had left, the Lord hardened Pharaoh's heart one last time. Pharaoh took his army and went after the Israelites. The Israelites were afraid because they were trapped between Pharaoh's army and the Red Sea. Moses told the Israelites, "Today you will see the salvation of the Lord. The Lord will fight for you, and you will never see these Egyptians again."

God told Moses, "Raise your rod, and the waters of the sea will divide. Israel will walk through the sea on dry ground. When you get to the other side, raise your hand. The waters will return to their place in the sea and drown the Egyptian army." God did just as He said. God's power caused the Israelites to fear and believe the Lord and Moses.

The Israelites Complain after Deliverance

How do my words show what is in my heart?

After God's amazing deliverance from Egypt through the Red Sea, the Israelites walked for three days without water. When they finally found water, it was bitter and they couldn't drink it. The people grumbled against Moses, saying, "What should we drink?"

Moses prayed, and God performed another miracle. God had Moses throw part of a tree into the water to make it good for drinking. Through this test, God made a rule for the Israelites. He told them, "If you listen to the Lord, do what He says is right, and obey all of His commands, I won't cause you to suffer any of the diseases I punished the Egyptians with. I am the Lord, your healer."

For a little while, Israel rested in Elim by twelve springs of water and under seventy palm trees. But then, God led them to a wilderness where they complained again. They were hungry and there was nothing to eat. They said they would rather have been slaves in Egypt and died in Egypt where they had food. They accused Moses and Aaron. "You brought us here to kill us!"

But God was testing their hearts. He sent them bread from heaven to see if they would obey His commands. Each day, they were to gather just enough bread for one day. But on the sixth day, they were to gather enough bread for two days. Moses and Aaron said, "In the evening, you will know that God brought you out of Egypt. In the morning, you will see the glory of the Lord." In this way, God would teach Israel that they did not live by bread alone, but by the Word of God.

? What was God doing to the Israelites by providing water and manna the way He did?

The Purpose of the Law for Israel

How can God's people bless the world?

The children of Israel reached the desert of Sinai. Moses went up Mount Sinai to speak with God. God said, "Tell the children of Israel, 'You have seen what I did to the Egyptians and how I carried you on eagle's wings to myself. If you obey me and keep my covenant, you will be a special treasure to me, like no other group of people. You will be a kingdom of priests and a holy nation.'"

possible location of Mount Sinai

Bible Truth

46 **What did God give Israel in the Mosaic Covenant?**

God gave Israel a law so that they could live wisely in their land and draw other nations to worship God.

Exodus 19:1–6
Deuteronomy 4:1–14

Moses came back down to the elders of Israel and told them what God had said. All the people replied together, "We will do all that God has spoken." God told Moses to prepare the people for His coming. He was going to come down on Mount Sinai. The top of the mountain was wrapped in smoke because God descended in fire. The mountain shook, there were trumpet sounds, and there was thunder and lightning. No one was to touch the mountain. If they did, they would die.

? **How could Israel be a kingdom of priests and a holy nation to God?**

The Ten Commandments

What does obedience to God's law look like?

God spoke so all the people could hear Him, "I am the Lord your God, who brought you out of Egypt, the land of captivity." Then He gave them the Ten Commandments.

I   "Do not have any other gods before Me."
II "Do not make, bow down to, or serve any idols."
III "Do not use God's name in vain."
IV "Keep the Sabbath day holy."
V   "Honor your father and mother."
VI "Do not murder."
VII "Do not commit adultery."
VIII "Do not steal."
IX "Do not lie to your neighbor."
X   "Do not covet what is not yours."

Immediately after God spoke, there was more thunder and lightning, fire and smoke, and the sound of a trumpet. The people were so afraid of hearing God's voice and seeing the spectacular scene on top of the mountain that they thought they were going to die. Moses assured the people that God was testing them. God wanted them to fear Him so they would not sin. The people stayed far away, but Moses was hidden from their sight as he went in closer to God at the top of the mountain. There, he received more commandments and laws.

CHAPTER

6

Israel Breaks God's Law

Symbolism of the Tabernacle

God gave Moses detailed plans for the tabernacle. He also gave the design for the items to be placed in and around the tabernacle. The word *tabernacle* means "dwelling place." It symbolized God's presence among the people. God's presence also partly restored the fellowship between God and humanity that was lost in the Garden of Eden.

How can I approach God?

Even so, barriers were made in the tabernacle to keep people from the holy places. Though God was near, these barriers showed that people still had to stay distant from God because of their sin.

The curtain of the holy of holies had golden cherubim woven into it. This brought to mind the cherubim that kept Adam and Eve away from the Garden of Eden and the tree of life after the Fall.

THE TABERNACLE

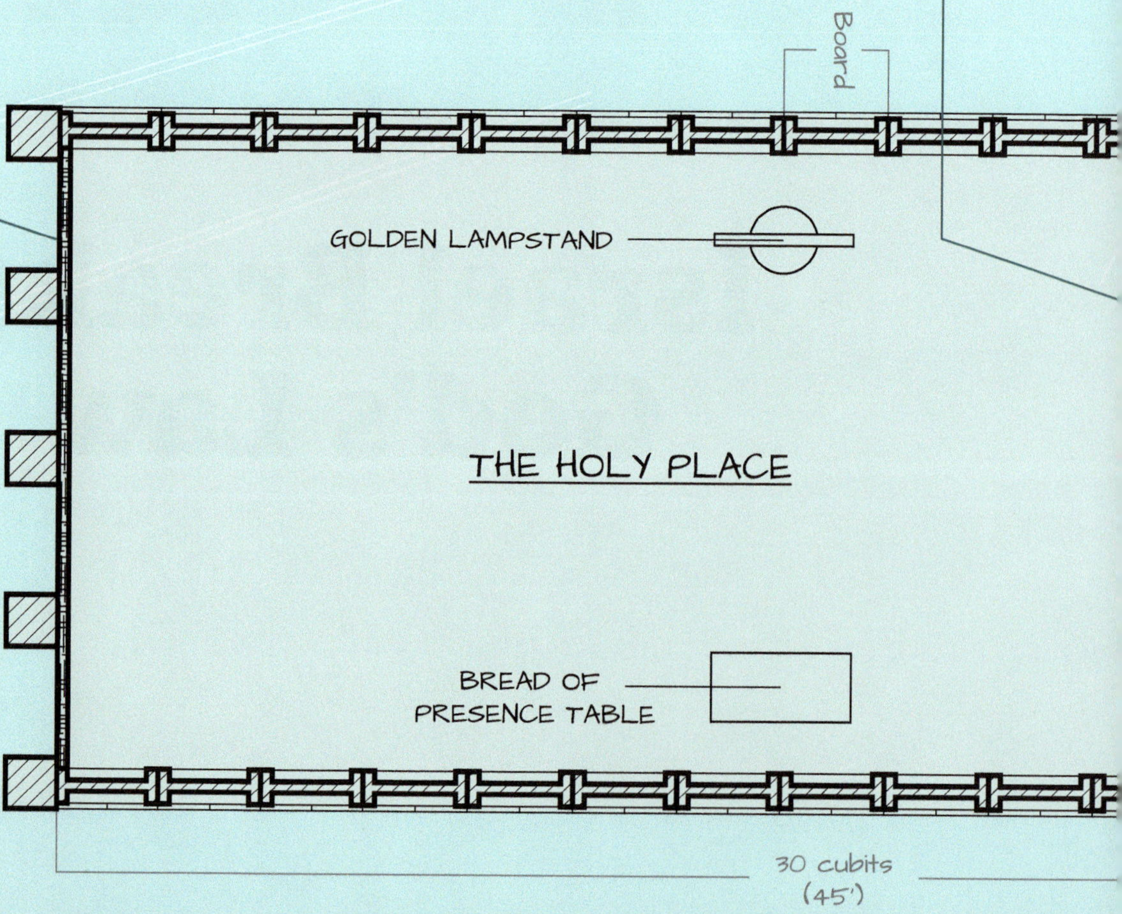

GOLDEN LAMPSTAND

THE HOLY PLACE

BREAD OF PRESENCE TABLE

30 cubits (45')

ARK OF THE COVENANT

The ark of the covenant was the most sacred piece of furniture in the tabernacle. It was built of fine wood and covered with gold, inside and out. The ark was hidden behind heavy curtains in the holy of holies, a room that was a perfect cube. The ark represented the throne of God and His presence with His people. On top of the ark was the mercy seat, which showed two golden angels facing each other. They were looking down and spreading their wings over the mercy seat. The mercy seat symbolized how God was on the throne between the angels.

Once a year, the high priest went into the holy of holies. With great care, he sprinkled the blood of the **atonement** on the mercy seat to atone for the sins of all the people. This was all to **foreshadow** Jesus shedding His own blood as a payment for the sins of mankind. When Jesus cried "It is finished," the curtain which hid the ark was torn in two. This showed that Christ Himself is the only person who could once and for all time atone for the sins of mankind. Only He could do this because only He is perfect and sinless.

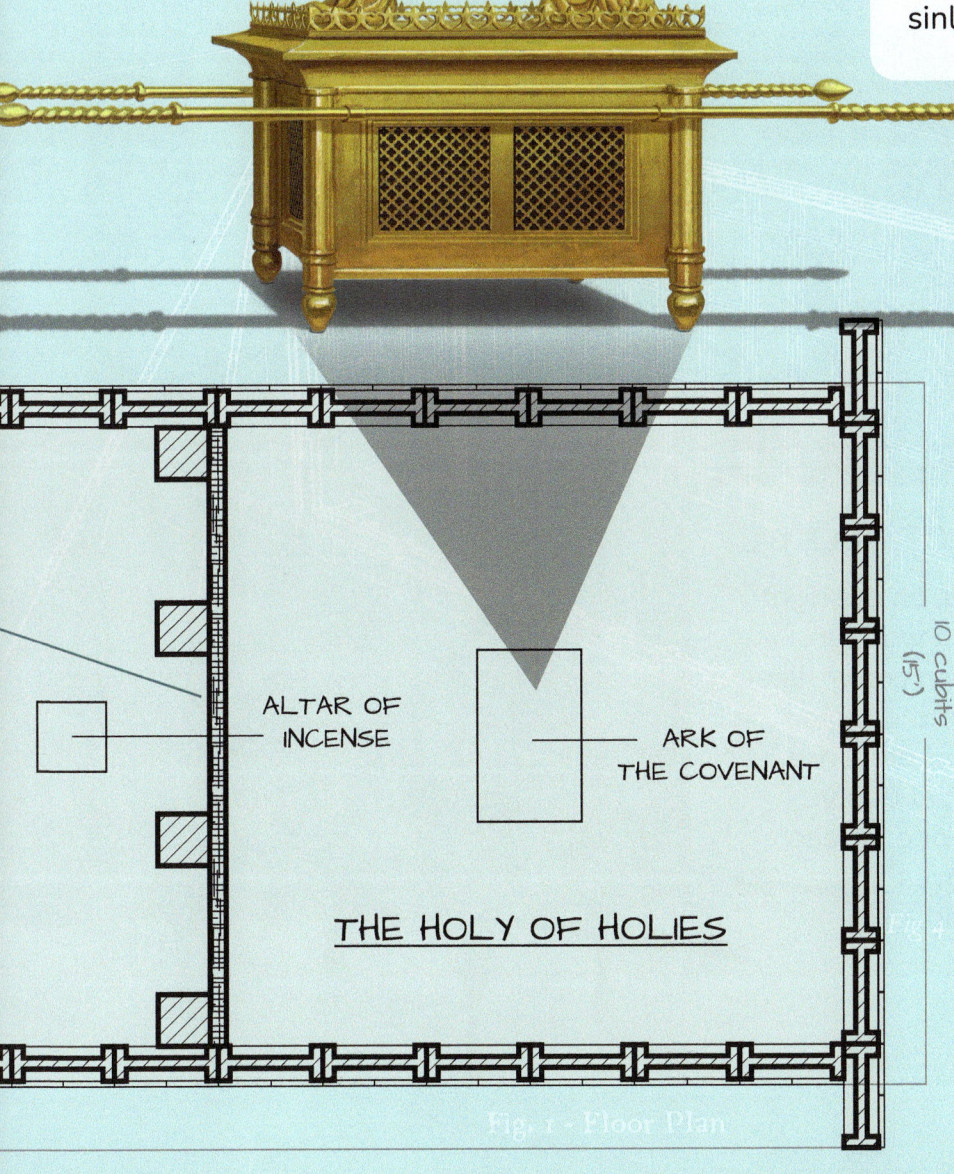

key terms

atonement
Atonement is making things right with God through a sacrifice for the sin that separates the sinner from God.

foreshadow
To foreshadow is to give a hint of something that is coming but has not yet been fully explained or revealed.

? What is foreshadowing?

GOLDEN LAMPSTAND

On the left wall of the tabernacle was a lampstand made of pure gold. Craftsmen formed the gold to resemble seven branches of an olive tree and their blossoms. A small oil lamp was placed on top of each branch. It was placed in the tabernacle's outer room, called the holy place.

The lampstand symbolized the tree of life. It showed that God was graciously providing a way for His people to have eternal life. The light from the seven blossoms on the lampstand also foreshadowed Jesus. Jesus would one day say that He is the Light of the World, and whoever follows Him will not live in darkness, but will have the light of God's life in them.

BREAD OF PRESENCE TABLE

Across from the lampstand, on the right wall of the holy place, stood a wooden table covered in gold. A golden crown-like design ran along the edges of the table. This table was for the bread of presence. Once a week, the priests placed twelve loaves of bread on the table, one for each tribe of Israel. The twelve loaves represented the people of God in the presence of God.

ALTAR OF INCENSE

The altar of incense* measured about one and a half feet wide on each side and three feet high. It was covered in gold and placed in front of the curtain to the holy of holies. The high priest burned incense on the altar both morning and evening. The smoke of the incense rising from the altar symbolized the prayers of God's people rising to the Father. The altar is a foreshadowing of the Lord's **intercession** for His church. We learn in the New Testament that Jesus intercedes continually for believers before the Father. His intercession is just like the incense burned continually before the holy of holies.

> **key term**
>
> ### intercession
>
> Intercession means to plead on behalf of another person. Jesus intercedes before the Father on behalf of God's children who approach the Father.

THE CURTAINS AND WALLS

The tabernacle had three large curtains. The first was called the gate of the court. This curtain was the only entrance into the courtyard where sacrifices were made. The second curtain separated the inside of the tabernacle from the activity and sacrifices in the courtyard. The third curtain separated the holy place from the holy of holies. This curtain was beautifully colored in blue, scarlet, and purple, and magnificent images of cherubim were sewn into the curtain. The first covering for the tabernacle was made of goat's hair. The second and third coverings were made of ram and goat skins. These coverings hid the inner curtain of the holy of holies from view. The boards that made up the walls were made of fine wood covered with gold.

 What did the tabernacle represent?

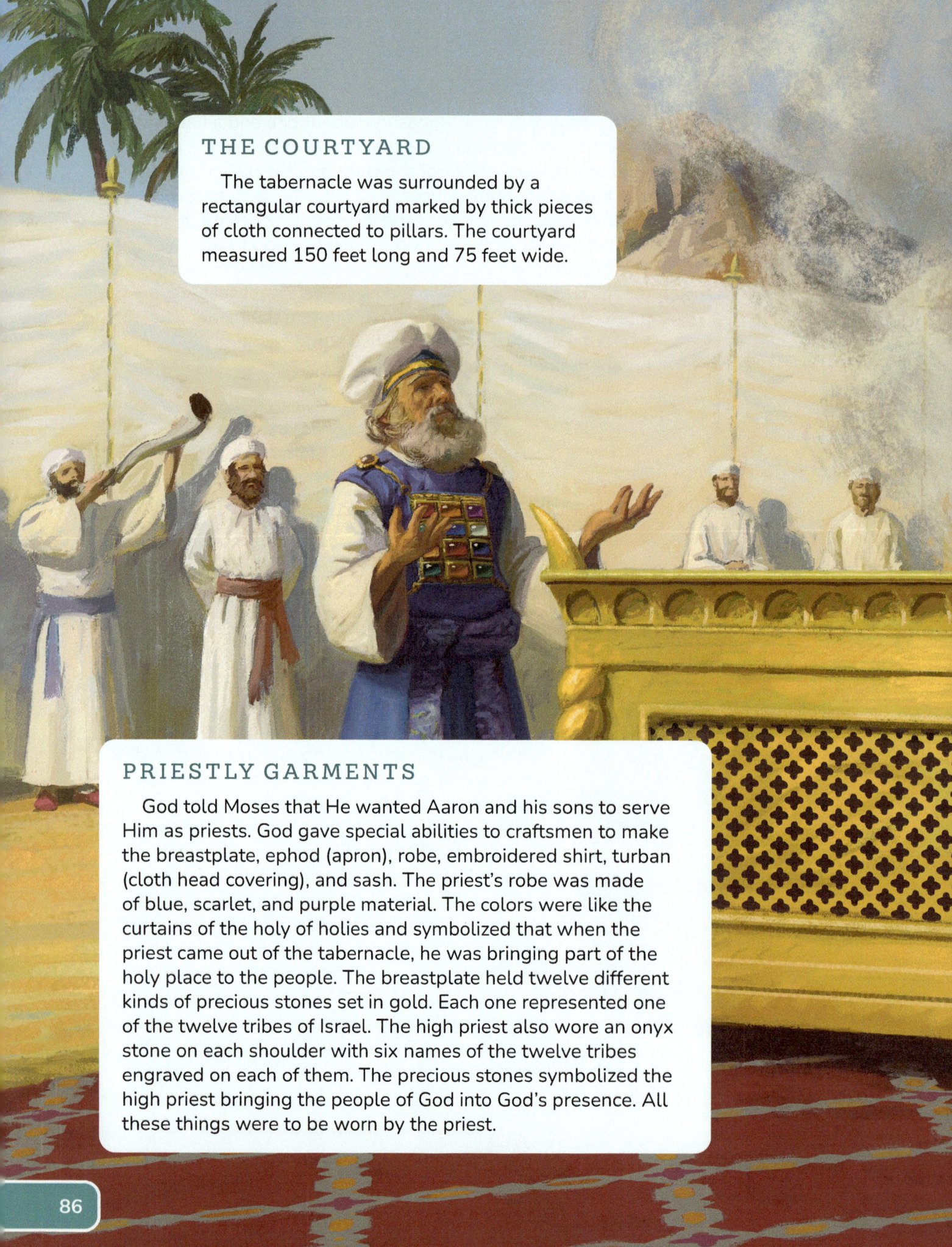

THE COURTYARD

The tabernacle was surrounded by a rectangular courtyard marked by thick pieces of cloth connected to pillars. The courtyard measured 150 feet long and 75 feet wide.

PRIESTLY GARMENTS

God told Moses that He wanted Aaron and his sons to serve Him as priests. God gave special abilities to craftsmen to make the breastplate, ephod (apron), robe, embroidered shirt, turban (cloth head covering), and sash. The priest's robe was made of blue, scarlet, and purple material. The colors were like the curtains of the holy of holies and symbolized that when the priest came out of the tabernacle, he was bringing part of the holy place to the people. The breastplate held twelve different kinds of precious stones set in gold. Each one represented one of the twelve tribes of Israel. The high priest also wore an onyx stone on each shoulder with six names of the twelve tribes engraved on each of them. The precious stones symbolized the high priest bringing the people of God into God's presence. All these things were to be worn by the priest.

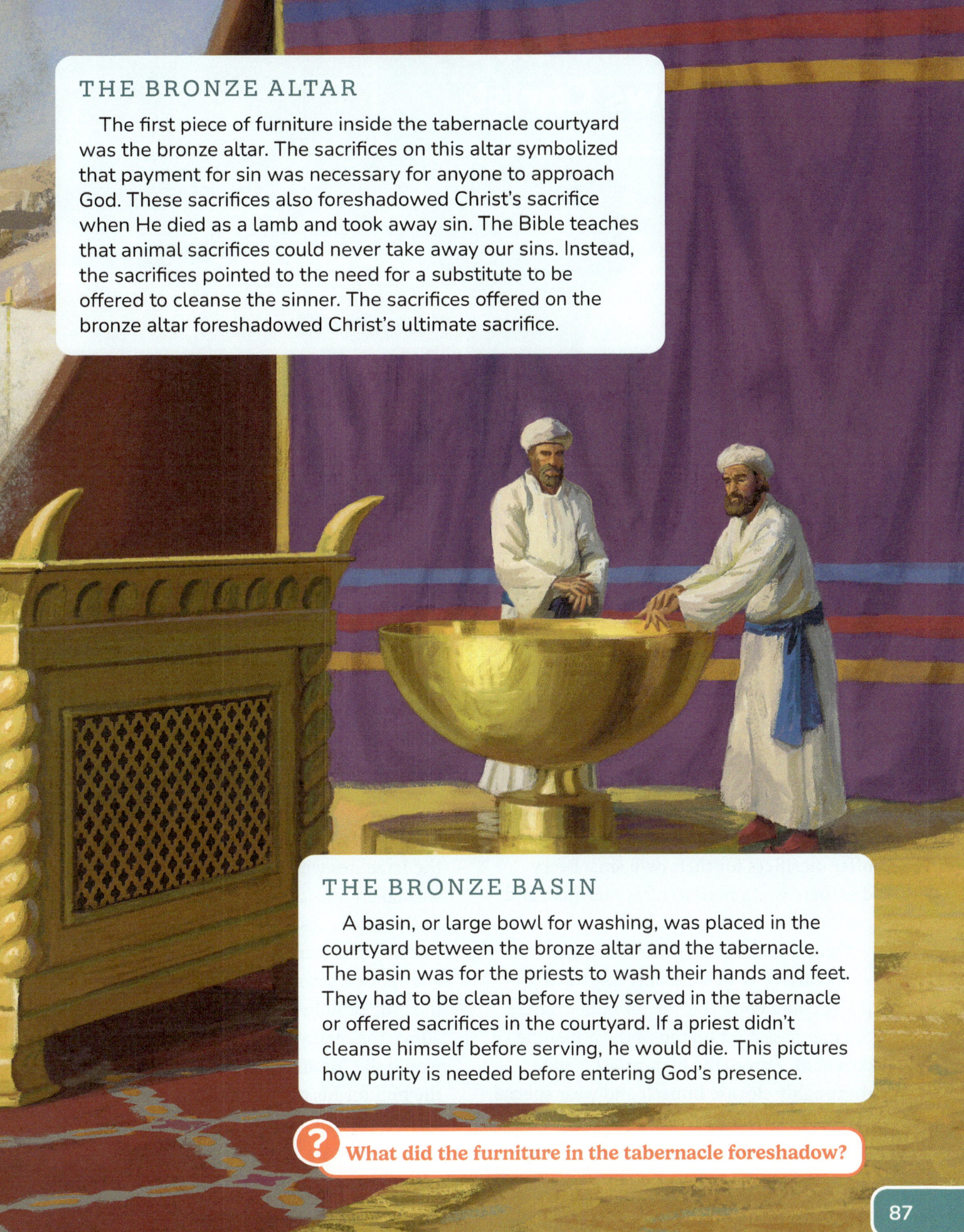

THE BRONZE ALTAR

The first piece of furniture inside the tabernacle courtyard was the bronze altar. The sacrifices on this altar symbolized that payment for sin was necessary for anyone to approach God. These sacrifices also foreshadowed Christ's sacrifice when He died as a lamb and took away sin. The Bible teaches that animal sacrifices could never take away our sins. Instead, the sacrifices pointed to the need for a substitute to be offered to cleanse the sinner. The sacrifices offered on the bronze altar foreshadowed Christ's ultimate sacrifice.

THE BRONZE BASIN

A basin, or large bowl for washing, was placed in the courtyard between the bronze altar and the tabernacle. The basin was for the priests to wash their hands and feet. They had to be clean before they served in the tabernacle or offered sacrifices in the courtyard. If a priest didn't cleanse himself before serving, he would die. This pictures how purity is needed before entering God's presence.

? **What did the furniture in the tabernacle foreshadow?**

Tabernacle Worship Foreshadows Christ

What does the tabernacle have to do with Jesus?

Fast Facts about

Leviticus

Author: Moses
Date: 1444 BC
Theme: The holiness of God and His desire for a holy people
Meaning of *Leviticus*: Matters of the Levites

Interesting Facts:
- It's referenced over fifteen times in the New Testament.
- Over ninety percent of Leviticus is in the form of direct speech from God.

Tabernacle worship foreshadowed Christ's coming. Every part of the tabernacle, even the sacrifices and priestly duties, pointed to Jesus' work on the cross to redeem sinners. The tabernacle showed that God cannot be approached without a blood sacrifice. God's holy and righteous presence is seen in every part of the tabernacle. The priests, who were dressed in clean and special clothes, helped present a sinful and unclean people to the holy and righteous God. But the priests also had to offer sacrifices for their own sins. Every day there was a need to offer sacrifices and perform ceremonies.

Once a year, the Day of Atonement would arrive. It was the only day the high priest could enter the holy of holies. There the mercy seat sat on top of the ark of the covenant. Aaron, the high priest, had to thoroughly cleanse himself and wear special clothes that he only wore on this day. He would offer a bull for his own sins. Then two goats were selected. One goat was offered as a sin offering for the people of Israel. Aaron put his hands on the second goat as a way of showing that the sins of the Israelites were being put on it. This goat was taken outside of the camp and released in the wilderness. This showed how the people's sins were removed from them. Aaron took smoky incense with him into the holy of holies so he couldn't see the area above the mercy seat clearly; otherwise, he would die. He first sprinkled the blood of the bull for his own sins on the mercy seat. Then he sprinkled the blood of the goat on the mercy seat.

Christ's Perfect and Final Sacrifice

John the Baptist called Jesus "the Lamb of God who takes away the sin of the world." John knew that the lambs sacrificed in the Old Testament foreshadowed when Jesus would offer Himself as a sacrifice on the cross. He was the perfect Lamb who came to be the ultimate sacrifice for our sins. Every animal that was killed pictured the seriousness of sin. Every animal that was killed foreshadowed Christ's perfect sacrifice, in which He took the place of the guilty sinner. The holy wrath of God had to be satisfied. Christ's perfect life, death, and victorious resurrection accomplishes that for all who place their faith in Him. Isaiah 53 spoke of God's plan to crush Christ for the sin of condemned and lost sinners. Israel's worship in the tabernacle foreshadowed God's glorious rescue plan for sinners through Christ.

Bible Truths

54 How is Christ the Priest?
Christ offered Himself as the sacrifice for our sin and intercedes with the Father for us.

Romans 3:25–26
Hebrews 2:17; 7:25–27

59 What is the atonement?
The atonement is Christ's satisfying divine justice by His sufferings and death in the place of sinners.

Romans 3:23–26; 5:8–11
1 Peter 3:18

The Golden Calf
MOSES INTERCEDES FOR ISRAEL

> Who can protect me from the punishment I deserve?

The People Turn to Idols

While God was speaking with Moses at the top of the mountain, the people below became restless. It had been forty days since anyone in the camp had seen or heard from Moses. They went to Aaron and said, "Make us a god to lead us." Aaron quickly gave in to the people. He said, "Bring me golden earrings from your wives and children." They brought the gold, and Aaron made a golden calf. He declared, "This is your god who brought you out of Egypt. Tomorrow is a feast to the Lord." The people of Israel got up early the next day to offer sacrifices and peace offerings to the golden calf. They feasted while worshiping the idol.

Moses Intercedes for the People

God told Moses to go back down the mountain because the people had sinned greatly against the Lord. He saw them worshiping the idol and heard their songs to a god made with their own hands. God told Moses, "Leave me alone so my anger may burn against the people. I am going to destroy these people and make a great nation from your descendants."

? When God saw Israel sinning with the golden calf, what did He say He was going to do?

Moses interceded for the people by saying, "Oh, Lord! Remember the promises you made to Abraham, Isaac, and Jacob, that you would make their descendants a great nation and give them this land. You are the God who keeps your promises. If you destroy your people, the Egyptians will think you brought them out of Egypt just to kill them." God listened to Moses' prayer and did not destroy the people.

Moses was furious when he saw the Israelites dancing around the golden calf! He was holding the two stone tablets on which God had written His laws. In anger and frustration, Moses threw the tablets down and broke them. He took the golden calf, melted it, ground it up, and dumped it in the water. He made the people drink the water. Moses went to Aaron and asked, "How did these people get you to make this calf?"

Aaron replied, "The people wondered what happened to you. I told them to bring their golden earrings. I threw the earrings into the fire, and out came this calf."

Moses shouted, "Whoever is on the Lord's side, come to me." The tribe of Levi stood with Moses. They then went through the camp and killed three thousand men who would not turn from the evil they had done.

Even though God was not going to destroy the people and begin again with him, Moses knew that God would still judge the people for their sin. Moses told them, "You have sinned greatly. Now I will go to the Lord. Perhaps I can make atonement for you." Moses went back up the mountain and confessed that the people had sinned greatly. He told God he was willing to face eternal death so the people could be forgiven. But the Lord told Moses that he could not die for the sin of the people. But as a punishment, God sent a plague on Israel.

? How did Moses respond to God's intentions to destroy Israel?

God then told Moses to lead the people to the Promised Land, a land flowing with milk and honey. But because of their sin, God said He would not go with the people. If He went with sinful people, He would consume them. God would send an angel before them to defeat the Canaanites. The people would get the land, but they would not have God with them. When the people heard this devastating news, they began to mourn.

Moses called out to the Lord, pleading with Him to come with them into the land. The Lord said, "My presence will go with you, and I will give you rest." Moses then asked the Lord to show him His glory. The Lord promised to make His goodness pass before Moses. The next morning, He called Moses up to the mountain. He passed before him and declared, "The Lord, The Lord God, merciful and gracious, longsuffering, and abundant in goodness and truth, keeping mercy for thousands, forgiving iniquity and transgression and sin, and that will by no means clear the guilty." Moses worshiped the Lord there and prayed for God to forgive His people.

God then renewed the covenant that the people had broken. He also wrote the commandments on the stones again. After forty days, Moses returned to the camp. The people were afraid of him because the glory of God continued to shine on his face, so Moses covered his head and gave God's Word to the people.

Bible Truth

61 **What is Christ doing for us now in heaven?**
Christ is at the right hand of the Father interceding for believers.

Acts 7:55 • Hebrews 4:14–16; 7:25

Spying Out the Land

Why is it hard to trust God sometimes?

FastFacts about

Numbers

Author: Moses
Date: 1406 BC
Theme: God's promises to Abraham being fulfilled
Meaning of *Numbers*: Comes from numbering the people

Interesting Facts:
- The first numbering of the men of war to enter Canaan was 603,550.
- At the end of their 40 years of wandering for failing to trust God, the number of the men of war had decreased to 601,730.

Forgetting God's Faithfulness

God brought Israel from Egypt with mighty wonders. This matched up with the promises He made to Abraham, Isaac, and Jacob. He promised to give their descendants the land of Canaan. On the way to Canaan, God took care of every need. When they were in the wilderness, God gave them food and water. Their sandals didn't even wear out. They saw the blessings of God day after day. They had seen God's faithfulness repeatedly. But instead of being thankful, they complained. They forgot that God could be trusted to faithfully meet their needs and fulfill His promises to bring them into the land.

Who was Joshua?

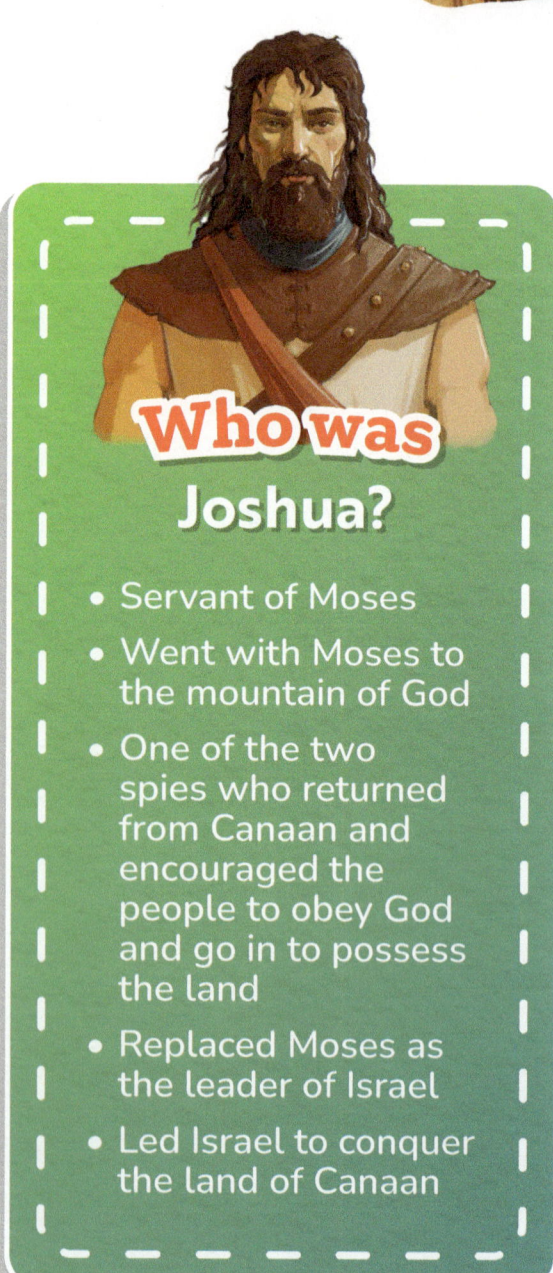

- Servant of Moses
- Went with Moses to the mountain of God
- One of the two spies who returned from Canaan and encouraged the people to obey God and go in to possess the land
- Replaced Moses as the leader of Israel
- Led Israel to conquer the land of Canaan

Weak in Faith

Two years after they left Egypt, God led the Israelites close to the land of Canaan. To prepare for the battles they would have to fight in the land, Moses sent twelve men to spy out the land. Before they went, Moses said, "Spy out the land. See if the people of the land are weak or strong and if there are few or many. Discover whether they dwell in tents or strong cities. Also, find out if the land produces good crops." Moses also told them to bring back some of the fruit of the land.

The Promised Land was abundant with pomegranates and figs. The spies even gathered one cluster of grapes so large that two men had to carry it on a pole between them. All that the land could produce was amazing to see. But the spies were also driven to fear by the great walled cities and giants that they saw. All the spies except Joshua and Caleb came back discouraged and convinced they could not take the land. Ten spies told the people, "We found the land flowing with milk and honey just as we have been told. But there are great walled cities and giants in the land."

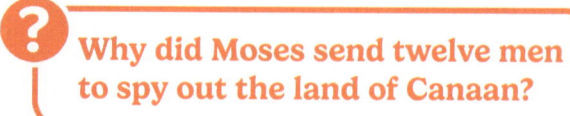

Why did Moses send twelve men to spy out the land of Canaan?

Joshua and Caleb disagreed with the report of the ten spies. They stood and said to all the people, "Let's go into the land and possess it. Surely the Lord will give it into our hands as He has promised."

The ten spies argued, "The people of the land are mightier and stronger than we are. It will be impossible to defeat them. How could we even dream of defeating the giants? Compared to them, we were like grasshoppers, and that is how they would see us. No, we cannot take the land."

The people wept that night. They began to grumble against Moses and Aaron, saying, "Why are we even here? It would have been better to die in Egypt or in the wilderness. That would have been better than having our wives and children become slaves in this land. Let's appoint a new leader and return to Egypt."

God's Judgment

Moses and Aaron fell on their faces and prayed for the people. Joshua and Caleb tore their clothes in great sorrow and cried out to the people, "The land is a good and fruitful land. If the Lord delights in us, He will certainly bring us into it. Don't rebel against the Lord. Though the people of the land are mighty, God is with us, and He has taken away any protection they have."

The people wouldn't listen and were ready to stone Joshua and Caleb. At this moment, the glory of the Lord appeared in the tabernacle in the sight of all Israel. God said to Moses, "These people have seen my signs and wonders over and over. I am angry at their disobedience. How long will it be until these rebels believe me? I'll send a plague to destroy them."

Moses fell on his face and asked God, "Why should the Egyptians be able to say You killed these people because You couldn't bring them into the land? Please forgive them and show Your power. Bring them into the land."

The Lord did not destroy the people. However, because of their lack of faith, God did judge the nation of Israel. Everyone twenty years old or older would not be allowed to go into Canaan because they didn't believe God. The ten spies who discouraged the people from following God died of a plague. Israel, who believed the report of the faithless spies, had to spend forty more years in the wilderness. That generation's children would inherit the land, but they wouldn't.

> **?** Why did the generation that left Egypt not get to inherit the Promised Land?

Moses Lifted Up a Serpent in the Wilderness

How can I be saved from my sin?

Israel Complains against God

Israel again grumbled and complained against God and Moses, saying, "Why did you bring us out of Egypt to die in the wilderness? There is no food or water, and we hate the manna God gives us."

God sent deadly serpents into the camp. Many Israelites were bitten and died. The people now realized that they had sinned against God by grumbling and complaining. They went to Moses and asked him to plead with God on their behalf. Moses prayed for the people. God told Moses to make a bronze serpent and put it on a pole high enough for all to see. Anyone who believed the Word of the Lord and looked at the bronze serpent would be healed of the serpents' deadly bite.

? What did those who were bitten need to do to be healed?

Bible Truth

68 **What is faith in Christ?**
Faith in Christ is trusting in Christ, who died and rose again, for our salvation.

Romans 4:20–21 • 1 Corinthians 15:1–5
Galatians 2:16

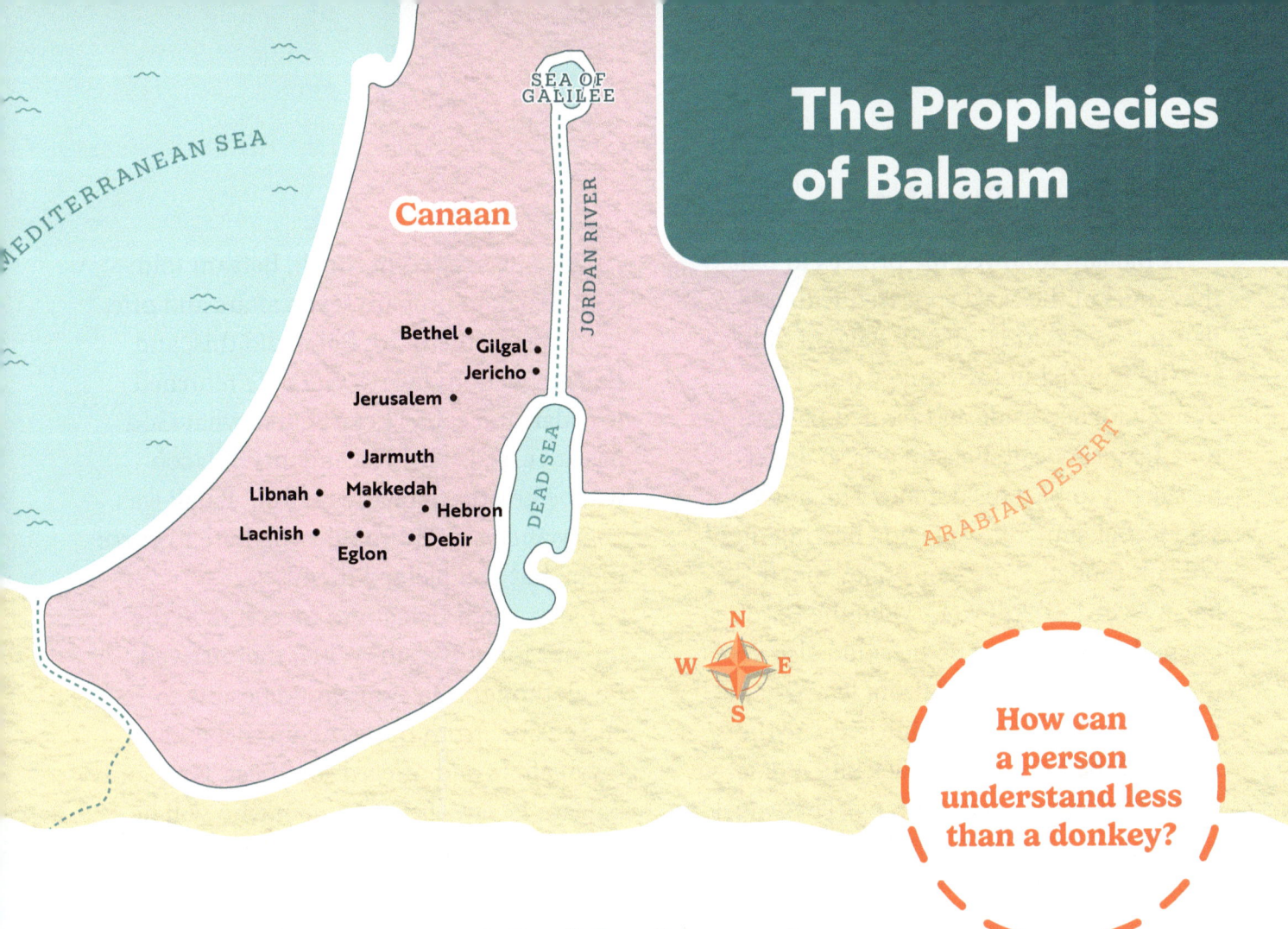

The Prophecies of Balaam

> How can a person understand less than a donkey?

The Nations Are Afraid of Israel

It would soon be time for Israel to possess the land. They drew close but were still on the eastern side of the Jordan River. As they journeyed, they were attacked by the Amorites and the people of Bashan. God strengthened Israel to defeat these armies and take their cities. The quick defeat of these nations brought fear to the heart of Balak, king of Moab. He knew he would not be able to defeat Israel and he wanted them to be destroyed. King Balak sent messengers to the prophet Balaam saying, "I know that whoever you curse is cursed. Please come and curse Israel so I can defeat them in battle." Balaam said to the messengers, "Wait until the morning and I will tell you what the Lord says."

God went to Balaam and said, "Do not go with these men to curse my people, for I have blessed them." The next morning Balaam told the messengers, "God will not let me go with you."

Balak didn't like this answer, so he sent princes to Balaam, asking him to curse Israel. Balaam answered, "Even if Balak gave me his house full of silver and gold, I could only say what the Lord allows me to say." But Baalam really wanted that money, so he told the princes, "Let me see what else the Lord has to say." God told Balaam he could go, but he could only speak the message that the Lord gave him to speak.

Balaam's Donkey Speaks

As Balaam followed the princes to Balak, the Angel of the Lord appeared with a flaming sword in His hand. Balaam didn't see the Angel, but the donkey did. The donkey turned aside and pinned Balaam's foot against a wall. Balaam was so angry he started to beat his donkey. The donkey said to Balaam, "Why are you beating me?" Balaam replied, "You won't obey me. If I had a sword, I'd kill you." Then the Lord opened Balaam's eyes so he could also see the Angel of the Lord. Balaam learned that his donkey had saved his life because the Angel of the Lord would have killed Balaam if the donkey had kept walking. The Angel of the Lord commanded Balaam, "Only speak the words that I tell you to speak to Balak."

? Why did the Angel of the Lord appear to Balaam?

Once he arrived in Moab, Balaam told King Balak to prepare seven altars and offer sacrifices to the Lord. Balak did this, and Balaam went to talk to God. He returned to Balak and said, "I can't curse what God hasn't cursed. The descendants of Jacob will be greater than any nation." Balak was angry and said, "I brought you here to curse them, but you blessed them!"

Balak asked Balaam to meet him at the top of Mount Pisgah. When they arrived, Balak thought Balaam would be able to curse Israel from there. Again, Balak built seven altars and offered sacrifices. God told Balaam to say, "Is God a man who will lie and go back on the promises He has made? No sorcery can be devised against Israel. Instead, God has commanded a blessing, and I cannot reverse it. There is a shout of a king among them. Israel will devour their enemies like a lion."

Balak said to Balaam, "Stop! Don't bless them or curse them!" Balaam reminded Balak that he had to say what the Lord told him to say.

? Who had God already promised to bless?

Balak took Balaam to the top of Mount Peor. After Balak built seven altars and offered sacrifices, Balaam again spoke of how God would bless Israel. He spoke of Israel's camp being like the Garden of Eden. He also said that God would raise up a great King who would be like a lion and defeat all of the nations. Balaam prophesied, "Blessed is he who blesses Israel, and cursed be the one who curses him."

Balak was angry about the blessings given to Israel. He said to Balaam, "I brought you here to curse Israel. Instead, you've blessed them three times! Now, go back to your home!" Balaam answered, "Didn't I tell your messengers that even if you gave me your house filled with silver and gold, I could only say what the Lord has said?"

Balaam Tells of the Great King

Balaam told Balak to listen to God's message. Balaam said, "A star will rise out of Jacob, and the great King's scepter will come out of Israel. He is not only the king of Israel. He is the king of all the world." Instead of cursing Israel, Balaam announced that the great King would come from Israel and rule all nations. After finishing this prophecy, Balaam and Balak went their separate ways.

? What did Balaam say about not being able to curse Israel?

Bible Truth

45 **What did God promise in the Abrahamic Covenant?**

God promised to give Abraham a land and a seed and to make him a blessing to all people.

Genesis 12:1–3, 7; 15:1–21; 17:1–14

Blessings of Obedience and Curses of Disobedience

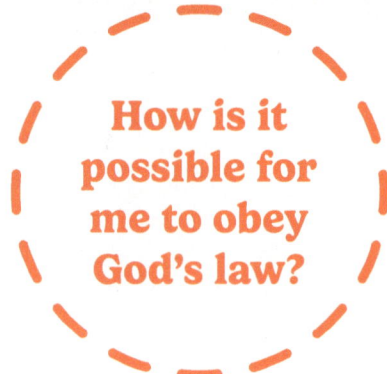

How is it possible for me to obey God's law?

Fast Facts about

Deuteronomy

Author: Moses (Deuteronomy 32:48–34:12 was written by someone else, possibly Joshua.)

Date: 1405 BC

Theme: Second giving of the law by Moses to the people

Meaning of *Deuteronomy*: Second law

Interesting Facts:
- Moses' last chance to warn, bless, and preach to Israel
- Moses' death is recorded.
- The Lord showed Moses the land that he could not enter before he died on Mount Nebo.

Remembering God's Law

Before Moses died, he preached a final sermon to Israel, which is found in the book of Deuteronomy. Israel had wandered in the wilderness for forty years. The generation of people who didn't believe God's promises had died. Moses wanted Israel to remember God's law so they would succeed and enjoy God's blessings.

 What did Moses command Israel to remember when they entered the land of Canaan?

Blessings and Curses

Moses told the Israelites of the blessings they would receive if they followed the laws of the Mosaic Covenant. He also warned them of the curses that would come if they broke the Mosaic Covenant by disobeying its laws. To help them remember to keep the covenant, Moses gave them a special command. After they crossed the river, they were to gather large stones and engrave on them the law of God. Then the tribes of Israel would stand on two mountains facing each other. Six tribes would stand on Mt. Gerizim to announce the blessings. Six tribes would stand on Mt. Ebal to announce the curses. After each curse, Israel would reply, "Amen" to confirm the people understood and agreed to God's commands. The curses were followed by announcing the blessings for obedience from Mt. Gerizim.

 What did the twelve tribes announce to each other from Mount Gerizim and Mount Ebal?

Moses told them that if they obeyed God with all their heart, did not follow idols, and repented when they did wrong, they would enjoy blessings. They would be safe, have healthy children, have plenty of food, be blessed with large herds and flocks, and win battles against their enemies. But if they worshiped idols, treated others wrongly, were immoral, hurt other people, and did not serve God with a joyful heart, they would suffer. These sufferings included poverty, famine, military defeat, sickness, and disease.

Moses also had bad news for Israel. The Lord already knew that Israel did not have a heart to hear and obey His words. There would be a small number of people who would obey the Lord and receive the blessing, but the nation itself would not keep the covenant. For this, God told them up front that they would come under the covenant curses. They would one day be driven out of the land that He was giving them.

> **?** What would happen to the blessings of God's covenant with the people if they disobeyed God's law?

A New Covenant Promised

One day, the Lord would give His people new hearts so they would love Him with all their hearts and all their souls and they would live for Him. Once the people obeyed God with hearts that loved Him, God would restore them and prosper them in the land. This was a promised new covenant in which people would love the Lord and have eternal life.

The Mosaic Covenant was different. In the Mosaic Covenant, people had to obey God to get the blessings. In the New Covenant, God blesses His people with new hearts so they can obey. However, Moses told the people that they did not need to wait until the New Covenant arrived to have new hearts that loved God. If they called out in faith to God right then, God would give them new hearts and eternal life.

Bible Truths

84 **Is God pleased with those who love and obey Him?**
Yes, God says, "I love them that love me; and those that seek me early shall find me."
Proverbs 8:17

85 **Is God pleased with those who do not love and obey Him?**
No, "God is angry with the wicked every day."
Psalm 7:8-13

CHAPTER 7

God Keeps His Covenant Promises

Joshua Leads Israel into Canaan

How can we know God is faithful to keep His promises today?

Fast Facts about

Joshua

Author: Joshua
Date: 1390 BC
Theme: Conquering Canaan for the Israelites' promised homeland
Meaning of *Joshua*: Salvation

Interesting Facts:
- First of twelve historical books
- Covers the entering, conquering, and occupying of Canaan (the Promised Land)
- Spread over three military campaigns

Introduction to Joshua

God allowed Moses to play a very important role in leading His people out of Egypt. Moses gave them God's law and helped them prepare for the conquering of the Promised Land, Canaan.

Moses' assistant was a man named Joshua. When Moses died, God told Joshua, "Moses my servant is dead. Arise, go over the Jordan River with all of the people of Israel. I will give you every place that the sole of your foot will tread upon. None of your enemies will be able to stand before you. Be strong and courageous and obey the law that my servant Moses commanded you. Do not turn right or left away from it. Meditate on the book of the law day and night. This is the only way that you will prosper. Be strong and of good courage. Do not be afraid. I will be with you wherever you go."

Rahab and the Spies

Joshua sent two men to spy out the city of Jericho. That night they stayed at the house of a woman named Rahab. But somebody told the king, "Two men from Israel came in to see our city so they can find our weaknesses and overthrow us. They're staying at Rahab's house." The king immediately sent men to Rahab. They asked her to bring out the men because they were spies. But Rahab said, "They did come to my house, but I didn't know where they were from. They have already left town, right before the gate was closed. If you go quickly, I'm sure you'll be able to catch them!"

However, Rahab knew the spies from Israel were in danger. She had already hidden them on her roof under stalks of flax. The king's men left right away and pursued the spies, just as Rahab had suggested.

Once the king's men left, she told the two spies, "I believe that the Lord has given this land to Israel. All who live on this side of the Jordan River are afraid because of you. We know about God's power over the Red Sea and how God defeated mighty kings for you. When we heard these things, our hearts melted in fear. Everyone's courage was lost. I know that the Lord your God is God in heaven and on earth."

? Whom did God raise up after Moses to take His people into the Promised Land?

Rahab also asked them for protection. "Because I have shown mercy to you, please promise me that you will return that kindness to me and my father's family. Give me a sign to guarantee that all of my father's family will live."

She told them to hide in the mountains for three days until their pursuers gave up the search.

The spies promised her, "If you don't tell anyone about our business here, we will keep your family safe when the Lord gives us this land. Tie this scarlet cord in your window as a sign to Israel that everyone in your house should be spared. If any of you leave the house for any reason, we will not be responsible for what happens to them."

Rahab tied the scarlet cord in her window, which was part of the city wall, and trusted the words of the spies.

For three days, the two spies hid in the mountains until they were sure all danger had passed. They told Joshua, "Truly, God will deliver the city into the hands of Israel. All the people of the land fear us."

> **?** Who in Jericho feared God and protected the spies?

Crossing the Jordan River

The Jordan River

Joshua led Israel to the bank of the Jordan River. This was not a good time to cross. At this time of year, the river overflowed its banks. God gave Joshua directions on how to cross. Leaders of Israel spread out among all the people and gave them those directions. "Prepare yourselves, for the Lord has given you Canaan. When you see the priests carrying the ark of the covenant, you must follow it. However, keep about three thousand feet away from it." Joshua then told the people to make sure that they were set apart to God. The Lord was going to do wonders before them the very next day.

On that day, as God instructed, Joshua told the priests to take the ark of the covenant before all the people and to step into the river. The priests' feet were barely in the water when God stopped the river from flowing. As the water in front of them passed downstream, dry land appeared. Every single Israelite walked across the dry riverbed toward Jericho.

? How did Joshua know when it was time to cross the Jordan River?

A Stone Memorial

God told Joshua, "Tell one man from each tribe to carry a rock from the riverbed where the priests stood. Tonight, set the rocks up where you spend the night." Joshua told the people that when their children asked about why these stones were stacked by the riverbank, they would say that the waters of the Jordan were cut off before the ark of the covenant. They also set up twelve stones in the riverbed where the priests were standing.

After the priests touched the bank of the river, the river overflowed its banks again. God had brought His people safely into the Promised Land.

? Why did God have the Israelites set up twelve stones where they spent the night?

Bible Truth

45 **What did God promise in the Abrahamic Covenant?**
God promised to give Abraham a land and a seed and to make him a blessing to all people.

Genesis 12:1–3, 7; 15:1–21; 17:1–14

The Fall of Jericho

How can God be just and merciful at the same time?

Jericho was the first city that Israel would need to conquer. One day, while Joshua was near Jericho, a man with his sword drawn stood in front of him. Joshua asked, "Are you on our side, or are you with our enemies?" The man answered, "No, I am the captain of the army of the Lord. Take off your shoes; this is holy ground." Joshua did so because this was the Lord Himself.

Because the people of Jericho were afraid of Israel, every opening in the city wall was tightly closed. The Lord told Joshua, "I have given all of Jericho to you, even its king and mighty men. Tell all your soldiers to march around the city once each day for six days. The ark of the covenant will go with them, and seven priests will march in front of the ark while blowing on ram's horns. On the seventh day, march seven times around the city. After the seventh time, tell the seven priests to blow their trumpets and tell the people to shout. The walls of Jericho will fall flat so the soldiers can run into the city and conquer it."

Joshua directed the people as God had said. He told the people, "Be totally quiet as you march. Don't even say a word until I tell you to shout. Then shout!"

For six days, the people quietly marched once around the city and came back to camp at night. The priests blew their horns in front of the ark of the covenant as they marched with the soldiers. For six days, the people of Jericho watched in fear. On the seventh day, the soldiers marched around the city seven times, all the while being quiet. On the seventh time, as the priests blew the trumpets, Joshua told the people, "Shout, because the Lord has given you the city! Only Rahab and whoever is with her in the house may live because she kept Israel's spies safe. Don't take anything from the city, or else Israel will be cursed and have trouble because of it. Everything in the city belongs to the Lord!"

And just as God had said, the wall fell. Israel destroyed everyone in the city, along with their animals and possessions. The **climax** of the fall of Jericho is that Rahab and her family alone were saved. Amid God's judgment on the sinful inhabitants of Jericho, He showed mercy to Rahab and her family. Rahab's faith in Israel's God contrasted with the wicked living of the rest of her people. Now she was one of God's people.

> **key term**
>
> **climax**
>
> The climax is highest point in the plot of a story.

? What caused Rahab to protect the spies and therefore be shown mercy?

Achan and Ai

Why are secret sins so damaging?

Israel destroyed everything in Jericho—the people, the possessions, the animals. But a man named Achan took home some of the things that were supposed to be destroyed.

The small city of Ai was the next city for Israel to conquer. Because it was much smaller than Jericho, Joshua sent only a small group of men to fight. But this time, Israel was defeated.

Joshua was discouraged and talked with God. "Why did You bring us over the Jordan? We will be destroyed in this land. Then what will become of Your great name?"

"Israel has sinned," God said. "They disobeyed My covenant and stole things from Jericho. I will not bless Israel until the sin is punished. You will not be able to defeat any enemies until the stolen things are destroyed. Tomorrow, the Israelites will see who the thief is."

The next day, God revealed that it was Achan who broke God's law. Achan admitted what he did. "When I saw clothing and money, I wanted them, so I took them and hid them in my tent."

Joshua asked, "Why did you trouble the whole nation with your sin? Now God will trouble you." Israel's punishment on Achan was approved by God. They stoned him and his whole household, and they burned them with fire. This was the same way Israel was to destroy the wicked enemies of God.

When God saw that Israel corrected the wrongdoing, He assured Joshua of victory by saying, "I have given the kingdom of Ai to you." God told Joshua exactly what his army should do. Joshua divided his army in two. One group would pretend to flee from the city. Thinking they could defeat Israel, the army of Ai would run out of the city to chase them. Once the army of Ai left the city, the other half of Joshua's army would run into the city to destroy it. Then Joshua's fleeing soldiers would turn to fight and defeat the army of Ai.

The plan worked perfectly. Joshua's army burned the city, but God allowed them to keep the cattle and goods of the city this time. Then Joshua built an altar to God and read the Mosaic Covenant to the people. In this way, Joshua renewed the covenant with them and reminded them that God keeps His promises.

? **What bad things happened as a result of Achan's sin?**

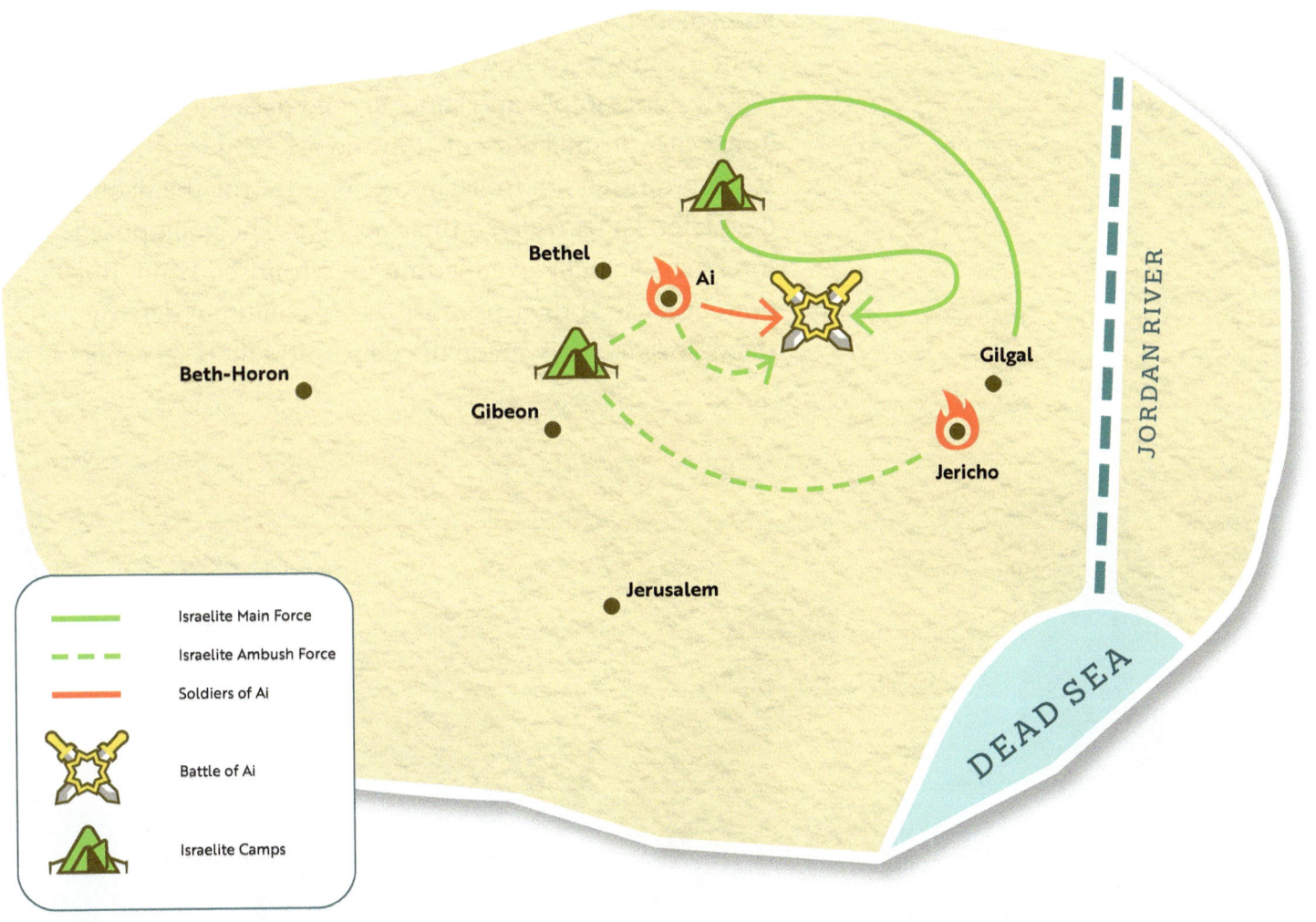

The Sun Stood Still

How does God's power back His promises?

The Gibeonite Deception

All the nearby kingdoms heard of Israel's victories over Jericho and Ai. The city of Gibeon decided to trick the Israelites instead of trying to fight them. Some men of Gibeon dressed in old clothes, gathered moldy food in old bags, and came to Israel. They asked Israel to make peace with them, and they lied by saying they were from far away. If Israel thought the men didn't live in Canaan, then Israel could make a covenant of peace with them. But Joshua wasn't sure. He asked them who they were and where they came from. The Gibeonites told Joshua, "Our bread was fresh when we left our city, but now it is stale. Our clothes and shoes are old because of our long walk." Joshua did not stop and ask God for wisdom. Israel promised not to harm them or destroy them. Three days later, Israel realized their mistake. Those supposed foreigners actually lived within the Promised Land. But now, because of their promise, Israel could not destroy them. Instead, they made the Gibeonites their servants.

? **What did Israel fail to do after hearing the Gibeonites' request?**

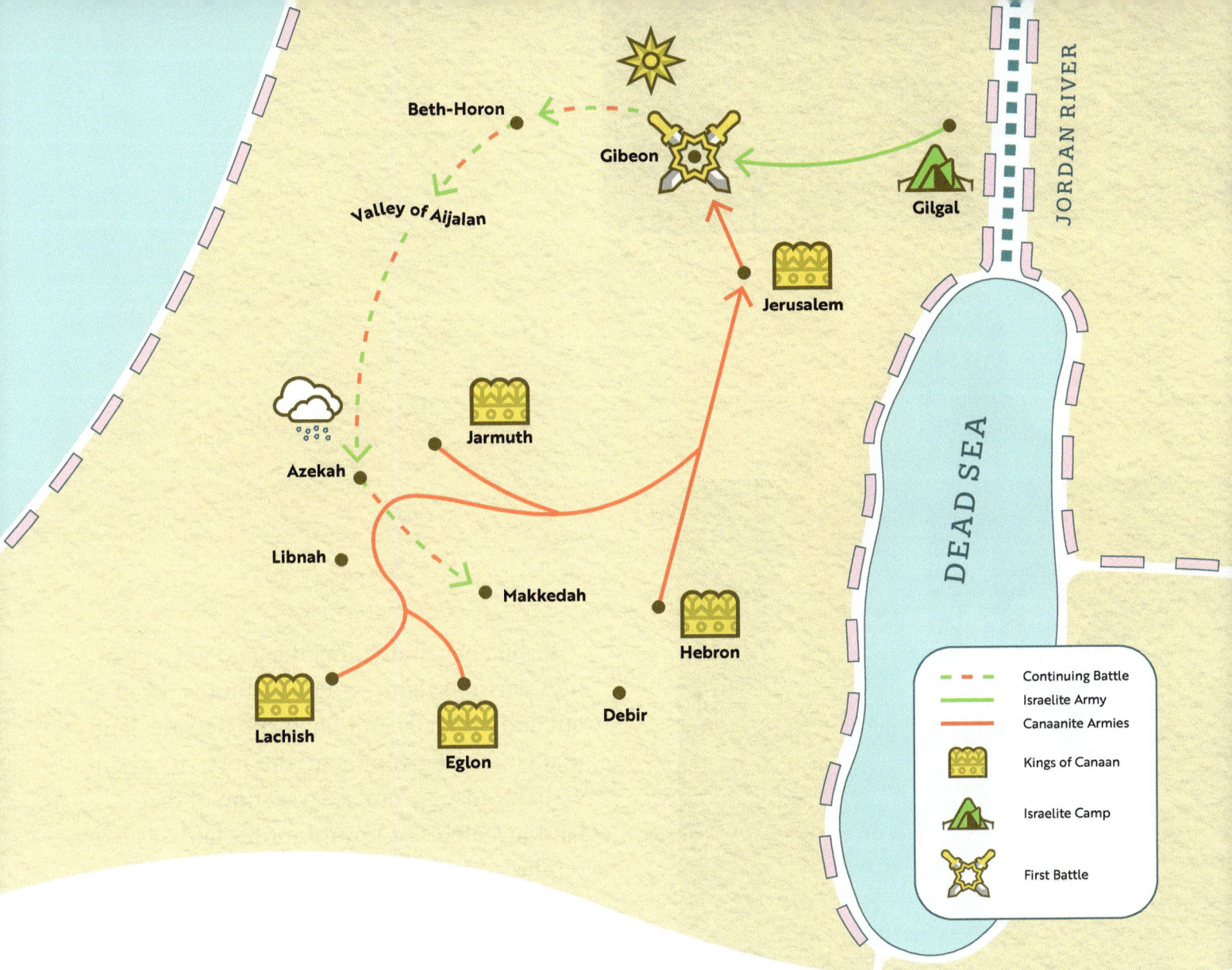

The Battle of Five Kings

The news of Ai's defeat and the Gibeonites' alliance with Israel caused neighboring kings to fear Israel even more. Gibeon was larger than Ai, and they were now on Israel's side. Five kings and all their armies joined forces to fight against Gibeon. Gibeon's king asked Joshua to help them. God told Joshua, "Do not fear, for I have delivered them into your hand." Joshua and his army traveled all night, and God confused the enemy. Some were killed on the spot while others ran away. As they ran, God rained great hailstones on them. The hailstones killed more enemies than the army did. Joshua had prayed to God for the sun and moon to stand still. God did this for Joshua, and the long period of light helped Joshua's army win. Again, the LORD showed that He would fight for Israel.

The five kings of those cities ran and hid in a cave. But they were found and killed after the battle. Because God fought for Israel, Joshua's army was also able to conquer all the kingdoms in the region. After these victories, Joshua and his army returned to the camp.

Caleb
A MAN OF ACTION

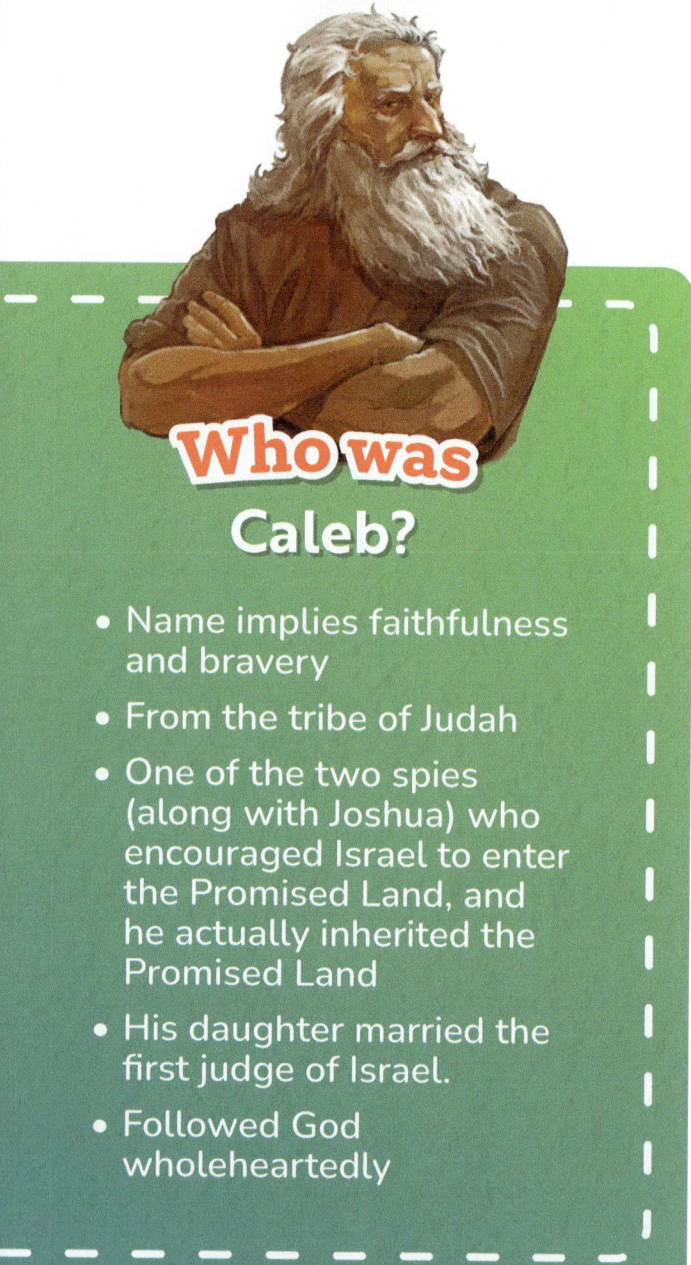

Who was Caleb?

- Name implies faithfulness and bravery
- From the tribe of Judah
- One of the two spies (along with Joshua) who encouraged Israel to enter the Promised Land, and he actually inherited the Promised Land
- His daughter married the first judge of Israel.
- Followed God wholeheartedly

What motivated Caleb to take action?

Joshua began dividing the land of Canaan into portions. Israel would begin to spread out and officially and finally possess the land that God had given them. But forty-five years earlier, Moses promised a section of that land to Caleb as a reward for his faith. Caleb reminded Joshua of this by saying, "I'm sure you remember what Moses, God's servant, said to you and me when we were in Kadesh Barnea. I was forty years old then. When we spied out the land of Canaan, I told Moses that we should obey God and conquer it. However, the other spies discouraged the people and put fear in their hearts. But I wholly followed the Lord my God. Because I believed God's promises, Moses promised me the land of Hebron for an inheritance. Because I wholly followed the Lord, that land would also be my children's inheritance."

How are God's promises claimed?

Caleb continued to speak. "The children of Israel have wandered in the wilderness for forty years since then. God has kept me alive these forty-five years since I spied out the land. I am now eighty-five years old, but I am as strong today as I was on that day that Moses sent me. The strength I go out to war with is the same level of strength I return with. Therefore, give me this hill country that God spoke of. I am claiming it as my inheritance. If the Lord will be with me, I will be able to defeat those who are living there now, exactly as the Lord had said all those years ago."

Joshua remembered Moses' promise and blessed Caleb. He gave the land of Hebron to Caleb as an inheritance. Joshua allowed him to have the land because Caleb wholly followed the Lord God of Israel. Before Caleb conquered it, it was called Kirjath Arba, being named after a man whom the people of the land greatly respected. Under Caleb, Hebron became a peaceful land and had rest from war.

modern-day Hebron

? **What does Caleb's inheritance teach us about the Abrahamic Covenant?**

115

Rest for God's People

A long time after these battles, when God gave Israel a **rest** from their enemies, Joshua spoke to the leaders of Israel. "I am now an old man," he said. "God has fought for you against other nations, and you have seen His power. I have divided the land for you tribe by tribe. God will continue to remove the nations from the land. It will be your homeland."

key term
rest

Rest is enjoying the presence of God without the disturbance of enemies. The defeat of Israel's enemies contributed to Israel being able to rest in the land.

What is true rest?

But Joshua also reminded them that they needed to keep the Mosaic law if they were going to stay in the land. "Be very courageous and obey all that God said. Do not give any attention to the idols of the people whom you defeat. Do not even speak their names. Love the Lord your God. Be careful not to disobey Him. Don't give your sons or daughters in marriage to idol worshipers from these other nations. If you disobey God's law, the Lord will remove His promise from you. The nations will cause you all sorts of troubles and pain. They will trap you and destroy you. You will lose the land that God has given you."

? What should God's people be courageous about?

Joshua continued his speech. "I will die soon, but you know in your hearts and souls that God has not forgotten His promises. All has happened as He said. But just as God has given you good, He will allow evil to come to you if you disobey. Then this will not be your home anymore. That is the price of breaking God's covenant and worshiping other gods."

Then Joshua gathered all the tribes of Israel to Shechem. He had a message from God. "Thus says the Lord, the God of Israel, 'I chose your fathers, even Abraham, who served other gods. I rescued you from Egypt through Moses and Aaron. I spared you and kept you safe from many enemy nations. I gave you lands, cities, and vineyards which you did not work for or build yourselves.'"

Joshua then challenged the people, "Fear God. Serve Him humbly. Choose now whom you will serve. But as for me and my household, we will serve the Lord."

The people said, "We would never forsake the Lord to serve other gods. We will serve the Lord. He is our God."

But Joshua cautioned them about saying what they knew to be the right thing. He warned them, "You are not able to serve the Lord." He warned them of the judgment that would occur when they sinned against God.

But the people insisted, "No, but we will serve the Lord."

Joshua warned them that they were being witnesses against themselves. They were making a covenant with God. They agreed with this covenant by saying, "We are witnesses." But this whole time, they had been worshiping various foreign gods. Joshua told them that they needed to abandon these gods if they were to make a covenant with the Lord.

A covenant was made, and Joshua had a large stone set up as a witness against them. Joshua died when he was 110 years old. Israel served the Lord as long as Joshua and the other leaders who remembered the works of the Lord were alive.

? **What choice did Joshua and the people make?**

CHAPTER 8

Israelites Do What Is Right in Their Own Eyes

Incomplete Obedience

What is a godly leader?

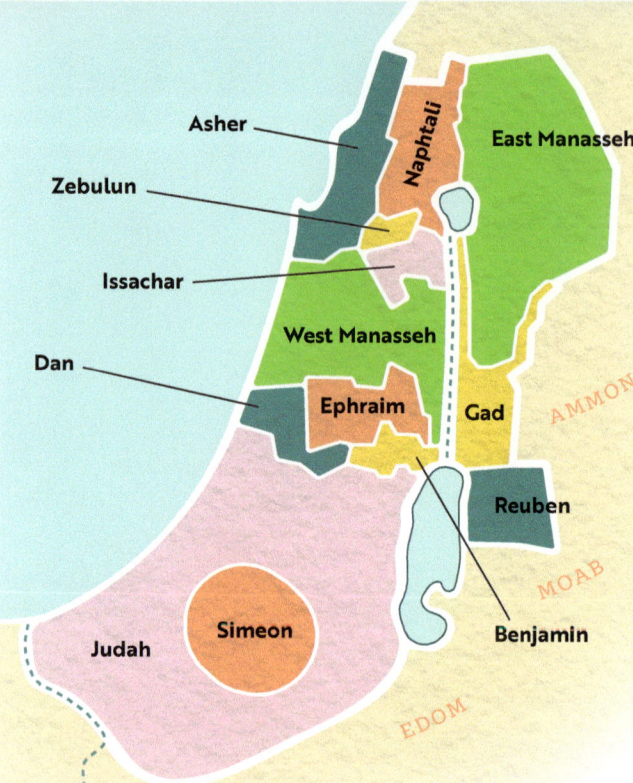

FastFacts about

Judges

Author: Samuel
Date: 1000 BC
Theme: Danger of people doing what is right in their own eyes
Meaning of *Judges*: Named for those Israelites God raised up to judge Israel

Interesting Facts:
- There were few godly leaders in Israel.
- Happens around the same time as the book of Ruth
- Time period in Israel's history in between the conquest of Canaan and the kings of Israel

Israel Continues the Conquest of Canaan

Joshua died before the land was fully conquered, so there was still much to do. Israel asked the Lord which tribe should begin conquering the land. God said the tribe of Judah should be first. Judah asked the tribe of Simeon to help them fight so they could each conquer their part of Canaan. The Lord fought alongside them, and they won many battles. They conquered most of Judah's portion of the land.

Israel Disobeys God

The Lord was with the tribe of Judah in its battles. God gave the tribe victory over most of the nations it fought against. But when the armies of Judah encountered the Canaanites who lived in the plains, they couldn't destroy them because the Canaanites had chariots of iron. Judah failed to trust that God would help them destroy all the wicked nations living in their territory. The rest of Israel followed Judah's example of partial obedience, and more and more nations were spared from destruction. Instead of destroying the people who lived in their land, they made them their slaves. Some of the tribes of Israel simply let the wicked nations live on one part of their land while they lived on another part.

? How did Israel disobey the Lord as they took possession of their territory?

God Judges Israel

The Angel of the Lord came to the people of Israel and reminded them how He had brought them out of Egypt and into this land. He reminded them that He had kept His covenant with their parents, just as He had promised. But God's covenant included curses if they broke the covenant, and they broke it by not destroying all the nations in the Promised Land. God would take these undestroyed nations and punish this generation with them. The nations would be like thorns and briars in their sides. Israel would lose the protection that God gave them from their enemies.

This generation ignored God's warnings about the dangers of disobeying Him. They did not think much about what would happen to them for disobeying. They worshiped Baal instead of God. Instead of being a nation of priests to the wicked nations, they became wicked like them.

God judged Israel and made them weak before their enemies. Now, instead of becoming prosperous, Israel was enslaved to those nations. In their misery, the Israelites cried out to the Lord. In His mercy, God sent leaders called judges to deliver Israel and defeat their enemies. But each time Israel found relief from their bondage, they went right back and served and worshiped the same false gods. Soon after, they would find themselves again enslaved to the Canaanites.

? Why did Israel fail to destroy all the Canaanite nations?

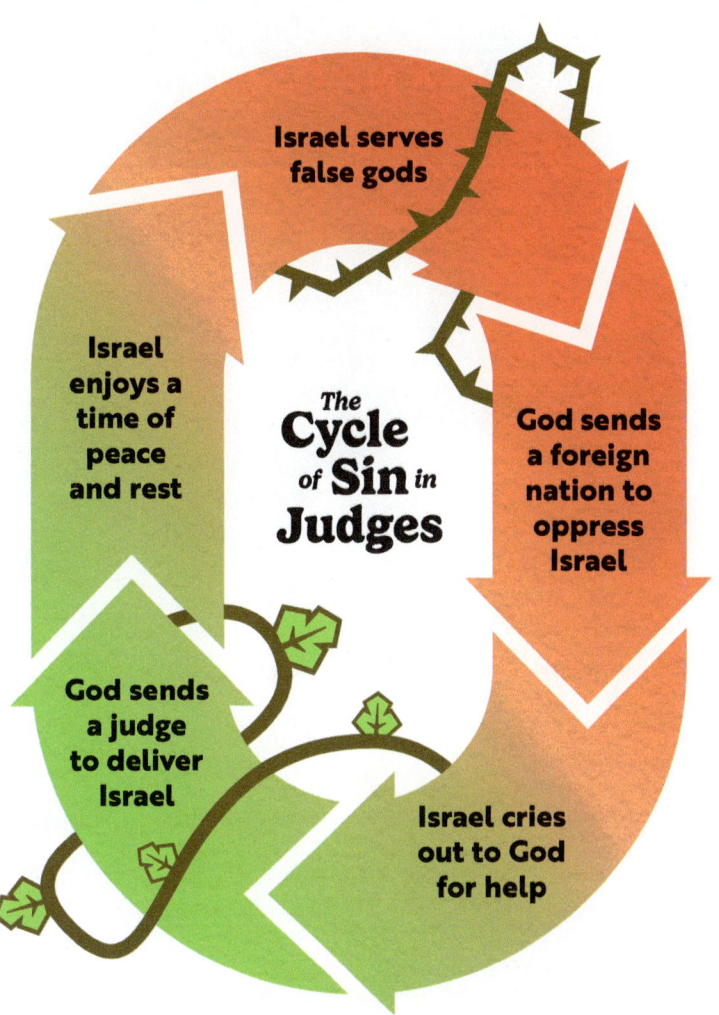

Bible Truths

30 **What is sin?**
Sin is failing to do what God commands or doing what God forbids.
James 4:17 • 1 John 3:4

39 **What effect did Adam's sin have on mankind's rule over the world?**
The world is now cursed, and mankind no longer seeks the good of others and the glory of God in his rule.
Genesis 3:16–19; 4:17–24

Deborah
A WOMAN OF COURAGE

Why did God use women to deliver Israel?

Who was Deborah?

- A prophetess of God
- The only female judge in Israel
- Mother in Israel
- A woman of faith and courage

A Time of Weakness

Israel cried out to God because the nations of Canaan were treating them harshly. God used Othniel and then Ehud to free His people. But when they lost these men's strong leadership, Israel turned away from the Lord again. Because of Israel's rebellion, God let the Canaanites take them over. After twenty years of cruel Canaanite rule, the people repented. God chose someone else to deliver His people once again. The prophetess and judge Deborah told Barak that God commanded him to gather ten thousand men to fight the Canaanites. God promised Barak great victory. But this promise was not enough for Barak. Sisera, the commander of the Canaanites, had a strong army with nine hundred iron chariots. Even though God commanded Barak to do this task, and even though Deborah said God would give him victory, he was afraid to fight against an army of chariots. He told Deborah, "I will not go unless you go with me." Deborah trusted God and said that she would go with him. But Deborah warned Barak that for his lack of faith, the glory of victory would not be his—Sisera would be defeated by a woman.

 Why didn't Barak accept the challenge from God that he heard from Deborah?

A Call to Battle

Sisera's men told him when Barak and his army arrived at Mount Tabor. Sisera called his mighty army and nine hundred iron chariots to battle. Deborah said to Barak, "Rise up! This is the day the Lord has given Sisera, the enemy of God, into your hand. The Lord has gone before you into battle!" As God promised, He helped Israel pursue the Canaanites, destroy their army and their chariots, and defeat them. Sisera left his chariot and ran from the battlefield. As he made his escape, he passed the family of Heber, who lived in Canaan. This family was part of a people who were at peace with Sisera's people. Jael, a woman from that family, invited Sisera to rest and hide in her tent. She gave him milk to drink and covered him with a heavy blanket. Sisera told her to stand at the door of the tent. If anyone asked if a man was inside, she was to say, "No." After Sisera fell into a deep sleep, Jael took a tent peg and drove it through the side of his head with a hammer. The captain of the Canaanites was killed by a woman, just as Deborah had said. Meanwhile, Barak continued to fight until he destroyed Sisera's king and won the day.

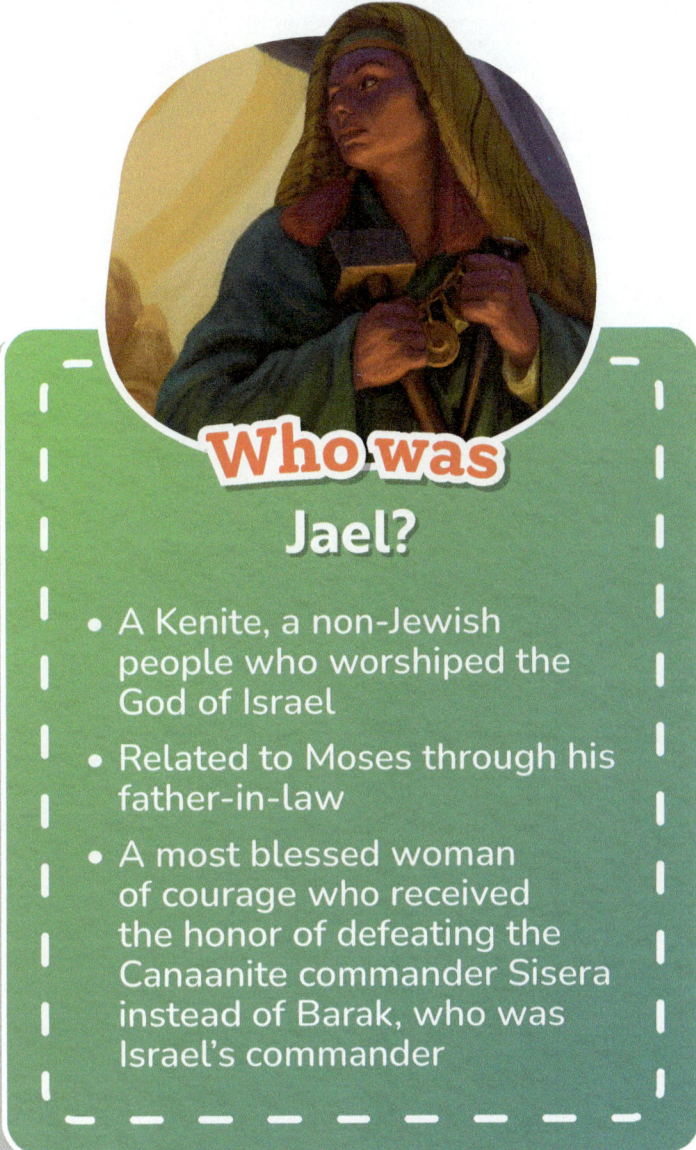

Who was Jael?

- A Kenite, a non-Jewish people who worshiped the God of Israel
- Related to Moses through his father-in-law
- A most blessed woman of courage who received the honor of defeating the Canaanite commander Sisera instead of Barak, who was Israel's commander

A Song of Victory

After Israel defeated Sisera's army, Deborah and Barak sang a song of victory. Barak must have found his courage in the battle to be able to sing this song. In the song, they praised God for helping Israel and celebrated those who fought the battle. The song mentions the two women who assisted in the victory, Deborah and Jael. Both were courageous women and are listed by name among the heroes of the battle.

? Who were the two unexpected heroes of this account?

Gideon
A FLAWED DELIVERER

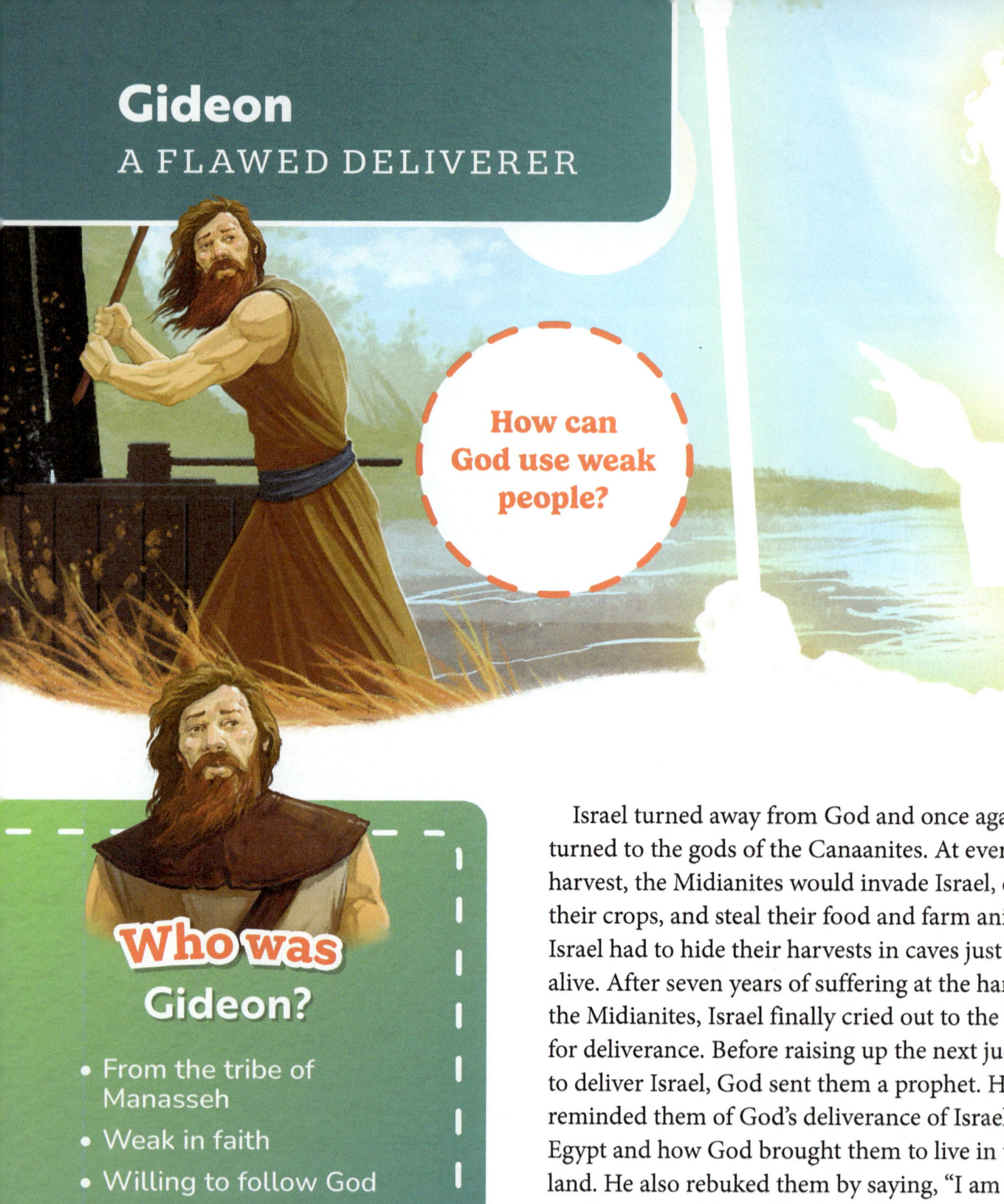

How can God use weak people?

Who was Gideon?

- From the tribe of Manasseh
- Weak in faith
- Willing to follow God
- Refused to be king but acted like one

Israel turned away from God and once again turned to the gods of the Canaanites. At every harvest, the Midianites would invade Israel, destroy their crops, and steal their food and farm animals. Israel had to hide their harvests in caves just to stay alive. After seven years of suffering at the hand of the Midianites, Israel finally cried out to the Lord for deliverance. Before raising up the next judge to deliver Israel, God sent them a prophet. He reminded them of God's deliverance of Israel from Egypt and how God brought them to live in this land. He also rebuked them by saying, "I am the Lord your God, who told you not to fear the gods of the Amorites in the land where you live. But you didn't obey my voice." God again confirmed why Israel suffered—they were disobedient.

God Calls Gideon to Deliver Israel

An Israelite named Gideon was secretly threshing wheat when the Angel of the Lord appeared to him. "You are a mighty man," the Angel of the Lord said. "The Lord is with you!"

Gideon was surprised at this message. "If the Lord is with us, why doesn't He do the great things for us like He did in the past? We've heard how the Lord brought us up from Egypt with miracles, but now He has forgotten us and turned us over to the Midianites."

The Lord replied, "I am sending you. Go save Israel from bondage."

But Gideon said, "How can I deliver Israel? My family is the weakest in the tribe of Manasseh, and I am the youngest among my brothers."

But the Lord insisted. "I will be with you. You'll win the battle over Midian as if you were only fighting against one man."

Unsure, Gideon asked for a sign. He brought a gift of food to the Angel of the Lord and set it down on a rock. The Angel of the Lord touched it with His staff, and flames burst from the rock, burning the food up. Gideon shouted, "I have seen the Angel of the Lord face-to-face!"

The Lord told Gideon to start freeing Israel by destroying the altar of Baal and the Asherah pole that stood in his own town. Gideon took ten servants with him, and they destroyed the altar. But they went at night because Gideon was afraid of his family and the townspeople. Sure enough, when they found the broken idols, the people of the city were outraged. They said that Gideon must die for destroying the altar of Baal and the Asherah pole. But Gideon's father defended him by saying, "If Baal is such a mighty god, let him fight for himself."

Gideon and the Fleece

The Midianites and Israel prepared for an epic battle. The Spirit of the Lord came upon Gideon. He sent messengers to other tribes, and many came to help fight the Midianites. Still, Gideon was weak in faith, so he asked the Lord to give him yet another sign that He was with him. Gideon placed a fleece on the ground. "Lord, show me a sign. When morning comes, let the ground stay dry, but let this fleece be wet." The next morning, the ground was dry and the fleece was wet. Still, Gideon doubted. That night, Gideon said, "In the morning, let the ground be wet and the fleece be dry." Even though Gideon should not have been testing God, God graciously did as he asked. He showed Gideon that He was with him.

> **?** Why did Gideon ask for signs that God would be with him?

The Lord Prepares an Army for Battle

Gideon gathered 32,000 men to fight. But God told Gideon, "There are too many men. Israel might boast that they defeated Midian on their own. Tell all who are afraid to leave and go home." A total of 22,000 men were afraid and went home. Still, God said that 10,000 Israelites were too many to fight the army of 135,000 Midianites. God told Gideon to bring them down to the water. "Those who get down on their knees to drink cannot go with you. Those who dip and drink from their hand are those I have chosen." There were 9,700 men who got on their knees to drink. Gideon's army now numbered only 300.

Knowing Gideon's fearfulness, the Lord told him to sneak into the enemy camp at night to hear what was being said. One Midianite soldier said, "I had a dream. A barley cake rolled down the mountain and knocked one of our tents down." Another replied that the dream was a sign that God had given Gideon the victory over the Midianites.

Encouraged, Gideon and his servant went back to their camp. Gideon commanded his army, "Arise to the battle! The victory is ours!"

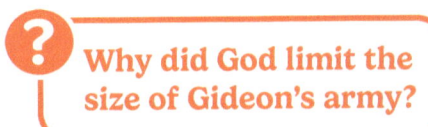

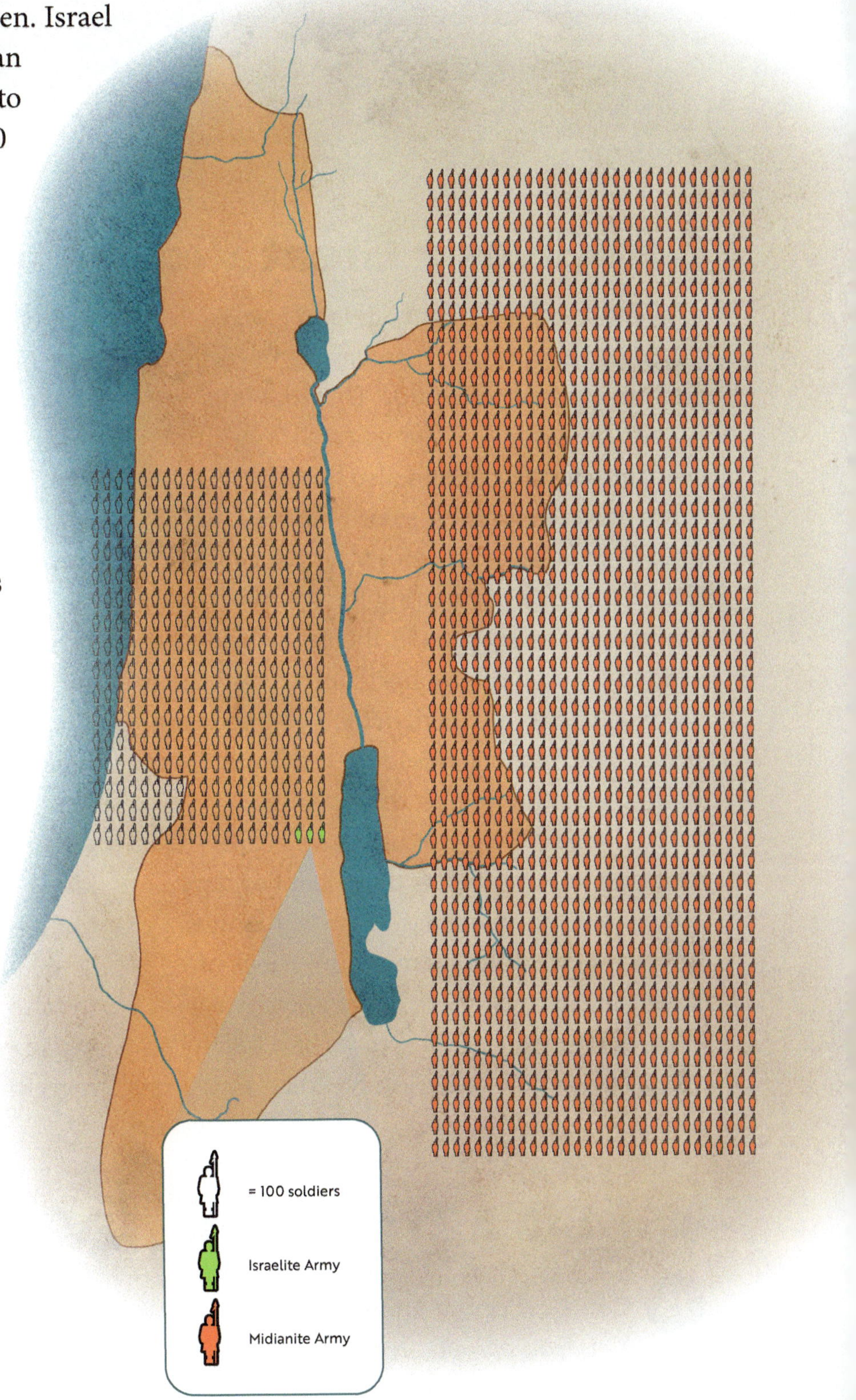

? **Why did God limit the size of Gideon's army?**

God Gives a Great Victory to Israel

While it was still night, Gideon gave each man a trumpet to carry, and also a burning torch in a pitcher. He said, "Do what I do." Gideon commanded that when they heard his trumpet, they should also blow their trumpets and shout, "A sword for the Lord and for Gideon!" The soldiers got in their places, quietly surrounding the camp of the Midianites as they slept in the valley below. Suddenly, Gideon blew his trumpet, and the 300 men did so too. Gideon and all his men broke their pitchers, raised their flaming torches, and shouted. In the darkness, the Midianites were confused and began attacking one another as they fled. For days, Gideon and his men chased the Midianites. He commanded the surrounding tribes of Israel to help track them down and destroy them. They eventually captured and killed two princes and two kings of Midian.

Israel then lived in peace for 40 years. The people asked Gideon to rule over them. Gideon told them, "I will not rule over you. Neither shall my son rule over you. The Lord shall rule over you." This sounded good, but Gideon asked for gold from the plunder* of battle, just as a king would. He collected 43 pounds of gold and made a special garment worn by priests, called an ephod, with it. Israel began to worship it and forgot God. Gideon also took many wives, just as the kings in those days would do. He named one of his sons Abimelech, which means "My father is king." Gideon said the right things. He said that the Lord should be their king. But he acted like a wicked king. He led the people in false worship. After his death, Israel began worshiping Baal again, completely forgetting God's deliverance from Midian.

Bible Truth

15 **Can God do all things?**
Yes, God can do all His holy will.

Psalm 135:6 • Daniel 4:35
Ephesians 1:11

Who did Israel worship after Gideon died?

Abimelech
A WICKED RULER

What makes a bad leader?

After Gideon's death, Abimelech spoke to his mother's family in Shechem and convinced them to make him king. He spoke to them of Gideon's other sons and said, "Would you rather be ruled by seventy men or by one who is your brother?" They all knew that choosing Abimelech as their king meant they would have to murder Gideon's other sons. They took up a collection of silver and hired worthless men to go with Abimelech to kill his brothers. Only Jotham, the youngest son, escaped. Abimelech was now king of Shechem. Jotham went up to Mount Gerizim, which was once the mount of blessings, and cried out to the city, "My father fought for you and freed you from the Midianites, and you have rewarded him by killing his sons. May fire appear and devour all of you!"

Three years passed. A man named Gaal wanted to rule, so he gathered men in the city of Shechem to fight against Abimelech. Abimelech heard about Gaal's plan and went to destroy Shechem before they destroyed him. He attacked people in the fields who weren't even prepared to fight. He attacked men who used to be his friends. In fear of him, about one thousand men and women of Shechem shut themselves in a huge tower. Without mercy, Abimelech set the tower on fire, and all the people inside died. Jotham spoke of this fire when he said "May fire come forth and devour you" in his curse. Abimelech defeated the neighboring city too. The people of that city hid in a tower that Abimelech also planned to set on fire. But a woman in the burning tower dropped part of a millstone on Abimelech's head. It broke his skull, and as he was about to die, he asked his armor-bearer to kill him so no one would say he was killed by a woman. His armor-bearer obeyed and killed him with his sword. When Abimelech's army saw he was dead, they went back to their homes. In this way, God brought judgment on Abimelech and Shechem for their murderous ways.

a millstone

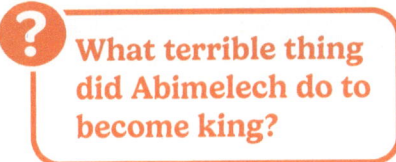

? *What terrible thing did Abimelech do to become king?*

Samson
A WORLDLY LEADER

Who was Samson?

- The twelfth and final judge in Israel
- A Nazirite his whole life
- A man of supernatural strength
- A man of faith
- Destroyed by his love for the world

How can I tell if I love the world more than God?

The Birth of Samson

Again, Israel turned away from the Lord. This time, they were ruled by the Philistines for forty years. Because God is merciful, He chose Manoah and his wife to bring about the next judge in Israel. The Angel of the Lord appeared to Manoah's wife and told her that she was going to have a baby boy. This baby was to be raised as a **Nazirite** from birth. The Angel of the Lord returned and spoke to Manoah as well. As the Lord promised, they had a son. They named him Samson, and the Lord blessed him.

key term
Nazirite

Nazirite vows were usually made for a set period of time. They had three requirements: no eating or drinking anything from the grapevine, including wine; no cutting of the hair at all; and no touching the body of anything that had died, human or animal.

Samson Marries a Philistine

Samson grew older and asked his father to arrange for him a marriage to a beautiful Philistine girl. His parents did not want Samson to marry the enemy of their people, but they didn't know God was going to use this against the Philistines.

Samson journeyed with his parents to the Philistine town of Timnath for his wedding. On the way, he took a detour by himself through the vineyards of Timnah. While he was in the vineyards, a lion attacked him. Samson killed it by tearing it apart with his bare hands. When Samson next saw the lion's dead body, it held a beehive full of honey. Samson took some of the honey and gave some to his parents.

During his week-long wedding celebration, Samson proposed a riddle to his guests. If these thirty guests could answer it, Samson would give them each an expensive change of clothes. If they couldn't answer it, they would each give him an expensive change of clothes. Remembering the lion filled with honey, he gave them this riddle: "Out of the eater came forth meat; out of the strong came forth sweetness."

Nobody could solve the riddle, so they threatened Samson's new wife. "Find the answer to this riddle or we'll burn you and your family alive in your house." Afraid, she begged Samson for the riddle's answer. Finally, Samson gave in and told her. She told her people, and with triumph they answered Samson's riddle, "What is sweeter than honey; what is stronger than a lion?" Samson was so angry that he killed thirty Philistines and gave their clothing to the men who answered the riddle. In a rage, Samson went back to his parents' home and left his new wife with her family.

Samson Defeats the Philistines

In the time of the wheat harvest, Samson returned to Timnath for his wife. Her father said, "I didn't think you would be back for her, so I gave her to your friend." Samson was very angry. He captured three hundred foxes. He tied two foxes' tails together and fastened a torch between them. He did this to all the foxes, then let them go in the dry fields of wheat. The Philistines' wheat harvest, vineyards, and olive trees were all burned up.

In revenge, the Philistines went and burned Samson's wife and her father to death. Then they threatened the tribe of Judah because of what Samson had done. Judah told the Philistines they would give Samson to them, and they tied his hands with strong, new ropes. When the Philistines came shouting to get Samson, he broke the ropes like they were straw. Then he grabbed the jawbone of a donkey and killed one thousand Philistines with it.

The Death of Samson

Even though Samson was a judge in Israel, he had a **worldly** heart. He fell in love with another Philistine woman named Delilah. The Philistines told her, "Find out the secret of Samson's great strength and we will give you a treasure in silver."

Delilah asked Samson, "Please tell me the secret to your strength. How could you be bound and not break loose?"

He answered, "If I am tied up with seven fresh bowstrings, I will not be able to break them."

As he slept, Delilah tied Samson's hands together with fresh bowstrings. The soldiers hid, ready to take him. When Delilah cried out, "The Philistines are here!" Samson easily broke the bowstrings. Delilah kept trying to find out his secret, but Samson lied to her each time.

key term
worldly
Those beliefs, values, thoughts, words, and actions influenced by Satan that characterize the lives of the unsaved.

What type of heart did Samson have?

Finally, Delilah cried, "How can you say you love me but tell me so many lies?"

Samson gave in. "If someone cuts my hair, I'll be as weak as any man."

When Samson fell asleep, Delilah carefully cut his hair. Just like every other time, the Philistines were ready when she cried out, "Samson, the Philistines are here!" Samson sat up, thinking he would easily free himself, but he quickly found that he had no strength to fight the Philistines. He was captured, blinded, and put to work grinding grain in the prison. Samson had lost his eyes, but his hair began to grow back.

To celebrate their victory over Samson, the Philistines decided to have a great feast to their god Dagon. About three thousand people were gathered in the temple of Dagon, and Samson was brought out to provide entertainment for them. A young boy led him by the hand. As they laughed and praised their god, Samson said to the boy, "Let me lean on the support pillars of the temple." Then Samson cried out to the Lord, "Please give me strength one last time. Let me die with the Philistines!" His strength returned and he pushed a pillar with each hand. The entire temple fell, killing all who were inside. Samson killed more people when he died than when he lived. Samson had judged Israel for twenty years.

? **What caused Samson's weakness?**

Hope in the Darkness

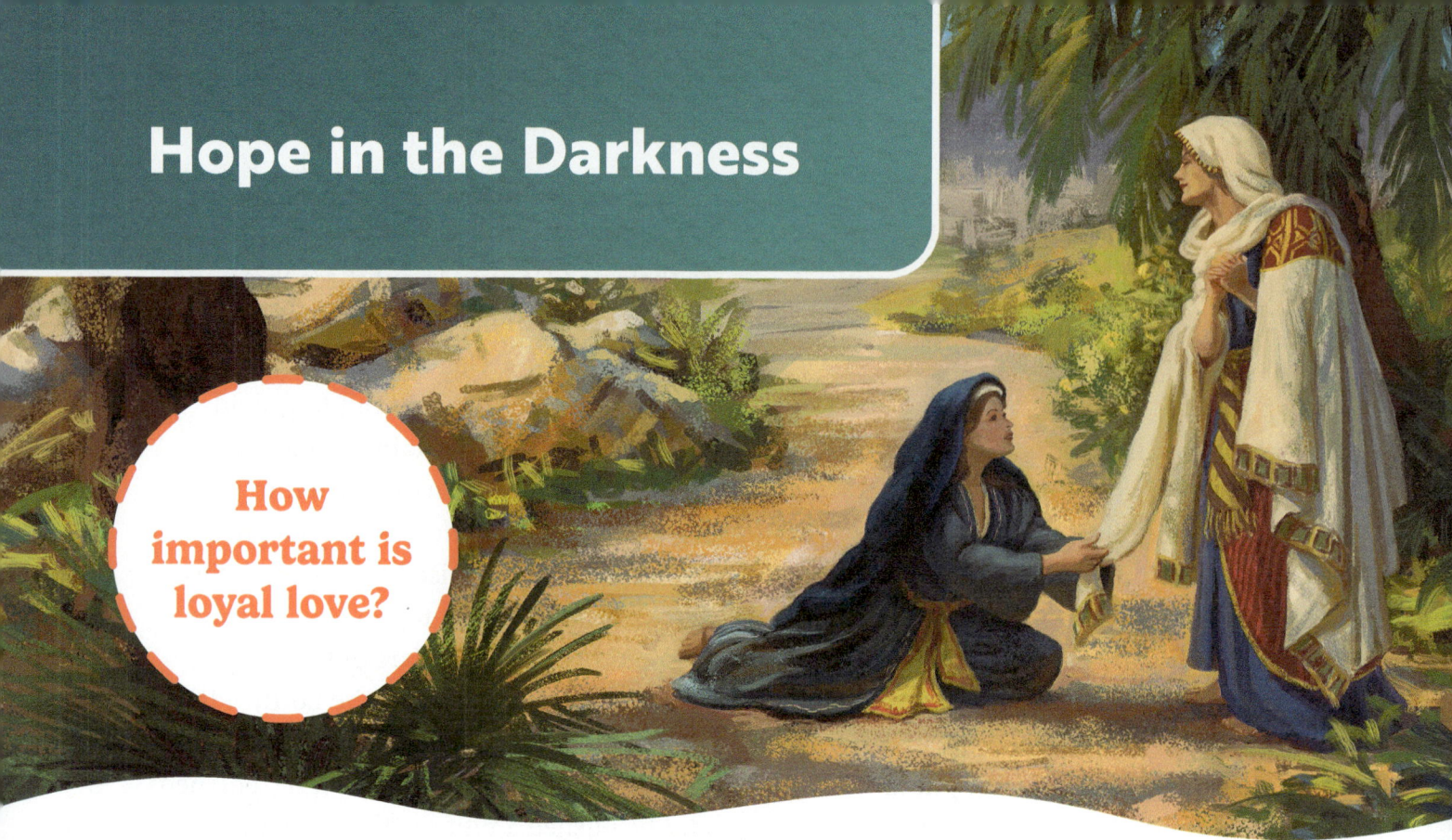

How important is loyal love?

FastFacts about

Ruth

Author: Samuel
Date: 1000 BC
Theme: Loyal love
Meaning of *Ruth*: Refreshment

Interesting Facts:
- The book of Ruth was set during the time of the judges.
- Ruth was a foreigner from Moab.
- She was King David's great-grandmother and ultimately an ancestor of Jesus.
- Ruth and Boaz imitate God's loyal love to Israel.

The Loyalty of Ruth

In the days when the judges ruled, there was a famine in the land. Elimelech and Naomi lived in Bethlehem, and they heard there was food in the neighboring country of Moab. They and their two sons moved there. They lived in Moab for about ten years. While they were there, both boys married Moabite women. One was named Orpah, and the other was Ruth. Then tragedy struck. Naomi's husband and sons died. Naomi, Orpah, and Ruth were now all widows, so they wept together in great sorrow. Naomi decided to return to Israel. She told Orpah and Ruth to return to their families. At first, they both refused and said they would stay with Naomi. Eventually, Orpah decided to return to her family. But Ruth refused to leave Naomi's side. She said, "Do not have me leave you. I will go where you go and live where you live. Your God will be my God, and where you die, I will die. Only death will separate us."

Everyone was surprised when Naomi returned to Bethlehem. Naomi's name meant "pleasant," but her life was now very hard. The women of Bethlehem wondered, "Is this Naomi?" With a heavy heart, Naomi said, "Don't call me Naomi; call me Mara. The Almighty has treated me bitterly." *Mara* means "bitter." Naomi blamed God for her trouble by saying, "I left here full and have come back empty."

? **What did Ruth say was the only thing that would separate her from Naomi?**

Boaz Shows Kindness

It was harvesttime in Bethlehem. According to the Mosaic law, the reapers were not to harvest the corners of the fields and were to leave what was overlooked or dropped. This portion of the harvest was left for widows, orphans, and the poor to gather.

Naomi sent Ruth to gather this leftover grain for them to eat. Ruth was working hard when Boaz, the owner of the field, arrived. He noticed Ruth among the workers and asked who she was. People said that she was Naomi's daughter-in-law and had been working very hard all day. Boaz told Ruth, "Come and work in my fields every day. Don't go to any other fields." When Ruth asked why he was so kind to a stranger like her, Boaz explained, "I've heard how you left your own people and how you have shown great kindness to Naomi. Rest and have your meal with my workers. Gather grain in my fields until the harvest is done."

Ruth was overwhelmed, and Boaz secretly told his workers to drop extra grain so Ruth would find it. Ruth told Naomi all about the kindness of Boaz. Naomi was overjoyed that Ruth was gleaning in the fields of her relative Boaz.

Naomi's Plan for Redemption

Earlier, when Naomi left Israel with her husband, they had sold their land until the year of redemption. This meant the land could be purchased back, but only by a near relative called a "kinsman-redeemer." It was important to Israel and to God that their land would stay with their family. Naomi told Ruth that Boaz was one of their potential kinsman-redeemers.

Because of the harvest, Boaz was busy overseeing the work at the threshing floor. Naomi told Ruth to put on her nicest clothing. Then she told her to uncover the feet of Boaz while he slept and to wait for him to tell her what to do.

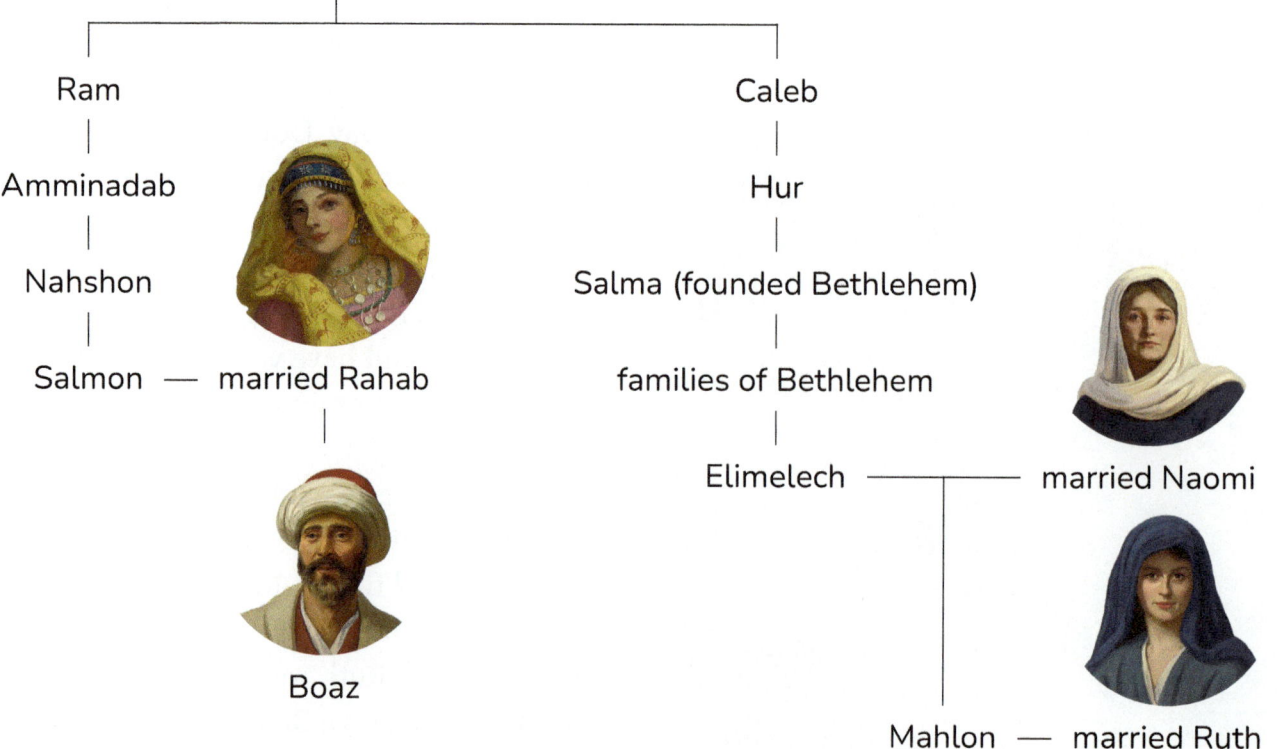

At midnight, Boaz rolled over and was startled to find a woman at his feet! He said, "Who are you?"

"I am Ruth," came the reply. "Protect your servant because you are a close relative and are able to redeem me."

Boaz said, "The Lord bless you! I will do as you have asked, but there is a closer relative who could redeem you. He gets the chance to redeem you first. I'll settle this tomorrow."

Boaz Redeems Ruth

The next day, Boaz gathered ten men to follow him and witness what he and the relative would agree on. He then went to the city gate and found the relative. Boaz explained the situation about Naomi's land. The relative said, "I cannot redeem it. Redeem the land yourself, Boaz."

Boaz was excited to tell Ruth that he was going to redeem the land and that they were going to be married. Naomi was also provided for. The Lord blessed Boaz and Ruth with a son, Obed. He was the father of Jesse, who was the father of David. The dark period of the judges ended with the light of a coming king. Ruth and Boaz showed a **loyal love** that is a picture of God's loyal love to Israel.

> **key term**
> **loyal love**
> Faithful, unfailing love; the love God has for His children.

 What great blessing was given to Ruth?

CHAPTER

The Kingdom and the King

Hannah
A SURPRISING REVERSAL

Why does God value humility?

FastFacts about

1 & 2 Samuel

Author: Unknown

Date: Approximately 915 BC

Theme: God's choice of David's family to lead Israel and of Jerusalem to be the place for divine worship in the temple

Meaning of 1 & 2 Samuel: Named after the judge and prophet from the time between the judges and the kings of Israel

Interesting Facts:
- Originally one book but split into two books when translated into Greek
- Begins with the birth of Samuel and ends with the sin of David's census and God's punishment of Israel for it

Hannah: Loved but Empty

Elkanah was an Israelite. He had two wives. The name of the first wife was Hannah. She couldn't have children. The name of the other wife was Peninnah, and she had children.

Every year, they traveled to Shiloh to worship the Lord and offer sacrifices. Elkanah gave Peninnah and her children portions to give for sacrifice. But he gave a larger portion to Hannah because of his special love for her, even though the Lord did not allow her to have children.

Peninnah often mocked Hannah because the Lord had closed her womb. Peninnah often did this when they went to the house of the Lord. Hannah became so sad that she couldn't eat. Elkanah tried to comfort her by telling her that he was better to her than ten sons would be to her.

? Why did Peninnah mock Hannah?

Hannah went to the tabernacle after mealtime. There she cried out to God. She promised God that if He gave her a son, she would arrange for her son to serve God his whole life. Her lips moved as she prayed, but no sound came out of her mouth. Eli the priest saw her and thought she was drunk with wine. She assured him that she was only seriously praying to God. Eli sent her away with his blessing. She left Shiloh rejoicing. Because she knew God had heard her prayer, her appetite returned and her sadness went away.

Hannah: Praising God

Hannah also thanked God. "My heart rejoices in the Lord. I praise you, God, for this blessing. You are the only holy Lord! You are the only rock!"

Then Hannah spoke of her enemy who mocked her. "Do not speak proudly anymore, because God knows everything. God can **humble** the strong and strengthen those who fall. The wife who had no children will have many. And the one with many children will become weak." Peninnah was finally humbled and put in her place while God lifted Hannah up.

Hannah's prayer was not just about herself and Peninnah. She was speaking about all the Lord's enemies. "The enemies of the Lord shall be broken to pieces," she said. "The Lord shall judge the ends of the earth; and he shall give strength to his King and exalt the horn of his Anointed One."

Hannah: Joyful through Prayer

As Eli had predicted, Hannah did have a son. She named him Samuel, which means "name of God." Because God had given her a child, she named him after God. She told Eli, "This is the child I prayed for. I will keep my promise to give him to the Lord for his whole life." Samuel bowed down and worshiped the Lord, showing his agreement to fulfill his mother's vow.

? What did Hannah promise God about her son?

> **key term**
> ### humility
> Humility is thinking less about oneself and more about others. To be humble is to recognize one's need for God. Pride is the opposite of humility.

? Who did Hannah rejoice in?

Eli
A FAILED PRIEST

What qualities are required for spiritual leaders?

Two Wicked Priests

Eli had two sons, Hophni and Phinehas, who served with him in the tabernacle. Even though they did the duties of priests, they loved evil. They did not follow God's laws about sacrifices. They stole from God and the people by selfishly taking a portion of the meat sacrifice. That was against God's laws. They disrespected their priestly role and God's laws. Hophni and Phinehas did many other wicked things as priests. They brought shame on their father, their job, their nation, and their God.

Samuel: A Godly Priest

Samuel was different. He obeyed God and was a blessing to everyone around him. Every year, Samuel's mother made him a special coat. When his parents came to offer their sacrifice, they would bring the coat to the tabernacle for Samuel. Eli told them, "Because you dedicated Samuel to God for a lifetime of tabernacle service, may the Lord give you more children." God gave Hannah five more children.

Eli's sons, however, continued in their wickedness. Eli told his sons that the people kept talking about their sins. He also warned them that they were sinning directly against God. But they ignored him and kept their sinful lifestyle. Their hearts were hardened. God had already decided to put them to death for their sins.

Who was Samuel?

- The son for whom Hannah had prayed
- Given back to the Lord for lifetime service
- A priest
- The last judge
- The first prophet of Israel
- Anointed the first two kings of Israel

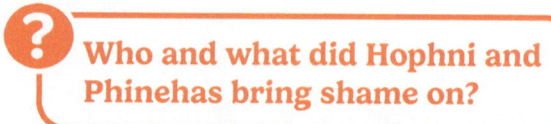

? Who and what did Hophni and Phinehas bring shame on?

The Lord Rejects Eli's Household

A man of God gave Eli a message from God about the privilege of being the priest. God asked Eli, "Why do you treat My work as though it is not important? Why do you honor your sons, but not Me? I will honor those who honor Me, but people who act as though I am not holy will not be honored. Because you have let your sons continue in sin, I will punish them and all those who come after them. All males born into your family will die early. Your two sons will both die on the same day. I will one day raise up a priest who will be faithful to Me. He will be my Anointed One forever."

? How did Eli treat God's work?

Bible Truth

30 **What is sin?**
Sin is failing to do what God commands or doing what God forbids.
1 John 3:4 • James 4:17

Samuel
CALLING A BOY

How can a child serve God?

Under Eli's watch, the boy Samuel faithfully served the Lord in the tabernacle. Even though Eli's eyesight was now dim and he allowed his sons to sin, God was preparing to provide Israel with a more spiritual priest who would be a light in the growing darkness.

God Calls Samuel

One night, Eli was resting and Samuel was lying down. In that time, God wasn't speaking directly to His people. When God first called out to Samuel, he obediently got up. Because he didn't expect God to be the one to call him, Samuel ran to Eli and said, "Here I am."

But Eli said, "I didn't call you. Go lie down again."

God called Samuel again, and again he ran to Eli. "Here I am; you called me." But Eli sent him to lie down again. Samuel did not yet know the Lord. The word of the Lord had not yet been revealed to him.

God called Samuel a third time. "Samuel! Samuel!" Samuel again went to Eli.

This time Eli realized that God was calling Samuel. "If God calls you again, say, 'Speak, for your servant hears.'"

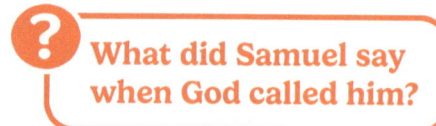
? What did Samuel say when God called him?

God Speaks to Samuel

God did call again, and Samuel answered, "Speak, for your servant hears."

God said, "I am going to do something in Israel. When people hear of it, their ears will tingle." God revealed to Samuel that He was going to fulfill His word by judging Eli's household. Eli knew of the blasphemous sins of Hophni and Phineas but didn't put a stop to them. Because of this, God would judge Eli, his sons, and the rest of their descendants. God made it clear that no sacrifice or offering could stop Him from going through with this punishment.

A Prophet in Israel

In the morning, Samuel was afraid to tell Eli what God had told him. Eli said, "Samuel, my son, what did God say to you? Do not keep it a secret from me." Samuel told Eli all that God said. Eli responded, "That is God's message. May He do what is good in His eyes."

God blessed Samuel and established him as His prophet in Israel. God was once again speaking regularly to His people through Samuel at Shiloh.

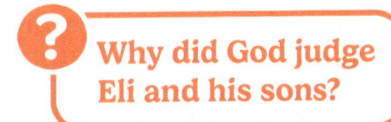

Why did God judge Eli and his sons?

Saul
ISRAEL DEMANDED A KING

Rejecting God: Rejoicing in a King

Why is what I want not always the best thing for me?

When Samuel was old, he made his two sons judges over Israel. But they were bad judges. They were interested in money. Instead of judging people fairly, they took bribes and judged unfairly. Israel's leaders told Samuel, "You are old, and your sons are not righteous like you. Appoint a king to judge us like the other nations." Samuel was upset to hear what the people asked of him, so he prayed to the Lord about it.

God told him, "Do what the people want. They have rejected me as their king and have served other gods ever since I delivered them from Egypt. And now they are rejecting you also. But warn them about the ways of the one who will rule over them."

Samuel told them God's message. "This will be what your king will be like. He will take your children to do his work. He will take your fields and orchards and give them to his servants. He will take a tenth of your crops for his officers. He will take your servants for himself. He will even take some of your animals, and you will be his servants. And when you cry out to God, He will not hear your complaints about how your king is treating you.

In their eagerness to have a king, the people of Israel ignored Samuel's warnings. "We will have a king rule over us so we can be like other nations. He will judge us, defend us, and fight our battles."

Samuel went back to the Lord and told Him about Israel's decision. God replied, "Do what they want; make them a king."

Who did the people of Israel want to be like?

Who did the people of Israel reject by demanding a king from Samuel?

Saul, the People's King

Saul was a very handsome and very tall man from the tribe of Benjamin. His good looks and height caused him to stand out from the rest of the men of Israel. One day, Saul and his servant searched for his father's lost donkeys. When they could not find them, Saul's servant suggested that they see if Samuel's wisdom and insight from God could help them find the lost donkeys. Before Saul arrived, the Lord had told Samuel to anoint Saul as the leader of Israel. Saul didn't even get the chance to tell Samuel why he was there. Samuel quickly told Saul that the donkeys were safe. He then told Saul that he was the person Israel wanted as king.

What was notable about Saul?

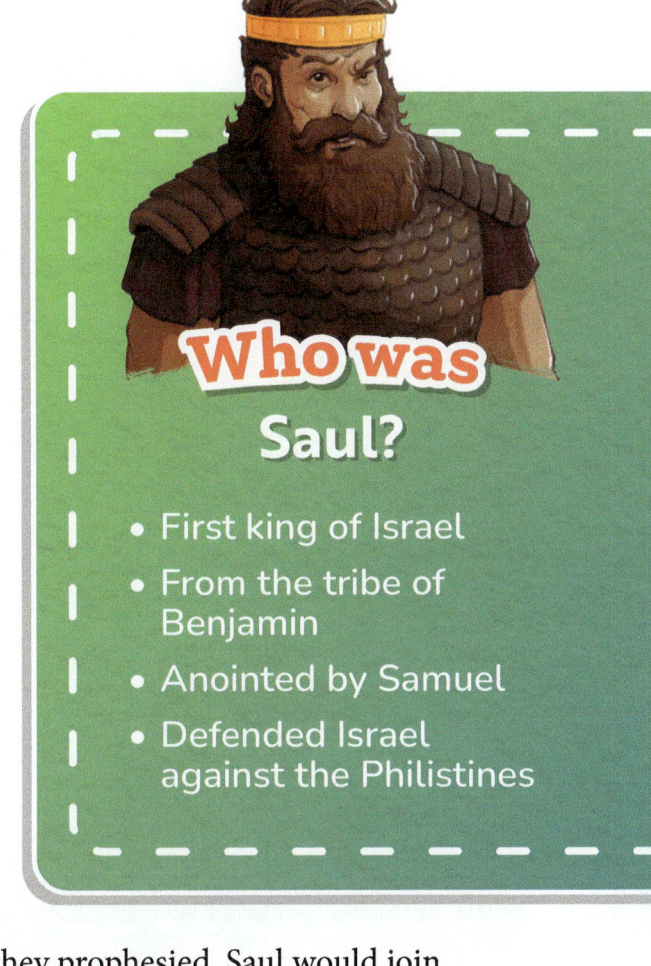

Who was Saul?
- First king of Israel
- From the tribe of Benjamin
- Anointed by Samuel
- Defended Israel against the Philistines

Saul didn't want this responsibility. He objected that his tribe and clan were the most unimportant ones in Israel. But Samuel poured oil on Saul's head to show that God had chosen Saul to be the king of Israel.

Samuel then gave Saul three signs to demonstrate that God had chosen him as king. First, he would meet two men who would tell him that the donkeys had been found. Second, he would meet three men on their way to worship. They would give him two loaves of bread. Third, he would meet a group of prophets.

When they prophesied, Saul would join them, and the Spirit of God would come upon Saul. The Spirit would empower Saul to do what he was supposed to do next. He was to attack the group of Philistine soldiers in his hometown of Gibeah. Then he was to go to Gilgal and wait for seven days for Samuel to come to offer sacrifices.

Everything happened as Samuel had said it would. But Saul did not tell anyone that he was going to become king, and he did not attack the Philistine soldiers.

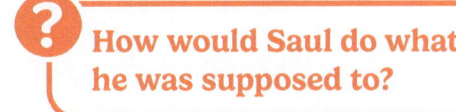
How would Saul do what he was supposed to?

When Saul failed to act, Samuel gathered the people of Israel at Mizpah for his special announcement from God. He spoke God's words. "I freed you from Egypt and from every kingdom that has come against you. But you have rejected your God, the very one who saved you from those who treated you unfairly. You said, 'No, we want a king to be over us.'"

When Samuel finished speaking, a king would be chosen from all the tribes of Israel. God guided the process so Saul would be selected. But Saul could not be found. He was not willing to obey the word of the Lord. But God made his hiding place known, and when Saul was found and stood up in front of the people, he was the tallest man among them. Samuel declared that the tall good-looking man before them was the one whom God had chosen. All the people shouted, "Long live the king!"

Saul went home, and God guided several men to go with him. But still Saul did not attack the Philistine soldiers in his town. He just went back to farming. Only after some relatives in another town were attacked did Saul finally start to rally Israel to fight its enemies. Only then did he really begin to rule as king.

Saul
UNBELIEF AND DISOBEDIENCE

What excuses do I make for sin?

Many years passed with Saul reigning as king in Israel. One day, Samuel said to Saul, "The Lord sent me to anoint you as king over Israel, so you must listen to what He says. Because Amalek attacked Israel when they came out of Egypt, God wants you to destroy every person and animal in that city. Do not keep anything alive."

Saul gathered 210,000 men and destroyed the city of Amalek, as well as the towns in its territory. But he went against God and let King Agag live. Saul's soldiers also let the best of the livestock live. God saw Saul's sins and how he turned from completing God's commands. The Lord spoke to Samuel about Saul's disobedience. He said, "I regret that I made Saul king." In anger, Samuel cried out to God all night before confronting Saul.

Partial Obedience

When Samuel arrived the next day, Saul proudly announced that he had done what the Lord had told him to do. But Samuel replied, "Then why do I hear the bleating of the sheep and the mooing of the cows?" Saul blamed his men and made an excuse that the people kept the animals alive for sacrifices to the Lord.

Samuel challenged Saul. "Does God love burnt offerings and sacrifices as much as He loves obedience? Listen! Obedience is better than sacrifice! Rebellion is as sinful as witchcraft, and stubbornness is as bad as idolatry. Because of your disobedience, God has rejected you from being king over Israel."

Full Rejection

King Saul confessed his sin to Samuel and wanted everything to stay the same. But Samuel told Saul, "Since you have rejected the word of the Lord by disobeying Him in this way, God has rejected you from being king."

Saul desperately reached out to grab Samuel as he turned to leave. But when he did this, he tore Samuel's robe. Samuel told Saul, "The Lord has torn the kingdom from you. He has given it to one of your neighbors—one who is better than you."

Samuel demanded that King Agag be brought to him. Agag thought that maybe his life would be spared. But Agag had been a cruel king and had killed many people. Samuel told him that he would die by the sword, and Samuel himself killed Agag.

Samuel departed from Saul. He did not see Saul ever again. The Lord was sorry that He had made Saul king of Israel. Despite Saul's failure and rejection by God, Samuel mourned for him.

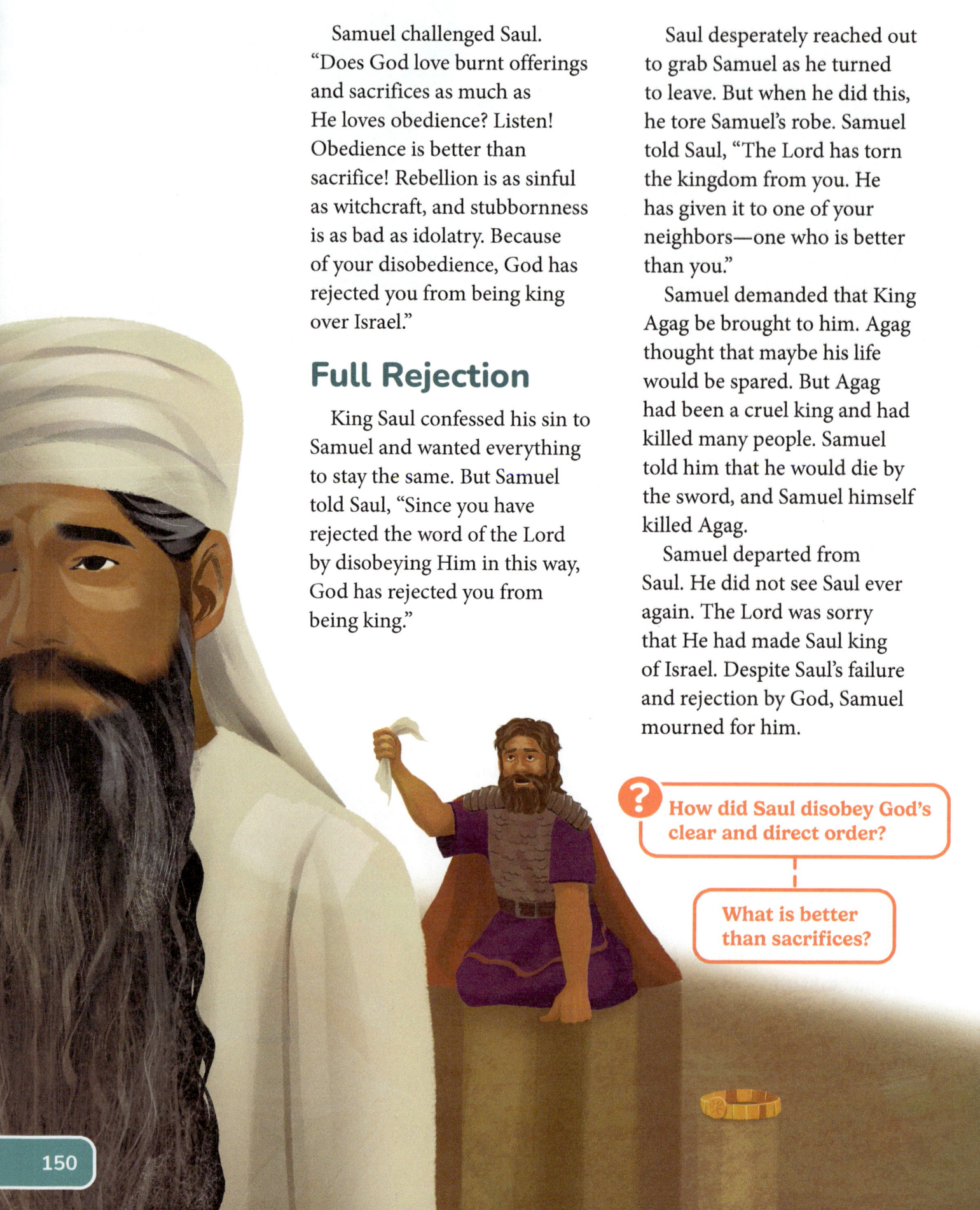

? How did Saul disobey God's clear and direct order?

What is better than sacrifices?

David
ANOINTED TO BE KING

What makes a good king?

God asked Samuel, "How long are you going to be sad about Saul? I have rejected him as king over Israel. I am going to send you to Jesse in Bethlehem. You will anoint one of his sons to be the next king."

But Samuel was afraid that Saul would kill him if he knew what he was doing. Saul still wanted to be king, and he wanted his sons to be kings after him. So God told Samuel to take a calf with him to Bethlehem. Once there, he could sacrifice to God and invite Jesse to join him in the sacrifice. This way, Saul wouldn't wonder why Samuel had gone to Bethlehem.

Who was David?

- Youngest of seven sons
- A shepherd
- Killed a giant who defied God
- A victorious warrior
- Israel's exemplary king
- A murderer
- A man after God's own heart
- Wrote almost half the book of Psalms

Samuel did exactly what God told him to do. When Samuel arrived, people were afraid and asked why he had come. Samuel answered, "I came to sacrifice to the Lord." He told Jesse and his sons to come to the sacrifice. When Jesse's family came, Samuel looked at Jesse's oldest son, Eliab, who was tall and good-looking. Samuel thought to himself, "For sure, the Lord's anointed is right here."

But God told Samuel, "Do not consider his looks or height. I have rejected him. The Lord doesn't see only what people see. People look at appearance, but the Lord looks at a person's heart."

Then one by one, Jesse's seven sons passed before Samuel to see if one of them was God's choice. But Samuel said to Jesse, "No, the Lord has not chosen any of these. Are all your sons here?"

"Not all of them," Jesse replied. "The youngest one is taking care of the sheep."

Samuel said, "Bring him here. We have to finish this task before we do anything else."

When David, Jesse's youngest son, came in, Samuel could see that he had beautiful eyes and was handsome. The Lord told Samuel, "Get up and anoint him, for he is the one." Obediently, Samuel anointed David with oil while his brothers looked on. Immediately, the Spirit of the Lord came upon David. Having finished what God told him to do, Samuel left.

? **Why did Samuel think Eliab was God's choice?**

Why wasn't David brought to meet with Samuel?

What is more important to God, one's outward appearance or one's heart?

David
CONFIDENT IN GOD

How can a shepherd defeat a warrior in battle?

A Giant Warrior and a Small Shepherd

There was war in Israel. The armies of Philistia and Israel faced each other on two opposing mountains. The Philistine champion was a terrifying man named Goliath. He was over nine feet tall and was decked out in full soldier gear and armor. His twelve-foot spear alone weighed over thirty-three pounds. Goliath even had a man to carry his shield and walk in front of him.

Goliath demanded to fight a champion from Israel. The loser's nation would be servants to the winner's nation. Goliath blasphemously mocked the one true God. This all made Israel shake in fear. No one in all of Saul's army was brave enough to fight Goliath.

David's three oldest brothers were soldiers in Saul's army, but David was not. He was at home with his aging father and tending to their flocks. One day, his father sent him with supplies to his brothers. When David arrived, he saw Israel's fear and heard Goliath mock the God of Israel.

David asked, "What will be done for the man who kills this Philistine and takes away this dishonor from Israel? Who is this Philistine who defies the armies of the living God?"

David's oldest brother angrily scolded him for coming, but when word of David reached King Saul, he sent for him. Saul took one look at him and told him that he was too young.

David protested. "I have killed a lion and a bear in order to protect my sheep. God will keep me safe from this Philistine, just as God has kept me safe from those beasts."

Saul replied, "Go, and God be with you."

? Who was Goliath insulting?

What was the closest thing to military experience that David had?

A Shepherd and His Lord

Saul put his own armor on David, but David was not used to fighting in armor. This did not worry David, though. He took his rod, sling, and five smooth stones from the stream as he faced Goliath.

Goliath cursed David by his gods. "I'm going to feed your dead body to the birds and wild beasts."

But David responded, "You come with sword and spear, but I come to you in the name of the Lord of hosts. God will deliver you into my hand. I will strike you down and cut off your head. I will feed your armies' dead bodies to the birds and wild beasts. Then all people on earth will know that there is a God in Israel. The battle is the Lord's to win."

As David ran toward the Philistine, he put a stone in his sling and slung it. It hit Goliath square on the forehead and sank in, and Goliath fell facedown. David ran up and used Goliath's sword to cut off his head. When the Philistines saw that their champion had been defeated, they ran away.

? Who was humbled in this story?

David
PATH TO THE THRONE

Hunted by His Own King

David often served Saul by playing music for him and by leading in battles for him. He also became close friends with Saul's son Jonathan. But when Saul heard the people praising David more than they praised him, he became jealous and hated David.

One day as David played his harp for the king, Saul threw a spear at him. David escaped. Then Saul sent David to fight the Philistines, hoping that the Philistines would kill him. But God was always with David.

King Saul commanded his own men and his son Jonathan to kill him. God warned David, so David and his men fled to the wilderness. Though Saul hunted David daily, God protected David. Jonathan refused to hunt David and instead encouraged him. "Don't be afraid. You will be Israel's king."

? What encouragement did Jonathan give David about his kingship?

Saved by His King's Enemy

Once, David and Saul were on opposite sides of the same mountain. Saul was getting very close to capturing David. But God was in control. A messenger came at just the right time and told Saul, "Go home right away! The Philistines have invaded your land!" Saul gave up the chase and returned home.

Why is it important to do the right thing at the right time?

Cave Mates

Saul didn't stop his hunt for David. One day as he was hunting David, he went into a cave to rest. He didn't know it, but David and his army were hiding in that same cave. David tiptoed behind Saul and cut off a piece of his robe. David was committed to keeping Saul safe. Even though David's men wanted him to kill Saul, David wouldn't allow his men to even touch the king.

After Saul left the cave, David called to Saul, "My lord the king!" and bowed. "Why do you believe those who lie, saying that I want to hurt you? I could've killed you in this cave, but you are the Lord's anointed. Even though you are trying to kill me, I spared your life!"

Saul answered, "David, you are righteous. May God reward you. I know that you will be the king of Israel." Saul asked David to promise to not kill all of his descendants when he became king. David swore that he wouldn't. Saul then went home, but David returned to the stronghold.

? What did Saul say God would do for David?

King Saul's Death

What's the best way to get to the top?

The King Is Dead

Saul did not stop hunting David, so David fled to the territory of the Philistines, where Saul wouldn't go looking for him.

King Saul faced a new problem. There was another war with the Philistine army. Israel was losing the battle. Many soldiers were dying, and even Saul's sons were killed. King Saul was badly wounded by the Philistine archers. Saul asked his armor-bearer to kill him before the enemy army found him. But his armor-bearer was too afraid to do what Saul asked. Saul then took his own life to save his pride and end his agony. The Philistines celebrated their victory by mistreating Saul's dead body. They also sent his armor into their cities and presented it to their false gods. However, some brave men from Israel retrieved the bodies of Saul and his sons. They buried their bones and fasted for seven days.

David Mourns Saul's Death

An Amalekite man told David, "I saw that Saul was wounded in the battle. He asked me to kill him because he was suffering. He would not have lived. So I killed him, took his crown, and brought it here to you."

David and his men tore their clothes in sorrow. They mourned for Saul, Jonathan, the rest of the dead soldiers, and the house of Israel until evening. David asked the Amalekite, "How were you not afraid to kill the Lord's anointed?"

David told a servant to execute the Amalekite who said that he had murdered King Saul. David had great respect for Saul, even though Saul showed only hatred for him.

? Why did David order the execution of the Amalekite who said he killed King Saul?

David Honors Israel's Royal Family

David was very sad to hear that Saul and Jonathan had been killed in battle. He said, "The glory of Israel is slain; how the mighty have fallen! Do not tell it in places where the Philistines will rejoice. The mighty are wickedly thrown aside. The sword of Saul was successful. Saul and Jonathan were pleasant, united, swifter than eagles, and stronger than lions. Weep over Saul who gave you ornaments of gold, oh daughters of Israel. Oh, how the mighty have fallen in battle! I am very saddened for you, my brother, Jonathan. Your friendship was pleasant. Your love for me was extraordinary. How the mighty have fallen, and the weapons of war perished!"

> **?** What emotion did David express when he heard about King Saul's and Jonathan's deaths?

CHAPTER

10

God's Covenant with David

David
ELEVATED TO BE KING

How does God use people to carry out His plans?

After the death of King Saul, God directed David to travel to the city of Hebron in Judah. The people there anointed David king over the southern region of Judah. But much of the northern part of Israel wasn't ready to submit to their new king. Many were still faithful to Saul and his family line. So at that same time, Abner, the commander of Saul's army, anointed Saul's son Ishbosheth as king over the northern region of Israel.

❓ What happened to David in Hebron?

Ishbosheth
Saul's son; made king in the north when Saul died

Abner
commander of Saul's army; killed Joab's brother

David
first made king in the south

Joab
commander of David's army

David's Rise to Power

As a result of this lack of unity, there was continual war between David and Ishbosheth. David's army grew stronger, but Ishbosheth's army grew weaker because of his poor leadership. Abner became frustrated with Ishbosheth and told him, "The only reason you're king is because of me. I'm going to give this kingdom back into the hands of David where it should be."

Abner sent a message to David that said, "If you make an agreement with me, Israel can be united." David agreed. But before Abner could return home, Joab, the commander of David's army, killed Abner to avenge the death of Joab's brother. As David mourned Abner, all of Israel understood that David was innocent of Abner's murder. News of Abner's death weakened the hearts of Ishbosheth and his kingdom. Because of this, two of Ishbosheth's captains came to his home by night and killed him as he slept. David had the two men killed for taking the life of Saul's son. Now that Ishbosheth's kingship was over, David was made king of all Israel.

God Fulfills His Covenant with Abraham

Israel's enemies, the Jebusites, were living in the city of Jerusalem. Because it was part of the land promised to Israel, David and his strong army drove out the Jebusites. David moved to Jerusalem, which was also called the stronghold of Zion, and he gave it another name: the city of David. David finally reigned over all Israel. His reign lasted forty years. God was fulfilling the promise to Abraham that kings would come from his family.

Bible Truth

45 **What did God promise in the Abrahamic Covenant?**
God promised to give Abraham a land and a seed and to make him a blessing to all people.
Genesis 12:1–3, 7 • 15:1–21 • 17:1–14

The Davidic Covenant

How does the Davidic Covenant relate to me?

David Recalled God's Goodness

God had chosen David as king years before he became king in Israel. When David was a young man tending his father's sheep, God sent Samuel to anoint him as king. Even though David had faithfully served his king, King Saul became afraid of David's popularity. David eventually had to run for his life. Now, years later, God placed the kingdom securely in the hands of King David. God gave David victory over all his enemies and over all the nations around Israel. David was determined to honor God for His kindness to him and to all Israel.

A Temple for the Lord

David told the prophet Nathan about his plan to honor God. "I live in a beautiful house made of cedar wood. But the ark of the Lord sits in a tent made of curtains. I would like to build a house where we can place the ark of the covenant." Nathan did not stop to ask the Lord about David's plan. He thought it was a good idea, so he told David to do what was in his heart and that the Lord was with him.

That night, God spoke to Nathan. "Tell David not to build me a house. Ever since I delivered Israel from Egypt, I have lived in a tent. And at no point have I commanded anyone to build me a house."

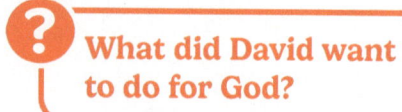

? What did David want to do for God?

God's Covenant with David

The Lord spoke to David through Nathan. "I took you from shepherding sheep. I gave you victory over the enemies of Israel. I will give you a great name like other great kings who came before you. But the other kings will be forgotten. Also, I will be with Israel and give them their own land. They will be a nation at rest. They will never be driven out of their land again." Instead of David building the Lord a house, the Lord promised David that He would build a house for him. God said, "This house will not be a wooden building, but a royal family that will not pass away." The Lord also promised David, "I will build a kingdom for your son. His kingdom will be an everlasting kingdom, and he will build a temple for my name."

God made it very clear that, though His promise would include David's sons, any unfaithfulness would still be corrected and punished. But God promised to never take away His loyal love for David and his seed. God told David that when his son sins, He will discipline him with problems at home and battles against enemies. But God was talking about more than just David's son—He was also talking about a Son who would come many years later. "He will be the Son of David, but I will be a Father to Him. I will never remove my loyal love from Him. I will establish your house, kingdom, and throne forever."

? What did God say He was going to do for David?

? What does God mean by building David a house?

David's Prayer

David was greatly humbled by all that God said. He replied, "Who am I, and who is my family that we should reign over Your people?" He remembered his own weakness and said, "Lord, you know what I am and who I am." David praised God with a full heart by saying, "Lord, you are great. There is not another God like you. You are the true God, and there is no other god." David also pleaded with God. "Let Your word come to pass. Please build my house. I am only bold enough to ask this because of Your great promises. May You bring to pass all that You have said, and may my house be blessed forever as You have promised."

? How long would David's kingdom last?

Bible Truth

47 **What did God promise in the Davidic Covenant?**
God promised that the Seed of David would rule over the entire world for the glory of God and the good of others.

2 Samuel 7:8–16
1 Chronicles 17:7–14
Psalm 89:3–4, 19–37

The Davidic Covenant
PSALM 2

Why is it crucial to submit to the Messiah?

key term
Messiah

Messiah is the Hebrew word that refers to Jesus Christ as the anointed prophet, priest, and king spoken of in the Old Testament.

Fast Facts about
Psalm 2

Author: David
Date: 975 BC
Theme: Obedience to the Lord's Anointed, the Son of God

Interesting Facts:
- This psalm speaks of David's descendants and how they will reign from Jerusalem, just like God had promised.
- This psalm looks ahead to when the Davidic Messiah will rule all nations forever.

David wrote Psalm 2. The promises of the Davidic Covenant went beyond his son Solomon. They would be fulfilled by the **Messiah** whom David wrote about in this psalm. The coming of the Messiah was certain. He will rule over all the kings of the earth and will put down all their rebellion against God.

Man's Rebellion

Since the reign of the Son is certain, David begins Psalm 2 by saying, "Why do the kings and nations rage against the Lord and against His Anointed? The rulers of the earth have revolted against the Lord and His Son, saying, 'Let's break free from the Lord's authority. The kingdoms belong to us. We don't need God telling us what to do.'" These kings are deceived into thinking that they can successfully rebel against God.

God's Response

David further writes that as kings rise in rebellion against God, He is not troubled or afraid. He knows their weakness and pride. God laughs at and mocks their show of strength. They will all be overthrown, and God announces His coming victory. David tells of the great coming King who will sit on the throne in Jerusalem.

? *Who is the King of Zion?*

God's Call

The Messiah, the King, then speaks. He announces a decree that the Lord has made to Him. "You are My Son. Today I have begotten You." This statement refers to the Davidic Covenant, in which God promised to be a Father to David's heirs and promised to make the Davidic King His Son. Psalm 2 reveals that this King will not rule over only Israel. The Father gives the earth and all its nations to His Son. There is no limit or boundary to the Son's kingdom. Those who resist His authority will be destroyed and shattered like a dish that falls to the floor. Therefore, David writes that instead of fighting against God, leaders should listen to what the King has to say and submit to Him. God's call through the psalmist is for sinners to serve the King, worship Him, and reject the rebellion that leads to destruction. God blesses all who take refuge in Him.

Bible Truth

55 How is Christ the King?
Christ rules over us, will come to judge the world, and will establish His kingdom on earth.

Psalm 2:6–8 • Acts 2:34–36
1 Corinthians 15:25

? Who does God give to the King of Zion as loyal subjects?

Absalom
A FAILED CONSPIRACY

How does God's discipline show His love?

David's Failure as a Father

Absalom was one of King David's sons. He had to leave the country because he killed his brother Amnon for mistreating their sister, Tamar. After several years, David permitted Absalom to return to Jerusalem, but David wouldn't see him for two years. Finally, Absalom spoke to Joab, David's general. "Why did the king bring me to Jerusalem if he doesn't want to see me?" Joab would not answer Absalom, so Absalom had Joab's field set on fire. Joab eventually spoke to the king about his son. David finally allowed Absalom to see him and kissed him when they met. This signaled that David had restored Absalom.

? What did King David not allow Absalom to do when he first returned to Jerusalem?

Absalom's Rebellion

After this, Absalom plotted to overthrow his father. He presented himself as a powerful man by parading around the city with chariots, horses, and men who did what he told them to do. When people came to the king for judgments, Absalom would meet them first. He acted as a friend who cared. He took their hands, listened to their complaints, and agreed with them. He'd say, "If I were made to be judge in Israel, I would give everyone the justice they deserve." With his fake concern, he won the hearts of Israel.

? How did Absalom treat those who came to see the king?

Absalom's Conspiracy

It had been about nine years since Absalom killed his brother. He asked his father for permission to go to Hebron, the city where David had been presented as king. Absalom told his father that he needed to go there to fulfill a vow he had made to serve the Lord. David told him to go in peace. Absalom took many men with him who didn't know of his conspiracy. When Absalom arrived in Hebron, he secretly sent men throughout Israel. He told them, "When you hear the sound of the trumpet, tell all the people, 'Absalom reigns in Hebron!'"

? Where did Absalom go to begin his rebellion?

David's Soldiers Fight for Him

Soon, a messenger came to David with news that Absalom had rebelled against the king and had taken Hebron. Absalom was heading toward David to overthrow Jerusalem. David was a man of war, so he went into action. He gathered his household and his loyal soldiers, and then he moved out of the city. David wept as they went up the Mount of Olives toward the wilderness. The high priest brought the ark of the covenant to go with David. But David sent the ark back, saying, "If I find favor in the eyes of the Lord, He will bring me back to Jerusalem to see it again."

Advice from His Counselors

Absalom sent for Ahithophel, who was one of David's counselors. His counsel was so respected that many said it was like the voice of God. He was not loyal to David, so he willingly joined Absalom against him.

David asked his friend and loyal counselor, Hushai, to stay in Jerusalem. David instructed Hushai, "Pretend to pledge loyalty to Absalom. Give him bad advice that goes against the words of Ahithophel."

Absalom and his men wanted to know how best to defeat David's army. Ahithophel advised, "Attack David now. If you go now, you will scatter David's army." They asked Hushai for advice as well. Following David's instructions to confuse Absalom, he said, "You know that your father is a mighty warrior, and his men are fierce in battle. Wait until all Israel has joined you against David. Then you will easily defeat him." Absalom said, "The counsel of Hushai is better than Ahithophel's." Hushai's counsel would be followed instead of Ahithophel's, just as God planned. God was actively defending Jerusalem and bringing down Absalom.

Defeat of Absalom

David prepared to lead his men into battle, but his men would not let him fight. "If you are killed, the battle is over. You must stay in the city!" Ever the loving father, David asked for his men to deal kindly with Absalom. The battle began in the thick woods of Ephraim. Absalom's army was badly defeated. As Absalom rode on a mule in battle, his thick hair got caught in a tangle of tree branches. His mule ran off, leaving him hanging from the tree.

Joab heard that Absalom was seen hanging from a tree, so he went and personally killed Absalom. After the battle was over, David mourned his son. "I wish I had died instead of you, oh Absalom, my son, my son!"

David was eventually brought back to Jerusalem as king over Judah. He also eventually gained the allegiance of the northern tribes of Israel. Absalom was humbled and was killed. David was humbled, but according to God's faithfulness, he was restored.

> **?** How did Israel respond to David after the battle?

CHAPTER

11

A Kingdom Divided

Solomon Chose Wisdom

FastFacts about

1 & 2 Kings

Author: Unknown

Date: 6th century BC

Theme: Israel suffers many times for its repeated sinfulness, but there is hope because the line of kings hasn't ended and God is still ready to forgive those who repent.

Meaning of Kings: Named after all the kings of Israel and Judah

Interesting Facts:
- Originally one book but split into two books when translated into Greek
- Starts with the death of David and the reign of Solomon
- Tells how the kingdom divided
- Ends with the destruction of Jerusalem by Nebuchadnezzar and the fall of Judah's last king, Zedekiah.

What makes someone wise?

Solomon Begins to Reign

When David grew old, he proclaimed that his son Solomon would be the next king of Israel. Solomon's older half-brother, Adonijah, tried to get Israel to crown him king instead. However, his efforts came to nothing. Before his death, David made sure that all the people knew that God had chosen Solomon to be king.

At the beginning of his reign, Solomon unwisely married Pharaoh's idol-worshiping daughter. Solomon loved the Lord, but not with all his heart. For the most part, he was obedient to what his father David taught him about God.

Who was Solomon?

- Son of King David
- Third king of Israel
- Reigned for 40 years
- Wrote Ecclesiastes, Proverbs, Song of Solomon, and two psalms
- Built the first temple in Jerusalem
- A teacher of wisdom

Solomon's Request

King Solomon went up to Gibeon to offer sacrifices to God. The temple had not yet been built, and the people would offer sacrifices in certain high places. Solomon offered one thousand burnt offerings to the Lord.

The Lord appeared to Solomon in a dream, asking what Solomon wanted for God to give him. Solomon answered, "You have been very merciful to my father and merciful by allowing me to be king. But I am like a child, not knowing what to do. You made me king over Your chosen people, who have become too many to count. Help me wisely decide what is right and wrong as I govern this great multitude."

God was delighted with Solomon's request. "I'm very pleased that you asked me for **wisdom** rather than for a long life, riches, or the death of your enemies. You asked for understanding to know good judgment, so I will give you an understanding heart. As a result, there has never been nor will there ever be anybody like you. I will also give you the riches and honor you didn't ask for. There will be no other king like you while you live. And if you obey my words, as David your father obeyed, I will give you a long life."

Solomon woke from his dream and went to Jerusalem. There, he stood in front of the ark of the covenant and offered burnt offerings and peace offerings to the Lord.

> **key term**
> **wisdom**
> Wisdom is the skillful use of knowledge to live successfully and rightly.

? What did God give Solomon?

Wisdom at Work

Two women who lived in the same house came to King Solomon to settle a serious argument. Both women had newborn babies, but one woman's baby had died while she was sleeping. When she awoke and saw that her baby was dead, she switched her baby with the other woman's living baby. But when the other woman woke up and saw the dead baby, she knew it wasn't hers. Each woman insisted that the living baby was her own. They came to Solomon arguing. "My child is alive. Hers is dead!"

King Solomon responded by asking for a sword. "Cut the living baby in half," Solomon commanded. "Give each woman one half of the baby."

Immediately, one woman cried out, "Do not hurt the child! Give it to her!"

The other woman said, "Let neither one of us claim the baby. Go ahead and cut him in half!"

By this, King Solomon understood who the real mother was. He gave the baby to the woman who would never want her baby to be harmed. All Israel heard how Solomon had settled this argument and knew that God had blessed him with great wisdom.

Wisdom Tested

The Queen of Sheba heard about Solomon's wisdom from the Lord. She wanted to see this wisdom for herself. She prepared hard questions to test him with, then she traveled to Jerusalem. She was very impressed by his wise answers. She was also amazed at the house he built, his meals, the behavior and clothing of his servants, and the burnt offerings he offered. All of this left her in awe.

Wisdom Praised

The Queen of Sheba told King Solomon, "I didn't believe the good reports about you until I saw and heard you for myself. The men and servants who hear your wisdom are blessed. Now I understand that I had not heard even half of all your glory! Because the Lord loves Israel forever, He has made you king so that you will do what is right for His people."

As a sign of her respect, the Queen of Sheba gave Solomon a very large gift of gold, spices, and precious stones. Solomon gifted her with whatever she wanted before she returned home.

> **?** What was the Queen of Sheba impressed with upon meeting Solomon?

The Building of God's House

Where is God's presence with His people now?

Construction of God's House

It had been almost five hundred years since Israel had left Egypt. It was now the fourth year of King Solomon's reign. He started building a house for the Lord. He knew that God had promised his father David that he, as David's son and the next king of Israel, would build a house for the Lord. The building of the temple would be done with great care and would be directly overseen by Solomon himself.

The Lord spoke to Solomon during the building of the temple, "If you live according to My commandments, I will do what I promised to your father. I will dwell among you, and I will not leave you."

? What did Solomon have to do to experience what God had promised?

The Inner Sanctuary

It took seven years to build the temple. Solomon used the design he received from his father David to build the temple. Since the temple was a permanent building, it was larger than the tabernacle. The inner sanctuary, called the holy of holies, was cube-shaped and about thirty feet wide on each side. All the room's surfaces, as well as the whole house, were covered with gold. The holy of holies had two gold-covered cherubim in it. They stood beside each other, and their outstretched wings touched both walls. The doors had carvings of cherubim, palm trees, and flowers. Everything was covered in gold and featured the finest workmanship available.

The Ark in the Temple

When the temple was finished, Solomon gathered Israel's leaders together. The priests and Levites carefully brought the ark of the covenant and the holy objects into the temple. King Solomon and the people with him sacrificed to the Lord. The number of sheep and oxen that they sacrificed couldn't be counted.

Finally, the priests brought the ark of the covenant into the holy of holies and set it under the wings of the cherubim. The cherubim's wings covered the ark.

When the priests left the holy place, a cloud filled the house of the Lord. The priests could not do their duties because the glory of the Lord had filled the house.

? What filled the temple?

Solomon's Blessing

Solomon told the people, "Blessed be the Lord, who spoke to my father David and has done what He promised. God chose David to lead Israel. My father wanted to build a house for the Lord. But God told him that I, David's son, would build a temple. Today, I am the king of Israel, as God promised. I have built this house for the Lord. I have made a place for the ark that contains the covenant that the Lord made with our fathers when He brought them out of Egypt."

Solomon's Prayer of Dedication

Solomon knelt in front of the altar of the Lord, lifted his hands to heaven, and prayed, "O Lord, God of Israel, there is no God like You. You are merciful and faithful to Your word. Continue to provide a king over Israel, and faithfully answer Your people's prayers for forgiveness. Condemn the wicked but bless the righteous. When Your people's sin removes them from their land or stops the rain from falling, hear their prayer for forgiveness. Put them back in their land and send the rain again. Fearing You is what will keep them in this land and make them prosperous in it.

"Answer Your people's prayer for victory over their enemies. But if they sin and You allow them to be captured, and they repent with all their heart and soul, let their captors have compassion on them. Forgive them and answer their prayer. These are Your people, whom You chose out of all the nations of the earth."

Solomon stood and praised the Lord for His faithfulness. He asked for God's continued presence with them. Solomon prayed that they would love and obey God and keep all His commandments. Lastly, he asked that God would make His name great in the earth and remember his prayer.

Solomon's Sacrifices

The king and his people offered another 142,000 animal sacrifices and dedicated the house of the Lord. The celebration lasted for two weeks. The people returned to their homes with glad hearts because God showed goodness toward His people.

> **?** What would lead to the Israelites being captured and removed from their land?

Solomon Disobeyed God

If You Obey, Your Kingdom Will Remain

The Lord appeared to Solomon and said, "I have heard your prayer and have set apart the temple for My glory. If you and your descendants obey Me, I will make sure that you have a descendant to sit on the throne. But if you sin and Israel turns to worship idols, I will remove Israel from the land and cast them out of My sight. This temple will crumble into a pile of rubble. Everyone who passes by and sees the empty land and the destroyed house will know that Israel has been punished this way because of their sin."

Why do we need a greater King?

? What did God warn Israel about?

Tons of Gold, Thousands of Horses, and Hundreds of Wives

Solomon partnered with Hiram, king of Tyre, to get supplies and workers for all his building projects. Solomon even partnered with Hiram to build a fleet of ships that could sail to Ophir and bring back large quantities of gold every year. He had some of the gold pounded into shields to decorate his houses. He also made a gold-covered ivory throne that had a golden lion on each side of it. He even made golden drinking cups. His wealth was beyond comparison. Solomon was greater than any king in both riches and wisdom. People from around the world wanted to hear his wisdom and see his riches.

Solomon had 1,400 chariots and 12,000 horsemen in different cities. Silver was as common as stone, and expensive cedar wood was as common as any other wood. Solomon imported thousands of horses and even traded horses with neighboring nations.

God had told the Israelites, "Do not marry women from other countries because they will turn your heart to worship false gods." But Solomon greatly loved having all his foreign wives, who were from at least six other nations. He had a total of one thousand wives. Many of his wives were not followers of the God of Israel. They turned Solomon's heart away from God and led him to worship false gods. He was not true in his love for God like his father David had been. Solomon committed the serious sin of idolatry by worshiping Ashtoreth, the goddess of the Sidonians, and Milcom, the abomination of the Ammonites. He used some of his riches to build high places so his wives could worship their false gods.

God was angry and said, "Since you haven't kept the covenant I made with you, even though I appeared to you twice, I will tear the kingdom from you and give most of it to your servant. Because I respect David your father, I won't do this until you are dead and your son is on the throne. However, I will give one tribe to your son for David's sake and for the sake of My chosen city, Jerusalem."

Because of Solomon's sin, God raised up two enemies who hated Israel, Hadad and Rezon. These two men and their followers were the beginning of the unrest and lack of peace that Solomon would experience as king.

? **What did Solomon do as a result of marrying foreign women?**

So far, who has been the only faithful person of those involved in the Davidic Covenant?

Jeroboam and the Man of God

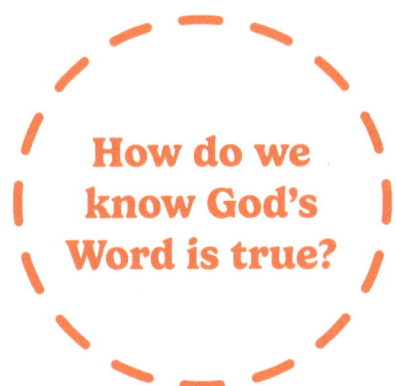

How do we know God's Word is true?

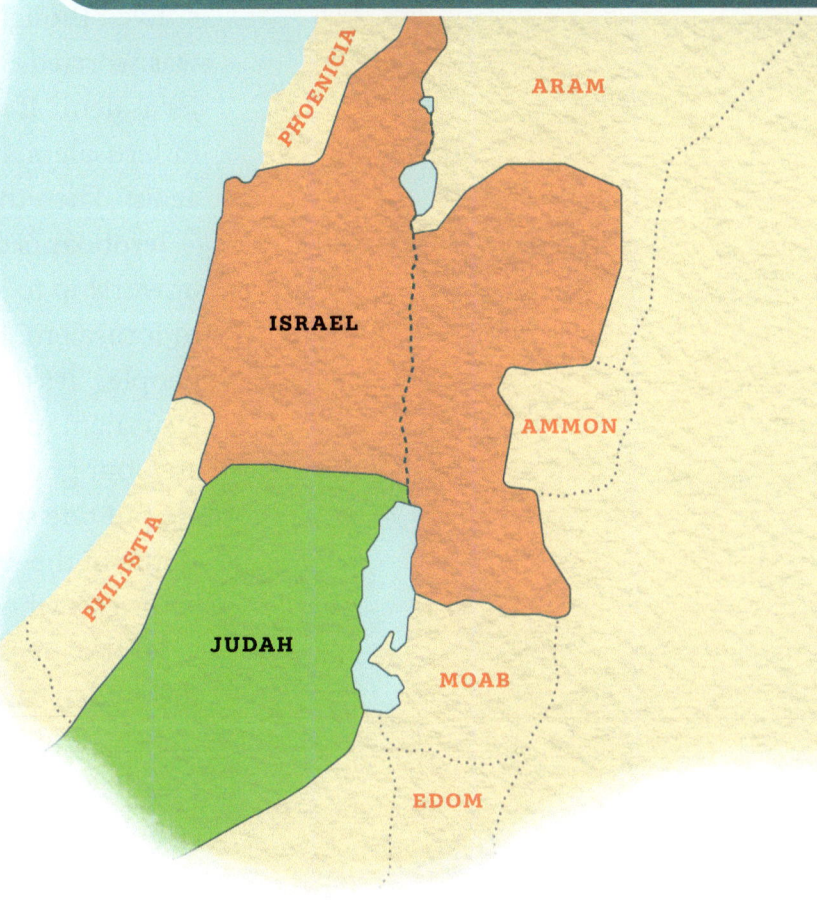

Israel Divides

God raised up Jeroboam against Solomon. Jeroboam was a servant of Solomon who was put in charge of many things through his hard work. A prophet named Ahijah came and talked to Jeroboam alone. The prophet tore the new robe he was wearing into twelve pieces and gave ten of those pieces to Jeroboam. He told Jeroboam that God had said, "I will tear the kingdom away from Solomon and give you ten tribes. But Solomon's son will still have one tribe for David's and Jerusalem's sake. I have chosen Jerusalem from all the tribes of Israel and will keep My name there. Israel has forsaken Me by worshiping other gods and disobeying My commandments."

How had Israel forsaken God?

Jeroboam Receives Ten Tribes

The prophet continued God's message. "If you obey Me and do what is right as David did, I will bless you. I will establish you and give Israel to you. As for David's seed, they will have trouble, but not forever."

Solomon heard about this meeting and sought to kill Jeroboam. But Jeroboam ran away to Egypt and stayed there until Solomon's death.

Solomon died after reigning in Jerusalem for forty years. After Solomon's death, his son Rehoboam was crowned the next king. But when Jeroboam heard of Solomon's death, he came back to Israel. Rehoboam was harsh with Israel from the start of his reign. The northern ten tribes followed Jeroboam, and Judah in the south followed Solomon's son Rehoboam. The prophet Ahijah's words were fulfilled, just as the Lord had spoken by him.

Jeroboam's Idolatrous Plan

Even though he controlled most of Israel, Jeroboam was worried. "What if these people desire to go back to Jerusalem? If the people sacrifice in the house of the Lord in Jerusalem, they will be convinced to follow Rehoboam again. Then they will turn on me and will kill me."

Jeroboam's counselors told him to make a new place of worship to keep the people from wanting to go back to Jerusalem. He made two calves of gold and told the people, "It's too much for you to travel all the way to Jerusalem to worship. Look at these golden statues. These are your gods that brought you out of the land of Egypt." He put one statue in the southern town of Bethel and one statue in the northern town of Dan. He also chose men to be priests who were not from the tribe of Levi.

Jeroboam established a day for feasting and celebrating the golden calves he had made. He copied what was done rightly in Judah at the temple. But the place, the idols, the altar, the sacrifices, and the priesthood that Jeroboam established were not at all according to the law of God.

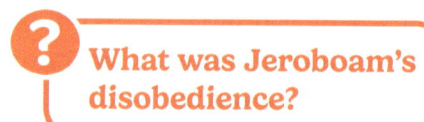

? What was Jeroboam's disobedience?

A Man of God Confronts Jeroboam

Because of Jeroboam's great sin, God sent a prophet with a message for him. He found Jeroboam making offerings at the altar in Bethel. The man of God cried out, "O altar, altar, the Lord says, 'A child named Josiah will be born in David's family line. He will sacrifice these false priests on you, and human bones will be burned on you.'"

Then the prophet said, "This is the sign that the Lord has spoken. This altar will be torn down, and the ashes will be poured out!"

Jeroboam did not like what the prophet said. He pointed his finger at the man of God and cried out, "Grab him!" Immediately, Jeroboam's hand was stuck in that position. Everyone watched as the altar split, and the ashes poured out exactly as the man of God had said.

The king pleaded, "Pray to the Lord that my hand will be healed." The man of God prayed, and the king's hand was healed immediately.

The Word of the Lord Is True

Though the king wanted to reward him, the man of God refused the king's offer. This was because God had commanded him to not eat or drink. God even told him not to return home the same way.

An old prophet that lived in Bethel heard about what happened and went to find the man of God. The old prophet invited the man of God to come to his house and eat and drink. The man of God declined the invitation, but the old prophet persuaded him with a lie. "An angel told me that God says you are supposed to eat and drink with me at my house." The man of God disobeyed what God had told him and went with the man. While they were eating and drinking, the word of the Lord came to the old prophet. He told the man of God, "Because you have disobeyed the Lord and not kept His commands, you will die and be buried away from your home." After their meal, the man of God got on a donkey and left. A lion attacked and killed him on the road. The old prophet said, "The Lord did what He said He would do if the man of God disobeyed Him."

> **?** How was the word of the Lord proven true to Jeroboam?

CHAPTER **12**

Faithful God, Unfaithful People

A Famine in the Land

Why should I worship only God?

God Sends a Famine to His People

Ahab was the seventh king of the Northern Kingdom of Israel. The Northern Kingdom remained separated from the Southern Kingdom of Judah. Ahab married Jezebel, the daughter of the Sidonian king Ethbaal. The Sidonians worshiped Baal, the false god of the Canaanites. Jezebel was faithful to Baal and became known for her wicked and cruel ways. Foolishly following his wife's example, Ahab forsook the Lord and became a worshiper of Baal. Ahab ruled with great wickedness, more than all the kings that were before him. He led Israel away from God. He set up an altar and temple to Baal in Samaria.

God sent Elijah to Ahab with a strong rebuke for worshiping a false god. "Hear the word of the Lord as I stand before Him. There will not be dew or rain in the coming years until I command it."

? Who was Baal?

Baal

Baal was a false god worshiped by the Canaanites. They believed he was responsible for sending the rain. According to their beliefs, the dry season was when Baal died and couldn't rise to send rain. Each year, the goddess Anath would rescue Baal from the underworld, and together they would supply the fruit of the fields. Baal was represented by a bull (strength) and also by a lightning bolt (rain and fire). Baal couldn't send lightning to burn the sacrifice of his prophets. However, fire fell and burned Elijah's sacrifice when he prayed to the Lord.

Who was Elijah?

- A great prophet of the Lord
- Prophesied in the Northern Kingdom of Israel
- Rebuked Ahab for leading Israel to worship Baal
- Used by the Lord to demonstrate the weakness of Baal and the power of God
- Anointed Elisha as a prophet at the end of his ministry

A Drought, a Widow, and a Resurrection

Just as Elijah had said, the rain ceased, and crops began to fail. Without rain, famine would soon follow. God told Elijah, "Hide by the brook Cherith close to the Jordan River. I have commanded the ravens to feed you there." Every morning and every evening, ravens brought bread and meat for Elijah to eat. He rested and drank from the brook. But after a time, the brook dried up because there was no rain. Food and water were becoming more and more scarce in all of Israel.

However, God prepared a place for Elijah in the city of Zarephath. Zarephath was in Sidon, the homeland of Jezebel and Baal, outside the land of Israel. The Lord chose a widow there to take care of Elijah. When Elijah arrived, he saw the widow and asked for a cup of water and a piece of bread to eat. But she replied, "I am searching for sticks to make a small fire. I will bake bread from the last bit of flour and oil I have. My son and I will eat it and then die."

Elijah insisted that he be fed. "First bring me a piece of bread, then you and your son can eat." With great faith, the widow made bread for Elijah. He said, "Listen to this promise of God: Your flour and oil will not run out until the Lord sends rain again on the land." God's power to provide during a famine showed the weakness of Baal's power to send rain and make things grow.

After a time, the widow's son became ill and died. In grief, the widow cried, "Have you come to judge me for my sins and kill my son?" Elijah prayed to the Lord, and He heard his prayer. The child came back to life and Elijah presented him to his mother alive. The widow said, "Now I know that you are a man of God and that the word you speak is true."

> **?** What miracle did God work for the widow's son?

God against Baal on Mount Carmel

Elijah Confronts Ahab

After three and a half years, God sent Elijah to go to Ahab again. God told Elijah that He was going to send rain and end the drought. Ahab and his servant Obadiah were searching for green grass and water that would keep their animals alive. To speed up their search, Ahab and Obadiah split up to cover more ground. Obadiah saw Elijah and asked if it was really him. Elijah said, "Tell Ahab I have come to speak with him." The servant was afraid to tell Ahab this. What if Ahab came and Elijah wasn't there anymore? But Elijah assured him, "I will see Ahab today."

Obadiah fetched Ahab. Seeing Elijah, Ahab called out. "Is that you, Elijah? The one who troubles Israel?"

Elijah corrected him. "It is your worship of false gods and neglect of the Lord that has brought this trouble on Israel. Gather all Israel, as well as the 450 prophets of Baal and the 400 prophets of Asherah whom your wife cares for, and meet me on Mount Carmel."

> **?** How long did God withhold the rain in Israel?

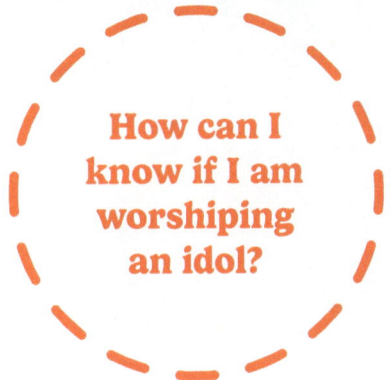

> How can I know if I am worshiping an idol?

Only One True God

King Ahab sent a message throughout Israel to gather the people and the prophets of Baal on Mount Carmel. On this mountain where Israel worshiped Baal instead of God, God's mercy would be revealed. By showing His power over Baal, His people would again be stirred to worship Him. Elijah called out to all those gathered on Mount Carmel, "How long will you wait to decide between God and Baal? Make up your mind! If the Lord is God, then serve Him. But if Baal is god, then serve him." The people did not give a response.

> **?** What did the people of Israel need to believe about Baal?

The Contest

Elijah announced the terms for a contest between God and Baal. He started by saying, "I alone am left as a prophet of the Lord, but Baal has 450 prophets. Let the prophets of Baal prepare a sacrifice. You are many, so you can go first. Cut the sacrifice in pieces and place it on the wood, but don't light a fire for it. I will also prepare a sacrifice to the Lord and will not light a fire for it. When the sacrifices are ready, Baal's prophets will call out to him. I will also call upon the name of the Lord. Whoever sends fire is the true God." This sounded good and fair to all the people.

The prophets of Baal prepared the sacrifice for their god. All morning, they jumped around and on the altar, crying, "Baal, answer us! " But nothing happened. Baal was silent.

At noon, Elijah began to mock the prophets by saying, "Maybe Baal can't hear you. Perhaps you should call louder. Since he is a god, he's probably quite busy. Maybe he's gone on a journey. Then again, he might be asleep. If you call a little louder, you might be able to wake him up." In the afternoon the prophets of Baal cut themselves in a desperate attempt to get Baal to act and send fire. They cried out to Baal all day until the evening. Still, there was no voice, nor was there any fire.

Now it was Elijah's turn. Elijah called the people to himself. Elijah rebuilt the altar of the Lord that had been knocked down and destroyed. He built it with twelve large stones to represent the twelve tribes of Israel. He also dug a deep trench around the altar. Elijah arranged the wood on the altar, cut the ox in pieces, and put it on the altar. Elijah then told the people, "Bring four large containers of water. Pour them on the sacrifice and on the wood." To leave no doubt, Elijah said, "Do it a second time."

Then, to everyone's awe, he said, "Do it a third time." The sacrifice and the wood were soaked, and the overflow filled the trench with water. Elijah wanted the people to understand that it was utterly impossible for this sacrifice to burn.

The people stood silently, waiting to see what God would do. Elijah came to the altar and prayed so all could hear. "Lord God of Abraham, Isaac, and Israel, today let everyone know that You are the true God. Let them know that I am your servant and have done these things at Your command. Please answer me so Your people will know that You are the true and living God."

? What did Elijah challenge the prophets to ask Baal to do?

The Lord, He Is God

Immediately after Elijah prayed, God caused fire to fall from the sky and completely burn up everything—the sacrifice, the wood, the stones of the altar, even the water and the dust around the altar. The people understood that this was the hand of God. They fell on their faces and cried out, "The Lord, He is God! The Lord, He is God!"

Elijah then had some men take the prophets of Baal away and put them to death. God was the clear winner of this contest, and He alone is God.

? What did God do that no other God could do?

Naboth's Vineyard

What makes a bad ruler?

Ahab's Sin

The vineyard growing next to Ahab's palace was well-kept and beautiful. It belonged to a man named Naboth, but Ahab wanted it for himself. Ahab said to Naboth, "I'm willing to buy or give you a better vineyard for your vineyard." Naboth replied, "May the Lord prevent me from giving you the inheritance I received from my fathers. It cannot be done!" Ahab was displeased and went back inside the palace. He lay down on his bed and turned to the wall, pouting like a child. Ahab refused to see anyone or eat any food.

Jezebel heard about this and went to find out why. "What has disturbed you in such a terrible way?" she asked. Ahab explained that he wanted to buy Naboth's vineyard, but Naboth refused. Jezebel replied, "Aren't you the king? I'll get this vineyard for you." Jezebel wrote letters to the city leaders in the king's name, saying, "Invite Naboth to a banquet and seat him in a place of honor. Also, invite two evil men to accuse Naboth of blaspheming God and the king. Then take him out and stone him."

? Why wouldn't Naboth sell his land to Ahab?

Ahab could have stopped all this, but he didn't. At the banquet, the evil men accused Naboth of cursing the king and God. Just as planned, Naboth was taken out of the city and stoned to death. Jezebel told Ahab the vineyard was now his. Ahab wasted no time going out and seeing his new vineyard. But Elijah met him there and said, "You killed Naboth and are taking his land. Hear the word of the Lord: 'I will completely destroy all of your family. Also, in the same place where the dogs licked up the blood of Naboth, they will lick up your blood. As for Jezebel, she will be eaten by dogs near the city walls.'"

Ahab tore his clothes and pretended to regret his sins. He wasn't truly sorry; he was only afraid of God's judgment. However, God showed mercy and held back the judgments on his family until a later time.

? **Who refused to stop Jezebel's evil plan against Naboth?**

Ahab's Death

Prophecy about Ahab's Downfall

Ahab had previously defeated King Ben-hadad of Syria twice in battle. When Ahab let God's enemy go home after the second battle, God said Ahab would lose his life for disobeying. Ben-hadad still kept a city belonging to Israel called Ramoth-gilead. Ahab was determined to win it back in battle.

Jehoshaphat, king of Judah, came to visit Ahab. Ahab asked him if he was willing to go to Ramoth-gilead and join him in battle against the Syrians. Jehoshaphat answered, "Yes. My soldiers will fight for you as if they were your own soldiers." Jehoshaphat added, "Let's ask the Lord's will before going into battle." In response to this, Ahab gathered four hundred of his prophets to hear their counsel. They said the Lord would give him victory. They advised him to fight.

Jehoshaphat knew these men were not true prophets of God. He asked if there was a prophet of the Lord that they could ask about this battle. Ahab said, "There is one, Micaiah, but I hate him because he never speaks a good prophecy about me." Still, Ahab sent for Micaiah. Ahab and Jehoshaphat put on their royal robes and sat on thrones in the city gate. Ahab's prophets continued to speak of victory in battle.

When Micaiah arrived, he pretended to agree with Ahab's prophets, but he was just mocking them and exposing their lies. He said to the kings, "Hear what God has said! Israel will be scattered in battle like sheep without a shepherd."

Prophecy Is Fulfilled

Ahab disguised himself and went into the battle. He was afraid of losing his life. Jehoshaphat stayed dressed like a king. Ben-hadad commanded the thirty-two captains of his chariots to fight only with Ahab. The captains saw Jehoshaphat, assumed he was King Ahab, and sought to kill him. When Jehoshaphat fled for his life, the men realized he wasn't Ahab and turned away. Even though Ahab had disguised himself, an enemy soldier shot an arrow at random and killed him. Later, Ahab's blood was washed from the chariot. True to Elijah's prophecy, the dogs came and licked up Ahab's blood where they had licked up Naboth's blood.

? What prophecy about Ahab was fulfilled by the dogs?

Elisha and the Shunammite Woman

How should I respond when I lose someone I care about?

Who was Elisha?

- Anointed as a prophet by Elijah
- Succeeded Elijah as prophet in the Northern Kingdom in Israel
- Asked God for double the power for ministry that Elijah had
- Performed twice as many recorded miracles as Elijah

Kindness

God used Elisha as a prophet in Israel after He took Elijah to heaven in a fiery horse-drawn chariot. As Elisha was traveling, a wealthy woman from Shunem in Northern Israel recognized him and invited him in for a meal. After that, every time he passed by her home, Elisha was invited to stop and have a meal with her and her husband. The Shunammite woman and her husband decided to build a room for Elisha. Now, when Elisha came for a meal, he also had a place to stay and rest.

Elisha decided he wanted to help the Shunammite woman because she was kind to him. She was a faithful Israelite who didn't ask for anything. Elijah asked his servant Gehazi what he could do for her. Gehazi noted that she had no son and her husband was old. Gehazi called the woman into the room, and Elisha told her, "I have wonderful news for you. A year from now, you will hold your own son in your arms." The Shunammite woman was stunned and thought Elisha was lying to her. But in a year, as Elisha said, she had a son.

? What was the great gift Elisha promised to the Shunammite?

196

Faith

When the child grew older, he went out to the fields to visit his father and his workers. While visiting, he got a terrible headache. "My head, my head!" cried the boy. His father told a servant to carry him to his mother. She held him until noon, when the boy died.

She placed him on the bed in the prophet's room. Without telling her husband what had happened to their son, the woman called to her husband, "We must find the prophet." Her servant took her by donkey to find Elisha. When she found him, she fell at his feet and wept. "Did I ask for a son? Didn't I say, 'Don't lie to me'?" Elisha understood by this that her son was dead, so he followed her back home. When he saw the dead boy in his room, he sent everyone out and prayed to the Lord. Elisha stretched himself over the boy. The boy sneezed seven times and opened his eyes. Elisha told the woman to pick up her son. With great joy, the Shunammite woman found her boy alive and held him close.

? **What did the Shunammite believe when her son died?**

Naaman and the Dirty River

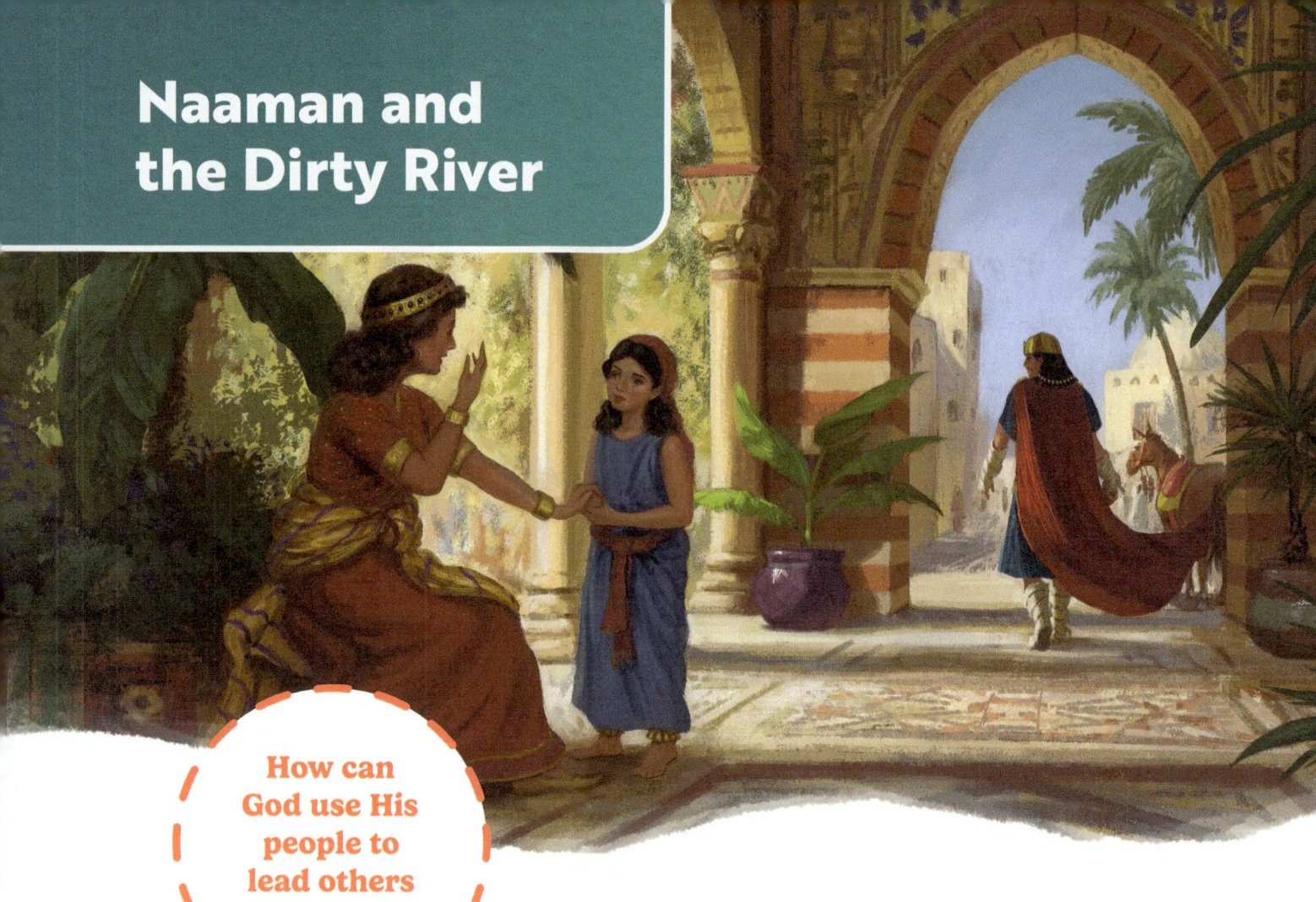

How can God use His people to lead others to Him?

Hope

Naaman served the king of Syria as the captain of the armies. Though he was a mighty man, he had leprosy. At the time, there was a young Israelite girl who served Naaman's wife. The girl said, "I wish my master could go to Samaria and see the prophet of the Lord. He would heal him of his leprosy."

The king heard the young girl's wish and decided he also wanted Naaman to be healed. He sent Naaman to the king of Israel with silver, gold, beautiful clothing, and a letter asking that the king of Israel heal Naaman of his leprosy. The king of Israel tore his clothes and said, "Who does the king of Syria think I am? Am I God, who has power to kill or to heal?"

Opportunity

Elisha heard that Naaman was asking the king for healing. He asked the king to send Naaman to him. When Naaman arrived at Elisha's home, Elisha didn't even go out to meet him. He sent his servant with a message, telling him to be healed by dipping seven times in the Jordan River. Naaman was expecting much more because he was the captain of his king's army. He wanted Elisha to come outside and make a show by placing his hands on him and crying out to God for healing. Naaman felt insulted by Elisha's instructions. He shouted, "Aren't there rivers in Damascus cleaner than this filthy Jordan River?" Naaman stomped away in a rage.

> **?** How did Naaman respond when he was told to dip seven times in the Jordan River?

Faith

Some of Naaman's servants said, "With respect, if the prophet had given you a great task to do, wouldn't you have done it? He has given you only a small task to dip in this river. Couldn't you just try it?"

Naaman set aside his pride and dipped seven times in the Jordan River. To his amazement, his leprosy disappeared. Naaman vowed to serve the Lord as the true God. The young, unnamed Hebrew servant girl in a foreign country led her captor to physical and spiritual healing.

> **?** What did Naaman receive when he obeyed Elisha?

Jehu the Executioner

Why do people think they can get away with doing wrong?

Coming Judgment

Ahab had been Israel's most wicked king. He and his wife Jezebel promoted the worship of Baal. Because of this, God's great judgment was about to come upon the family of Ahab and Jezebel. God would destroy all their sons and male descendants.

Judgment Begins

Elisha sent a prophet to anoint Jehu as king of Israel. The prophet found Jehu and anointed him. He gave Jehu a mission from God to destroy Ahab's family and stop their wickedness. Jehu gathered men and began by attacking King Joram, Ahab's son. Jehu shot Joram with an arrow, and his body was thrown in the field of Naboth. It was left there for the wild animals, as Elijah said would happen. Jehu and his men then went to the palace of Queen Jezebel in the city of Jezreel. Wicked Jezebel mocked them from a high open window. Jehu called out to her male servants, "Throw her down!" They threw Jezebel down to her death. Jehu and his men went into the palace to eat and drink. By the time they came out to bury Jezebel, they found that dogs had eaten her, just as Elijah had prophesied.

Ahab had seventy sons, all of whom God wanted destroyed. Jehu wrote a letter to the men of Jezreel, saying, "Anoint one of Ahab's sons to lead and protect Ahab's family." But since they did not want to fight Jehu, they asked him what he wanted them to do. Jehu said, "Bring me the heads of Ahab's sons." The men did as they were told and brought them to Jehu.

Jehu was now ready to destroy all the prophets, priests, and worshipers of Baal. He invited all the Israelite Baal worshipers to a magnificent sacrifice honoring Baal. All the Baal worshipers came to this celebration, anticipating this sacrifice to Baal. They squeezed into one building. Once inside, Jehu told his soldiers to go in and destroy them all.

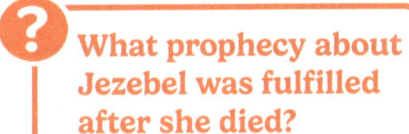

? What prophecy about Jezebel was fulfilled after she died?

How did Jehu stop the worship of Baal in Israel?

Jehu's Sin

Although Jehu killed Ahab and Jezebel's wicked family as God instructed, he didn't care to follow God. Jehu continued sinning by worshiping the golden calves set up in the Northern Kingdom by Jeroboam. As king, he continued to lead Israel in idol worship.

The Fall of Samaria and the Northern Kingdom

How should I deal with idols in my life?

No More Northern Kingdom

Hoshea was the last king of the Northern Kingdom of Israel, which was also called Samaria after its capital city. Hoshea reigned for only nine years. God had promised blessing if Israel obeyed His commandments. But if they chose to sin, there would be judgment. God had sent many prophets to warn them to leave their idol worship. Foolishly, king after king ignored their warnings. Hoshea did the same. He ignored the Word of God and led the people to do evil. They continued to serve idols, so God slowly withdrew His blessings from Israel. Shalmaneser, the strong king of Assyria, demanded that Hoshea and Israel serve him and pay him money and goods. Israel lived in fear of the Assyrians, so they paid money and goods to King Shalmaneser.

In the sixth year of his reign, Hoshea stopped sending money and goods. He didn't want to be a slave to Shalmaneser. Hoshea secretly asked the king of Egypt to partner with him against Assyria. When Shalmaneser found out, he captured Hoshea and threw him into prison. The Assyrians invaded the Northern Kingdom and spent three years waiting outside the city of Samaria to enter and defeat it. When Samaria finally surrendered, they were taken into captivity. Shalmaneser took those he captured and made them live in other countries. Then he brought people from other countries, all idol-worshipers, and made them live in Israel. His plan was to make it so Israel would no longer have their own country to defend and would be forced to live peacefully.

The Deeper Problem

God could have given Israel victory over Assyria if they had obeyed Him. Israel did not fully understand that God was allowing His people to be taken into captivity. They had refused to worship Him alone. They worshiped Him while worshiping golden calves and other false gods, including Baal, Asherah, Molech, and even the stars in the sky. The people hid in secret and burned incense to false gods. These false gods were the same false gods that the Canaanites worshiped. The Lord sent prophets to draw His people back to Him, but they wouldn't listen. They loved their sin and didn't care what God had said. True to His word, God allowed them to be cast out of their own land. They were taken into captivity in other lands.

> **?** What did God do to the Canaanites who worshiped idols?
>
> How did God deal with idolaters in Israel?

A Second Invasion

Shalmaneser's new people in Samaria had a problem. They were proud and paid no attention to the Lord, so the Lord sent lions to attack and kill them. The people sent word to Shalmaneser about this problem. He commanded an Israelite priest to leave captivity, go to Bethel, and teach the people about the ways of God so He wouldn't punish them with the lions. The priest taught the people from other nations to fear the Lord. However, there was another problem. The people thought God was just like their other gods. They added Him to their collection of gods, but they never turned to Him alone.

God used the prophet to speak with the people living in Samaria. He reminded them of the covenant He had made with them. But their disobedience continued. Their children and future generations combined fearing God with serving idols.

CHAPTER

13

The Southern Kingdom

Asa Inconsistently Followed the Lord

Was Asa a good king?

FastFacts about

1 & 2 Chronicles

Author: Unknown

Date: Approximately 450 BC

Theme: Israel was being taken into captivity* as judgment for violating the Mosaic Covenant, but a humble, repentant Israel would be restored to true worship of God, who would keep His covenant promises.

Meaning of *Chronicles*: a collection of records

Interesting Fact:
Chronicles begins by naming Adam and his descendants up until the time Israel returns to their land from being in captivity.

A Brief Explanation

The previous chapter focused on the kings in the Northern Kingdom. Israel in the north had a long list of wicked kings who did evil in the sight of the Lord. While the Northern Kingdom fell deeper and deeper into sin, the kings of the Southern Kingdom of Judah had their own struggles. Some of the stories in this chapter overlap with stories from Chapter 12. Some events are even repeated, such as the southern King Jehoshaphat's agreement with northern King Ahab and how Ahab was killed in the battle they fought together. Chapter 12 gave the view from the Northern Kingdom. Now, Chapter 13 gives the view from the Southern Kingdom.

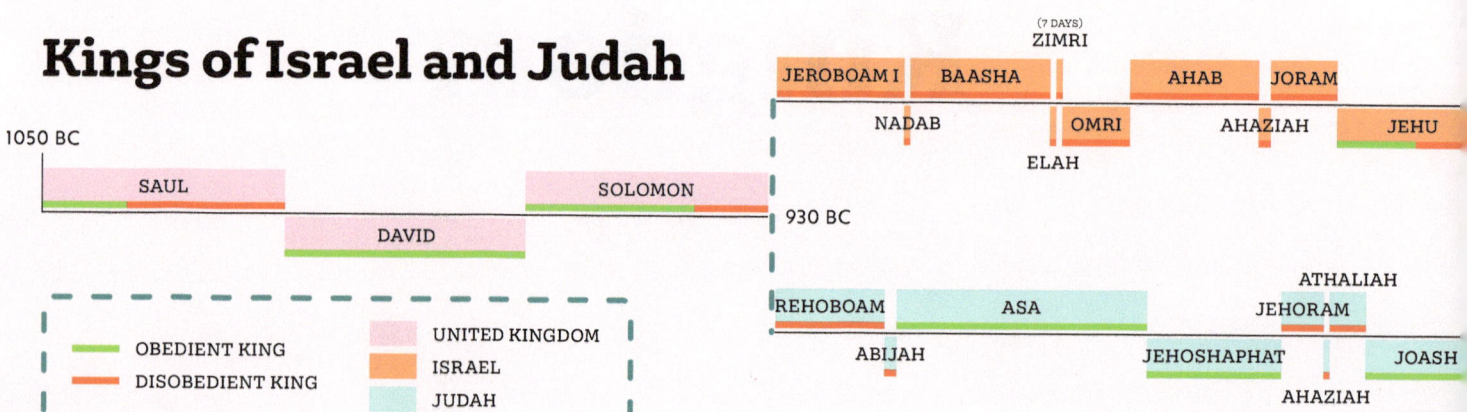

Good Start to Asa's Reign

David's great-great-grandson Asa was crowned king of Judah when he was twenty years old. He obeyed God by removing all the idols in Judah. He commanded the people to seek the Lord and obey Him. The people listened, so God gave Judah ten years of peace for their obedience. During this time, Asa tried to repair the temple and make Judah stronger. Asa told the people of Judah, "Because we have sought the Lord our God, He has given us rest on every side."

But then an army of one million Ethiopian men, along with three hundred chariots, came to fight against Judah. Asa knew he and his three hundred thousand men didn't stand a chance without God's help. He prayed, "Lord, You are the only one who can help us in this battle. We trust in Your name. You are our God. Do not let this army win over You." God fought against the Ethiopians, and Asa's army won.

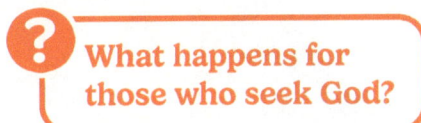

What happens for those who seek God?

Encouraged by God

God sent a prophet to Asa. The prophet said, "God is with you while you are with Him. If you seek Him, you will find Him. If you forsake Him, He will forsake you. For a long time, Israel has been without God, a priest, or the law. But when they turned to God and sought Him, they found Him. Be strong. Your work will be rewarded."

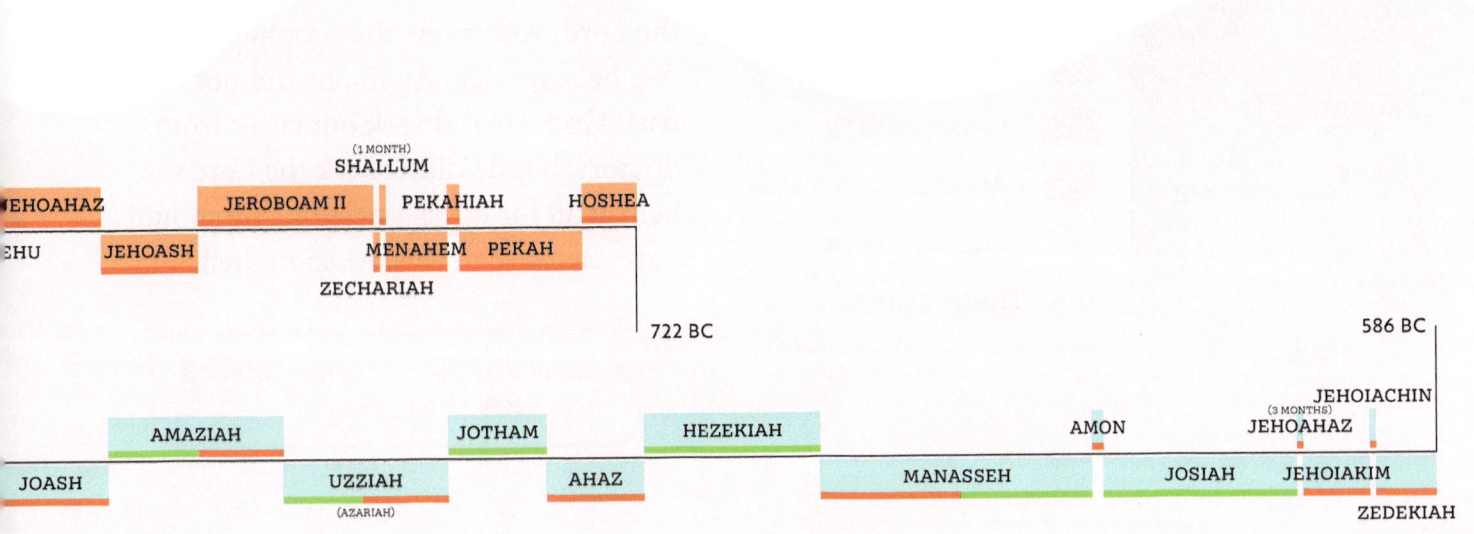

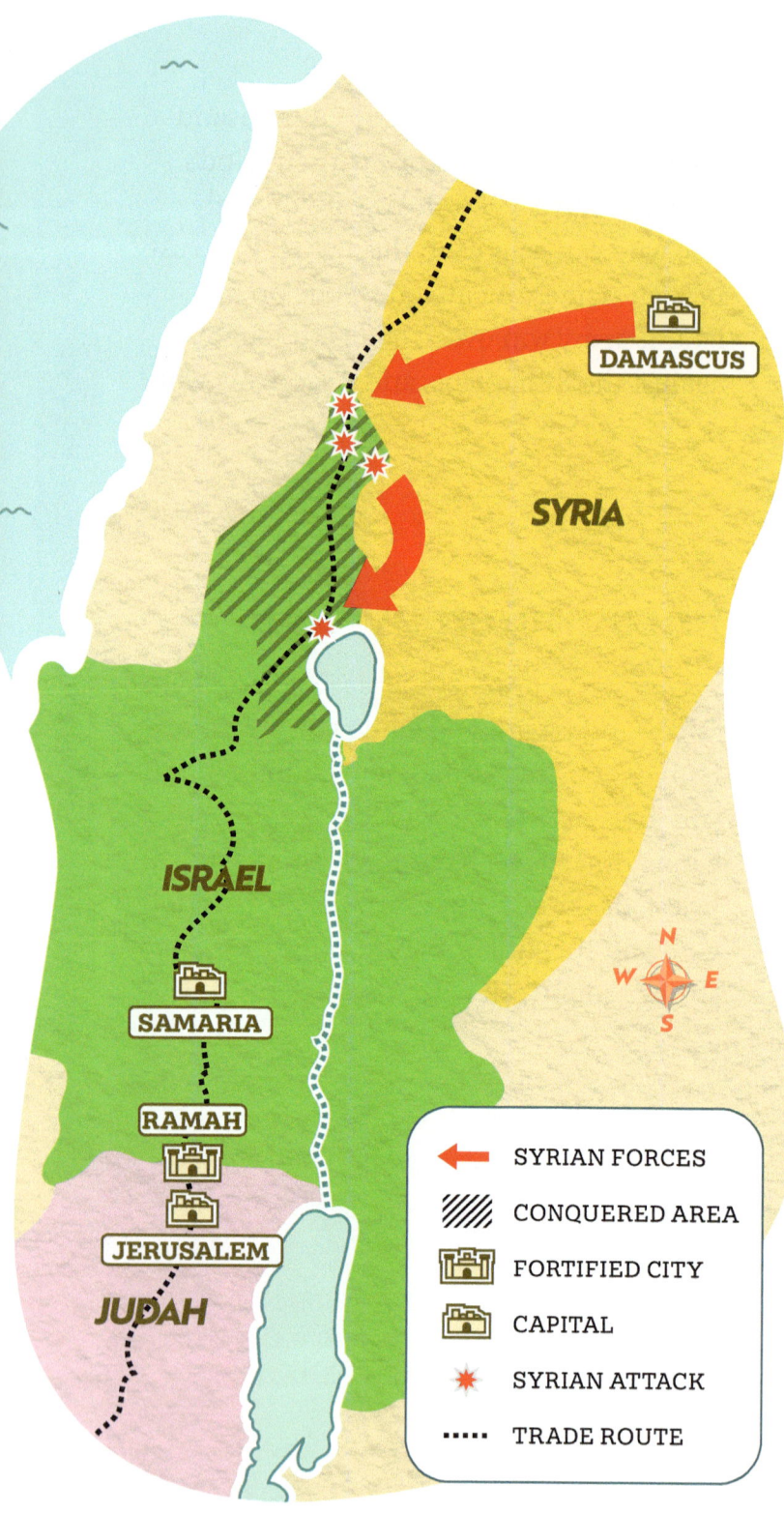

God's message encouraged King Asa. He got rid of the idols that they had brought back from the cities they had captured. He repaired the altar of God. All of Judah gathered to worship God. They sacrificed thousands of animals. They made a covenant to seek the Lord wholeheartedly. Asa even kept his mother from being queen because she worshiped an idol.

Even though the high places weren't removed, Asa had a true heart for God his whole life. All of Judah rejoiced in the peace they experienced because they sought God and found Him. God gave them twenty years of peace from their enemies.

But Baasha, the king of Israel, blocked a key trade route into Judah. Instead of seeking God's help, Asa paid the idol-worshiping king of Syria to fight Baasha. The plan worked. The Syrian king conquered parts of Israel, and Baasha stopped trying to block the trade route into Judah. But when God's prophet rebuked Asa for not trusting the Lord, Asa threw the prophet in jail. Asa became sick. Again, he did not trust God. He did seek out cures from doctors, but he didn't seek the Lord's help at all for his sickness like he should have. Because of this, he soon died.

? **How did Asa change toward the end of his reign?**

Jehoshaphat
THE FAITH OF A COMPROMISED KING

Why are friends so important?

God Will Not Be Fooled

Asa's son Jehoshaphat was crowned the next king of Judah. He began his reign by following God. He even sent priests throughout the land to teach the people God's ways. He tore down idols, and he made the cities and forts stronger. He became rich and was respected by the surrounding nations.

But Jehoshaphat partnered with Ahab, the ungodly king of Israel, to fight a battle. Ahab talked to his false prophets, who told him he would win the battle. But the prophet of God told Jehoshaphat that they would lose the battle and Ahab would die. Despite the warning, both kings still went to battle. Ahab was dressed like a normal soldier, but Jehoshaphat wore his royal clothes. God protected Jehoshaphat, but He guided a randomly shot arrow to hit Ahab in a weak spot of his chest armor. As prophesied, Ahab died in battle.

When Jehoshaphat returned to Jerusalem, a prophet asked him, "Should you love those who hate the Lord? God's anger is against you." Jehoshaphat determined to serve the Lord, and he encouraged the people to fear God and wholeheartedly be faithful to Him.

Later, three nations came to fight against Judah. Jehoshaphat and all the people gathered to seek God's help. Jehoshaphat prayed, "God of our fathers, aren't You God in heaven, and didn't You give this land to Abraham's seed forever? When Solomon built the temple, he taught us that we could pray to You when trouble came. He said You would hear us and save us. Now, our enemies want to take the land You gave to us. We can't beat them, and we don't know what to do. Our eyes are on You."

God sent a message through a prophet. "Do not be afraid," the prophet said. "You will not need to fight. Stand still and see the Lord save you. This is God's battle. The Lord will be with you." The king and all the people fell down and worshiped the Lord.

? What was wrong with Jehoshaphat's decision to partner with Ahab in battle?

Believing and Praising God

The next day, Jehoshaphat and the people praised God. "Praise the Lord; for His mercy endures forever!" At that time, God caused the enemies to fight among themselves until they were all dead. When the people realized that every one of their enemies was dead, they went and collected all the goods and valuables left behind by the armies. It took them three days to gather it all.

The people returned to Jerusalem rejoicing in the Lord. Jehoshaphat's reign of twenty-five years was free from war. He did right in God's sight. However, he did not tear down the high places of worship.

Sadly, later in life, Jehoshaphat partnered with another wicked king. Together, they planned to build ships for trade. A prophet told Jehoshaphat that his ships would be broken for partnering with a wicked man. And just as he said, the ships were wrecked.

? How did God fight for Jehoshaphat and Judah?

Joash Rejects God

What happens to those who reject God?

Jehoshaphat's grandson, King Ahaziah, was a wicked ruler who listened to the evil advice of his mother, Athaliah. When he died, Athaliah killed the king's descendants so she could rule over Judah. However, Athaliah's sister and Jehoiada the priest hid the king's infant son, Joash. After six years, Jehoiada secretly gathered the Levites and leaders. Together, they made a covenant in the house of God. A large group of men protected Joash as Jehoiada crowned him king at just seven years old. The people of Jerusalem rejoiced at the news. But Athaliah considered this act a crime. "Treason! Treason!" she screamed. But Judah knew who their rightful king was. Athaliah was executed, and young Joash was placed on the throne.

? **What did Jehoiada and the leaders do?**

Generous Followers

Joash reigned for forty years. While Jehoiada was alive, Joash did right in God's eyes. Joash wanted to repair the house of the Lord because Athaliah had ruined it through idol worship. He placed a wooden box outside for collections. People joyfully gave money daily. All the repairs were done excellently.

The people faithfully worshiped God by once again making burnt offerings to God. Because of all the good he did in faithfully serving the Lord, Jehoiada the priest was buried in the city of David among the kings.

God's People Worship Idols

After Jehoiada's death, some leaders came before Joash. He listened to their wicked advice and led the people to worship idols. God sent prophets so the people would repent, but the people refused.

God spoke to the people through Jehoiada's son: "Why do you disobey God? You will not prosper. God has forsaken you." King Joash did not remember Jehoiada's kindness to him. Instead, he commanded Jehoiada's son to be stoned. The son's dying words were, "May the Lord see and avenge!"

Because of Joash's wickedness, God allowed a small Syrian army to defeat the mighty army of Judah. They even killed many of the princes and leaders of Judah. Joash was also badly wounded. While he lay helpless in his bed, his own men came and killed him. This is how they got revenge for the stoning of Jehoiada's son. When Joash was buried, he was not put in a respected place with the other kings of Judah.

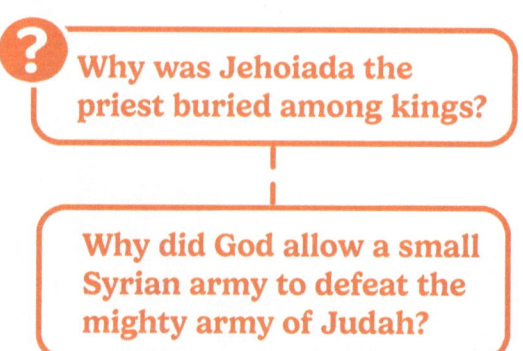

Why was Jehoiada the priest buried among kings?

Why did God allow a small Syrian army to defeat the mighty army of Judah?

The King Who Became Leprous

Strength

Uzziah was sixteen when he became king in Jerusalem. He was the king for fifty-two years. He was determined to seek God and do what was right. As long as he sought after God, he prospered. The Lord made Uzziah strong against his enemies. He became rich and was well known even as far away as Egypt. He had a strong and well-equipped army of 307,500 soldiers led by 2,600 powerful warriors. He provided his army with shields, spears, helmets, and chain armor, as well as bows and slings. In Jerusalem he set up weapons that could shoot arrows and throw stones. For all this, he became famous and great among the nations.

Pride and Punishment

When Uzziah's army was strong and defeating all their enemies, Uzziah became proud. This **pride** led to his destruction.

> **key term**
> **pride**
> Pride is thinking too highly of oneself and too little of others. To be proud is to depend on oneself and to give no credit to God. Pride is the opposite of humility.

Why is humility so important in a leader?

In his pride, the king also took on the role of a priest. He went into the temple of the Lord to burn incense. He knew that God's law said that only priests were allowed to do that, but his pride led him to make this sinful decision. Azariah and eighty priests went into the temple to confront Uzziah. They told him, "It is not your privilege or responsibility to burn incense to the Lord. This privilege is for the priests—the sons of Aaron. God Himself has set them apart to do this duty. You must leave here right away. You have done wrong. Burning incense to the Lord will not bring you any honor from Him." Those words made the king furious. But as he stood there in the temple, God sent His punishment—Uzziah's forehead was suddenly covered with leprosy. The priests hurried the king out of the sanctuary. Because of his leprosy, he could not return to his palace. Instead, he had to live alone. King Uzziah had leprosy until the day he died.

? What was Uzziah determined to do at the beginning of his reign?

Restoration under Hezekiah

What does repentance look like?

Cleaned and Reopened

By the time Hezekiah came to the throne, the temple had been closed for many years. Hezekiah's father, Ahaz, had set up idols and defiled the temple. Israel was experiencing God's wrath because they did not worship the Lord.

King Hezekiah was only twenty-five years old when he began his reign. He wasted no time repairing, cleaning, and reopening the temple. He told the Levites, "Set yourselves apart for the important task of making sure God's house is clean. Everything in this house must be acceptable to God. Our fathers have been unfaithful to our Lord. They have sinned and done evil. They have forsaken God and turned their backs on Him. They closed the doors of the temple's entrance hall, they let the lamps go out, and they have not burned incense or offered burnt offerings."

King Hezekiah was serious. He committed to avoid God's anger. He restored worship in the temple because he wanted God's blessing on the nation. After the temple was clean and ready, the king and other leaders went to the house of the Lord. This was where the priests sacrificed animals as a sin offering for the kingdom, for the sanctuary, and for Judah. There were so many sacrifices that the priests needed people to help them. The congregation worshiped the Lord, the Levites played their music, and the singers sang. At the end of their offerings, they sang, bowed, worshiped, and praised God together. It was a special day, and Hezekiah and all the people rejoiced.

? What did the people do after they offered the thousands of sacrifices?

Repentance and Rejoicing

Israel had not kept the Lord's Passover for a long time. Hezekiah wanted this to be a big celebration once again. He sent letters to parts of Israel, Judah, Ephraim, and Manasseh, inviting them to come to the Passover. He wrote, "Do not be stubborn like your fathers. Turn to God and serve Him so His anger will turn from you. God is merciful." Hezekiah showed the people that **repentance** is necessary for a right relationship with God. This meant that the people had to turn from their sin and delight in worshiping God.

> **key term**
> ### repentance
> Repentance is the act of being sorry for, asking forgiveness for, and turning away from sin.

Some laughed and mocked, but many humbled themselves and came. Together, they threw the idolatrous altars into the river. Though the priests had repented of sin and were able to participate in the celebrations, many of the people had not cleansed themselves before celebrating Passover. But God mercifully forgave the people for not cleansing themselves before participating in the Passover feast. For seven days, the people confessed their sin and sang praises to God. The occasion was so special that they decided to celebrate for an additional seven days. There had not been such a time of rejoicing in Jerusalem since the days of King Solomon. The priests and Levites blessed the people, and God heard their prayer.

> **?** What did the people do before they sang praises to God?

Blessings and Faithfulness

The people praised the one true God as they left that Passover celebration. In and around the cities of Judah, they tore down everything that was used in idol worship. Hezekiah told the priests and Levites to fulfill their service of burnt offerings and peace offerings, as well as to minister, give thanks, and praise the Lord. The joyful people gave so much to the Lord that the king had storerooms built to hold it all. He chose people to give out the food as needed to the priests and their families. The people gave so generously that there was more than enough for all the priests and their families to live on.

King Hezekiah did what was good and right in the sight of the Lord his God. Everything he did for the house of God, he did according to God's law. Hezekiah kept God's commandments and sought God with all his heart. Because he followed God, he prospered. Hezekiah's faithfulness to all of God's commands caused him to be unique among all the kings of Judah. There was no other king like him who did not stop following God and kept all His commandments. He even stood against the king of Assyria and would not serve him.

> **?** What is King Hezekiah known for?

The Siege of Jerusalem

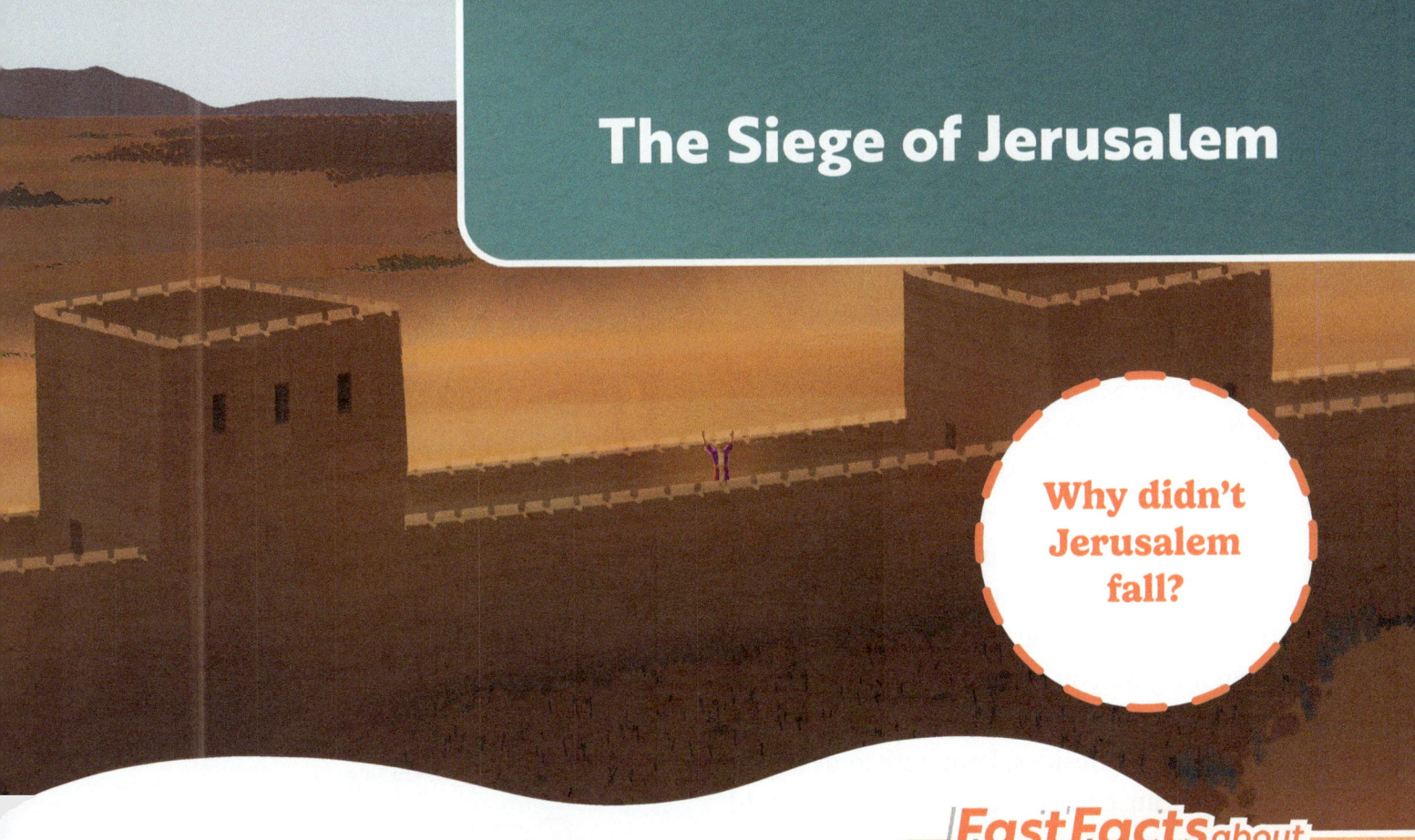

Why didn't Jerusalem fall?

Sennacherib Invades Judah

King Hezekiah had been king in Jerusalem for fourteen years. He obeyed God as King David had done. God was with him and blessed what he did. At this time, King Sennacherib of Assyria came into Judah with his armies and threatened King Hezekiah. Hezekiah tried to make peace by gathering money and gold and giving it all to King Sennacherib. He even stripped the temple of gold. But the Assyrian king was not satisfied for long. Soon, he threatened Hezekiah again.

This time, instead of giving money, Hezekiah arranged his armies around the city walls. He encouraged them by saying, "Be strong and courageous. Do not be afraid of the king of Assyria and his large army. We are mightier than they are. They trust in their own strength, but God is with us, and He is the one who fights our battles." With that encouragement from their king, the people of Jerusalem did not worry or fear because they were comforted with the words of their king.

Fast Facts about

Isaiah

Author: Isaiah
Date: Approximately 740 BC
Theme: God does all things for His own glory.
Meaning of *Isaiah*: The Lord saves

Interesting Facts:

- Quoted or referred to over eighty times in the New Testament
- Prophesied in the Southern Kingdom during the time the Northern Kingdom was defeated by Assyria
- Spoke directly about the person, work, and kingdom of the Servant of the Lord (the Messiah)

Sennacherib Blasphemes the Lord

King Sennacherib sent three of his officials and his whole army to Jerusalem. Hezekiah sent three men to meet with them and receive Sennacherib's message. One of the officials, Rabshakeh, asked, "Why do you have such confidence? If you are trusting in the power of Egypt, that is no good. That is trusting in a broken stick that will hurt you when you lean on it. If you are trusting in your God, that is no good either. Even if I gave you two thousand horses and you tried to put a rider on each one, you couldn't win. Besides, I am here to destroy Israel because your God is the one who told me to do it."

Rabshakeh was speaking loudly in the Jewish language to make the nearby people afraid. Hezekiah's three men asked Rabshakeh to speak in the Syrian language instead. But Rabshakeh continued to speak loudly in the Jewish language.

This time he addressed Hezekiah's army. "Don't let Hezekiah lie to you. He can't save you. Have the gods of any other nations been able to keep their nations from being captured by the king of Assyria? Where are the gods of all the nations we defeated? Will your Lord keep me from making you my slaves? Make an agreement with me, and you will have plenty of everything. Hezekiah cannot save you." Then his soldiers joined in, calling out against God and Hezekiah. They believed that the God of Israel was just like the gods of the other nations they had defeated.

The people of Judah did not answer because Hezekiah had commanded them to remain silent. The three men returned to King Hezekiah and told him what Rabshakeh had said.

> **?** What did the Assyrian king think would happen?
>
> Who did the king of Assyria think God was like?

The Lord Destroys Sennacherib and Saves Jerusalem

Hezekiah went to the house of the Lord and sent messengers to the prophet Isaiah. Isaiah responded, "Don't be afraid. Sennacherib, the king of Assyria, will die in his country. Don't be afraid of him who has spoken evil against God."

Hezekiah prayed. "God, You are the only God. You are the Creator of heaven and earth. Open your ears and eyes. The nations Sennacherib has defeated had idols that were simply pieces of stone and wood. Save us so the world knows you are the only God."

God answered Hezekiah's plea through Isaiah. "God has heard your cry and will fight for you." Then Isaiah told Hezekiah what God said about Sennacherib. "Your blaspheming and rebellion are against Me, the Holy One of Israel. You are proud. Your hatred is against Me. I will send you back from where you came."

That night, the angel of the Lord went into the Assyrian camp and killed 185,000 soldiers. Disgraced and defeated, King Sennacherib turned homeward to Nineveh. After returning home, Sennacherib was killed by his own sons while he worshiped in the temple of his false god. This fulfilled what God had assured Hezekiah of through Isaiah. Sennacherib had died in his own country.

? **How did God give the Israelites victory?**

The Coming King

How will the coming King be different from Israel's other kings?

The Righteous Reign of the Branch

The prophet Isaiah wrote an entire book of the Bible. In his book, he observed that Assyria had destroyed the Northern Kingdom and almost destroyed the Southern Kingdom. Isaiah said that God was using Assyria like an axe that was cutting down the forest of Israel and Judah. Eventually, even the Davidic kings would be cut down to a stump. But hope was not over for Israel. The stump of Jesse's family line, the line of David's father, would sprout a shoot. A Branch would sprout and would bear fruit. This Branch represents the Davidic Messiah. The Spirit of the Lord would rest upon this Davidic King. The Spirit would enable Him to rule with wisdom and understanding, counsel and might, and knowledge and fear of the Lord.

This coming King, this Branch, would delight in the fear of the Lord. He would be a perfectly just King. He would not make judgments relying on what He saw or heard. He would know all things and would make perfect judgments. When He would judge the poor, it would be with righteousness. He would make fair and just decisions for the humble. With His words, He would judge the wicked world. Righteousness and faithfulness would be at the center of His being and reign.

Jesus Is the Coming Davidic King

Jesus is the Branch that came from the family line of Jesse, through King David, to bear fruit. One day, Jesus will return to earth to rule over it in perfect righteousness. The Holy Spirit will enable Jesus, the Messiah, to rule with wisdom, understanding, counsel, might, knowledge, and in the fear of the Lord. He will treat the poor with righteousness and the humble with fairness. His spoken words will be enough to wipe out the wicked. Righteousness and faithfulness will be the two character traits He will be known for.

? How did God give the Israelites victory?

What would the Branch be known for?

Bible Truth

56 **What was the work of Christ?**
The work of Christ was to keep the law of God perfectly, to suffer the penalty of our sins, and to rise again on the third day.

Acts 10:39–43 • Romans 8:3–4
1 Peter 2:24

CHAPTER **14**

Fall of the Southern Kingdom

Manasseh
JUDAH'S MOST WICKED KING

The Sins of Manasseh

After King Hezekiah died, his twelve-year-old son Manasseh came to the throne. He reigned over Judah for fifty-five years. Unlike his father, who had faithfully served the Lord and was one of Judah's greatest kings, Manasseh was extremely wicked and unfaithful to God. Manasseh turned from the Lord. He worshiped the idols and false gods of the Canaanites. Even though his father tore down the altars to false gods, Manasseh foolishly built them back up again. He led God's people to worship Baal and even got involved in witchcraft. He put an idol of Asherah in God's temple, even though the temple was for bringing glory to God. He also built altars there to worship the planets and stars. There was no evil thing that Manasseh was not willing to do.

The most wicked and horrible thing he did was burning his sons as a sacrifice to the false god Molech. God was very angry at Manasseh's terrible wickedness and at how he turned the people of Judah away from Him.

God had promised blessings to Israel if they followed Him. If they obeyed Him, they would never be conquered and cast out of the land. However, because of their wickedness, they couldn't receive God's blessings. They sinned worse than the nations that lived in Canaan before they did. Now, God wanted to cast them out of the land. God spoke to them through His prophets, but the Israelites would not listen. As God had promised, judgment came for Manasseh and the kingdom of Judah because of their evil ways.

> How does God respond when I confess my sins?

> ❓ How did Judah's sin compare to the sins of the nations who were first cast out of the land?

Manasseh Repents

The Lord allowed commanders from Assyria's army to invade Jerusalem. They captured Manasseh and bound him with chains. They took him to Babylon. The king of Judah was humiliated and became their prisoner. His body became sick and weak. For the first time, proud Manasseh searched his heart. He had heard about the teachings of the Lord as a child, but he had ignored God's commands. He had laughed at the warnings of the prophets. Now, in his suffering, he finally admitted that he had sinned against God. Manasseh sought the Lord and greatly humbled his wicked heart. He cried out to the Lord, and in His mercy, God heard Manasseh's prayer.

Why was God willing to forgive Manasseh?

Manasseh is Restored

God was very kind to Manasseh and brought him back to his throne in Jerusalem. When he returned, he added to and improved the walls around the city of David. He also strengthened his kingdom by placing his commanders throughout Judah. Manasseh knew now that the Lord was the only God, so he threw all the idols in Jerusalem outside the city. Manasseh also went into the temple and tore down the altars to the false gods. He commanded all of Judah to worship only the Lord. But the people sacrificed to God at the high places instead of at the temple, where they were commanded to sacrifice.

When Manasseh died, his son Amon was crowned king. Sadly, Amon worshiped and served idols instead of worshiping God, just like his father used to do. He reigned for only two years before he was killed by his own servants.

Josiah and the Book of the Law

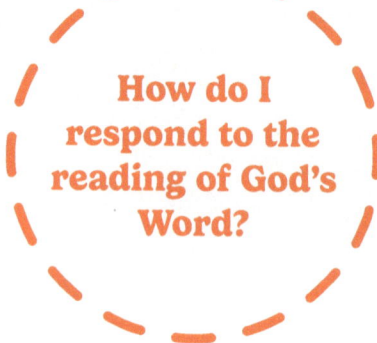

How do I respond to the reading of God's Word?

Josiah Seeks to Obey the Lord

Josiah was just eight years old when he became king of Judah. As a young man, he sought to learn the ways of the Lord. He did what was right in God's sight. He chose to follow the example of David rather than the wicked examples of Amon and Manasseh. In the twelfth year of his reign, he destroyed all the idols the people worshiped and ground the pieces to powder. The powder was scattered on the graves of those who had worshiped false gods. Josiah also destroyed all the altars that the people used for sacrificing to false gods.

God's Law is Found

In Josiah's eighteenth year as king, he sent men to repair the house of the Lord. Money was collected and placed in the temple to pay for the repairs. When the money was being brought out, Hilkiah the priest found the Book of the Law given through Moses. No one had seen it for decades—this was a great discovery!

The Book of the Law was sent to King Josiah and read to him. The king was shocked. Israel had sinned against God in big ways for many years. When the king heard about the curses and judgments coming to Israel, he tore his clothes in despair. He sent Hilkiah and several messengers to Huldah the prophetess. They said, "The king asks for a message from the Lord. Please tell us what will happen to us!"

Huldah told them the words that God spoke. "Judah has forsaken me and burned incense to other gods. I will pour out my burning wrath on Judah. All the curses that are written in the book will come upon these people."

What did the Book of the Law say was coming upon Judah?

Judgment Is Delayed

Huldah was also given a special message from the Lord for King Josiah. "You have humbled yourself and wept over these judgments. Because of that, I will delay these judgments and show mercy to you. I will certainly destroy Judah, but it will not be destroyed in your day."

Why was judgment from the Lord delayed?

Covenant Breaking

Fast Facts about

Micah

Author: Micah

Date: Approximately 725 BC

Theme: God is faithful to His covenant in both judging and restoring His people.

Meaning of *Micah*: Who is like the Lord?

Interesting Facts:
- Prophesied to both the Southern and Northern Kingdoms, but focused on Jerusalem
- Foretold the destruction of Jerusalem
- Called on all nations to hear his message
- Prophesied that the Davidic King would be born in Bethlehem

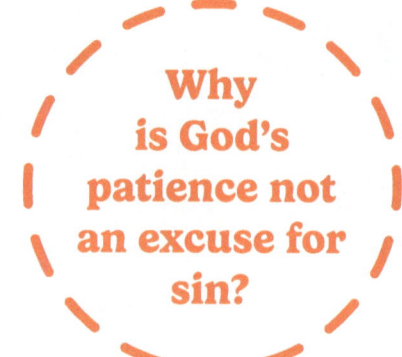

Why is God's patience not an excuse for sin?

Micah was a prophet who lived in the land of Judah. He ministered throughout the reigns of Jotham, Ahaz, and Hezekiah. The book of Micah is made up of three sermons. In these sermons, Micah points out Israel's sins and rebukes their evil ways. He warned of judgment to all who continued in sin, yet he also offered hope to all who would repent.

Sins of the Powerful

Micah preached against the evil works of powerful people in the land. These people would think up ways to steal from the weak and the poor. They stole land and houses. They even robbed people of their inheritances.

Micah also accused the powerful people of ignoring justice and loving evil things. He compared the way they treated the poor to the killing of animals.

The Lord planned disaster for the rich and powerful. They would be invaded by a powerful nation that would take everything from them. The inheritances they had stolen from their countrymen would also be stolen from them.

God's Judgment

During this time, the prophets of the Lord were considered fools. No one listened to them. Instead, the people listened to the false prophets. They flattered Samaria and Jerusalem with words of peace and prosperity. God declared that Samaria would be left like a pile of rubble in a field. The people ignored God's words. The false prophets would not admit the sin of Judah. They said, "The Lord is with us. He will protect us from all harm." They forgot the Lord's warning about breaking His laws. Moses had recorded that God would send disease and curses if they disobeyed His covenant. They would be cursed for their disobedience. Jerusalem itself would be plowed up. The temple would be destroyed. Mount Zion would become a high place to worship false gods.

How did the people view the prophets of God?

God's Covenant Endures

Judgment was coming for the sins of Samaria and Judah. But God also offered hope. God remembers all His covenants, including the promises made to Abraham and David. He would one day send a blessing to all the families of the earth. The blessing would be in sending the promised King who would be born in Bethlehem. This king would justly and perfectly rule all nations.

What did God provide for all who would repent?

Kings and Not-Quite-Kings
JEHOAHAZ, JEHOIAKIM, AND JEHOIACHIN

Why did God punish Judah?

God's promise to David was that he would have a son who would rule forever. Josiah was a godly king, but he was the last king in Judah who feared the Lord. God blessed Judah under Josiah's reign, and his sons who reigned after him all remembered this. They also knew how to continue that blessing. But the sons of Josiah were wicked and turned away from the Lord.

Pharaoh Neco

Jehoahaz

King Josiah had been killed in battle. He died trying to stop Pharaoh Neco of Egypt from joining with Assyria to fight Babylon. His son Jehoahaz was crowned king, but he reigned for only three months. Jehoahaz was wicked and did evil in the sight of the Lord. God allowed Pharaoh Neco to take Jehoahaz captive. Pharaoh Neco then required the nation of Judah to pay him tribute every year. They had to pay 100 talents of silver and one talent of gold. A talent weighed about 75 pounds. That made the tribute 7,500 pounds of silver and 75 pounds of gold. It was a large tax to pay. Jehoahaz never regained his throne in Judah. He died as a prisoner in Egypt.

Jehoiakim

When Pharaoh removed Jehoahaz from the throne, he made Josiah's son Eliakim the new king. Eliakim was twenty-five years old when he came to the throne, and he reigned for eleven years. Pharaoh Neco changed Eliakim's name to Jehoiakim. As king, Jehoiakim began taxing the people to pay for what Pharaoh demanded. Everyone was forced to pay. Sadly, Judah was once again being ruled by an evil king. Jehoiakim was worse than his brother. He hated the law of the Lord and was evil like many of the kings who had ruled before him. God sent many neighboring nations to fight against Judah because of their great sins. Soon, King Nebuchadnezzar of Babylon became stronger than Pharaoh. He took over as the real ruler of Judah. He came to Jerusalem, put Jehoiakim in chains, and took him to Babylon. Nebuchadnezzar also took some of the golden vessels from the house of the Lord and brought them to Babylon.

Jehoiachin

God had made a covenant with David to establish his kingdom forever. This covenant stated that kings would descend from David. It also said God would bless those kings richly if they obeyed His Word, but disobedience would be punished. This is exactly what had happened to Jehoiakim. The same thing would happen to Jehoiachin because of his wicked choices.

Jehoiachin was eighteen years old when he became king after his father. He also did evil in God's sight. He reigned for just three months before God removed him from his throne. When Nebuchadnezzar captured Jerusalem, he took Jehoiachin and more of the precious things from God's temple to Babylon. Nebuchadnezzar also carried away ten thousand men fit to be soldiers, craftsmen, and metalworkers. Only the poor and weak remained in Jerusalem.

The Davidic Covenant was clear that God would punish David's sons if they were wicked kings. God was also dealing with Israel for their sins. Judah and its capital of Jerusalem would not escape these judgments.

Israel and Judah became part of the Babylonian Empire

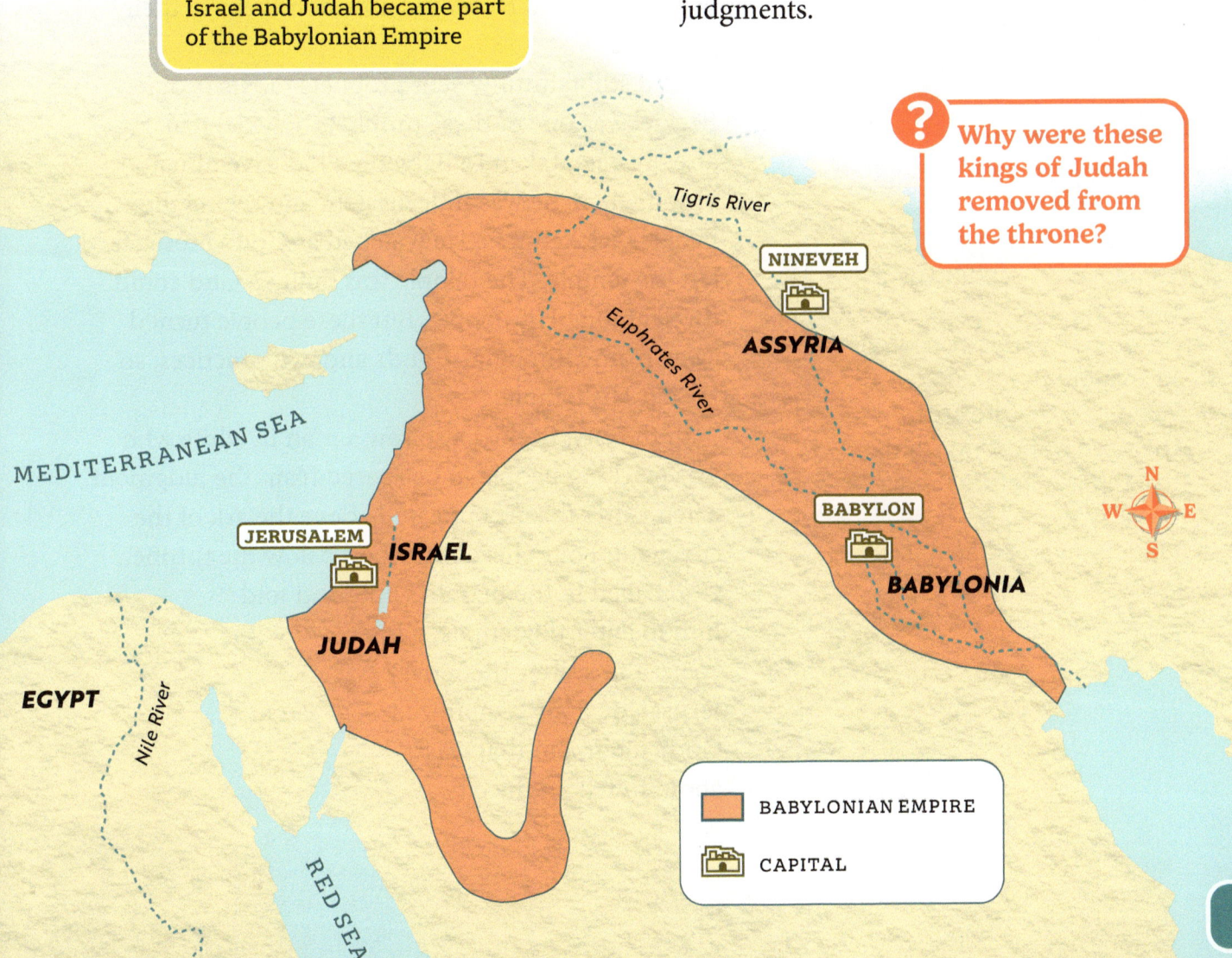

Why were these kings of Judah removed from the throne?

Jerusalem
BURNED AND PLUNDERED

FastFacts about

Ezekiel

Author: Ezekiel

Date: Approximately 570 BC

Theme: The holy God of Israel will judge Israel for breaking the Mosaic Covenant, but He will also restore His people and give them the Holy Spirit so they will be able to keep His law.

Meaning of *Ezekiel*: Strengthened by God

Interesting Facts:
- Ezekiel was both a priest and a prophet.
- God had him eat a scroll as part of his calling as a prophet.
- Foretold the destruction of Jerusalem
- Revealed the glory of the Lord departing from the temple before it was destroyed
- Had many spectacular visions

God Will Judge Sin

Why would God leave His people?

After taking Jehoiachin to Babylon, Nebuchadnezzar placed Zedekiah on the throne of Judah. He would be the last king of Judah and would reign for only eleven years. His heart also turned from God. He continued to lead Judah into wickedness. Judah had wholeheartedly turned from God's laws. It was now time for God to pour out His wrath on Judah. He would abandon them to their evil ways.

God still faithfully sent prophets to His people. Ezekiel was one of these prophets. Ezekiel had already been taken to Babylon. God gave him a vision where he was in Jerusalem and seeing the people's wickedness. He watched as God's presence left the temple. The temple was built so God could dwell among His people. But these people turned away from Him to false gods and evil practices, so He left His temple.

In the city, Ezekiel also saw a man in white who was marking people to be spared from the judgment. Then God's throne appeared above the ark of the covenant. Four cherubim stood below the throne. God called to the man in white and told him to enter the temple, gather coals, and scatter them over Jerusalem. This symbolized God's judgment that was about to fall on the city.

God's Presence Leaves the Temple

Ezekiel saw the glory of the Lord depart like a thick cloud out of the door of the temple. The cherubim rose up into the sky, and the glory of God rose high above them. God's glory left to the east of the city. Ezekiel became sad as he understood that God had abandoned Judah to its enemies.

In the ninth year of his reign, King Zedekiah of Judah rebelled against Nebuchadnezzar. In response to this rebellion, Nebuchadnezzar built a wall around Jerusalem and began a siege of the city. No one could go in or out. After a year and a half, there was a terrible famine, and the city was not able to resist any longer. Zedekiah knew that it was just a matter of time before Judah was overtaken. He took his sons and some soldiers and tried to escape. But the soldiers of Nebuchadnezzar found them, and Zedekiah's soldiers scattered. Zedekiah was captured, taken to Nebuchadnezzar, and forced to watch as his sons were killed. Then he was blinded, put in chains, and taken to Babylon.

The Temple is Destroyed

Nebuchadnezzar ordered Jerusalem and the temple to be destroyed. The city walls were torn down, and all the houses were burned. Even the king's house was burned. The temple was destroyed. All the temple's furniture and items of gold and bronze were taken to Babylon. This included the temple's massive bronze pillars and the large bronze basin, which were broken up and taken away. The bronze dishes, cups, and other things of value were taken from the temple. Then they set fire to the house of the Lord. Many people young and old were killed. Any remaining craftsmen or skilled workers were taken to Babylon as servants. God's warnings finally turned into His judgments that He had promised in the Mosaic Covenant.

> **?** What did God send when Judah disobeyed His Word?

Sent into Exile

How much does God hate sin?

Blessings and Curses

God's judgment on Israel and Judah should have not been a surprise. In the book of Deuteronomy, Moses said that God would bless Israel if they obeyed God's commands and followed Him with their whole heart. But Moses also told Israel that God would curse, or judge, them if they disobeyed His commands. Worshiping idols and following false gods were things that deserved punishment. The destruction of Jerusalem and removal to a foreign land were the worst things that could happen to God's chosen people, but that is exactly what happened.

? What would God do for Israel if they obeyed Him?

God's Just Judgment

The last three kings of Judah had to deal with King Nebuchadnezzar. He ultimately captured Jerusalem and took the people of Judah to Babylon.

The kings and people of Judah had been warned by Moses that their enemies would take them as slaves to another land if they kept up their wicked ways. They would have no strength to resist the invading armies. Enemies would swoop in like an eagle to conquer them. They wouldn't even be able to protect their children.

Their enemies would eat and drink all their wine, grain, oil, and cattle. The people trapped in Jerusalem would be so hungry from the lack of food in the city that they would do extreme things to avoid starvation.

God warned His people of even more curses. If they turned from Him by disobeying the laws of the covenant, they would experience the same diseases and plagues that He struck the Egyptians with. God would allow His people to be scattered into faraway lands. There, they would suffer greatly and live in constant fear.

Sadly, the people of Judah only mocked the prophets God sent to warn them. They also ignored the curses that Moses had said would come upon them for their great wickedness. There was nothing left for God to do but bring His just judgment. All of Israel was now defeated and living in fear, scattered among other nations.

? What did the Mosaic Covenant say would happen if Israel broke God's covenant with them?

The Promised New Covenant

How is the New Covenant different from the Mosaic Covenant?

Sadness Turned to Joy

Israel's judgment for breaking the Mosaic Covenant showed that a new covenant was needed. The Mosaic Covenant was God's law written on tablets of stone, but it did not change people's hearts. The people needed God to change their hearts so they would want to keep God's law. God sent Jeremiah to tell Israel of this New Covenant.

Fast Facts about **Jeremiah**

Author: Jeremiah
Date: Approximately 587 BC
Theme: God's justice and grace
Meaning of *Jeremiah*: The Lord will exalt

Interesting Facts:
- Written during the time Daniel was taken to Babylon
- Foretold the destruction of Jerusalem
- Written from Egypt to the people of Judah

New Covenant

The prophet Jeremiah wrote that a day was coming when God would make a new covenant with Israel and Judah. Other parts of the Bible reveal that this covenant would not be limited just to Israel. Believers from all nations would enter this covenant. God explained that the New Covenant would not be like the covenant that He made with Israel when He brought them out of Egypt. The blessings of the New Covenant would not depend on obedience to the law. The New Covenant would be different. Obedience to the law would come from being part of this covenant. God would write His law on the hearts of His people. He would be God to those in this covenant, and they would be His people.

In the New Covenant, God would guarantee the obedience of His people to His laws by giving them new hearts that want to obey. None of the people under the New Covenant would have to be taught about God because they would know Him as their Savior. This is because everyone under the New Covenant, from the youngest to the oldest, would know the Lord. They would not just know about the Lord; they would know Him personally. That is because each person under the New Covenant would have the law of God written on his or her heart. God would also forgive and forget their sins.

? In the New Covenant, where will God's law be written?

The Work of the Holy Spirit

God also gave His message about the New Covenant to the prophet Ezekiel. The Lord said that the unbelieving nations would see the holiness of His name. Israel broke all the previous covenants that God had made with them. God's people hadn't done a good job representing His holy name. But in the New Covenant, things would be different. God would cleanse and purify His people from all their sin. He promised to give each of His people a new heart and put a new spirit within them. Their hearts would be free from idolatry. God would remove their hard-as-stone hearts and give them soft hearts of flesh. Finally, He would put His Spirit in each person who would be part of the New Covenant. His Spirit would cause each one to know and want to obey God's law.

? What does the Holy Spirit have to do with the New Covenant?

Bible Truths

48 **Why did God promise the New Covenant?**
Israel could not keep God's law and came under His judgment.

Jeremiah 31:31–32
Hebrews 8:8–9

49 **What did God promise in the New Covenant?**
God promised to cleanse His people from sin and to give them the Holy Spirit so that they would obey God's law.

Jeremiah 31:33–34
Ezekiel 36:22–27
Hebrews 8:10–12

CHAPTER 15

Israel in Exile

Nebuchadnezzar's Humbling

Why would God make a man eat grass?

FastFacts about Daniel

Author: Daniel
Date: Approximately 540 BC
Theme: God's sovereignty over history
Meaning of *Daniel*: God is my judge

Interesting Facts:

- The book of Daniel records how godly people can have a real and positive impact on a country's government.
- The ministry of Daniel covered the whole seventy-year captivity in Babylon.

Who was Daniel?

- A descendant of David
- Righteous and faithful to God
- Interpreted two dreams for Nebuchadnezzar
- Survived the lions' den
- Government official in Babylon under several kings

The Winner Takes the Best

During Jehoiakim's third year of being king of Judah, King Nebuchadnezzar's army surrounded Judah. God allowed Nebuchadnezzar to capture the city. The king wanted the best of everything. He took the healthiest, wisest, smartest, and most respectable young men. He wanted to train them to serve in his kingdom. Daniel was one of these young men. He was taken to Babylon and renamed Belteshazzar. He stayed faithful to God and showed himself to be wise. King Nebuchadnezzar put Daniel's wisdom to the test many times.

God is in Control

One day, King Nebuchadnezzar had a troubling dream. He gathered all the magicians and the people who looked for messages from the stars. He thought they would know what his dream meant. But none of them could interpret it. When Daniel entered the room, the king told him the dream. He knew that Daniel was a wise man and was confident that Daniel could tell him what the dream meant.

"In my dream," said Nebuchadnezzar, "I saw a very tall and strong tree. It could be seen by the whole earth. Its leaves were beautiful, and its fruit was enough to satisfy the whole earth. Animals rested under it, and birds nested in its branches.

"Then I saw an angel come down to earth. He said, 'Cut that tree down. Cut its branches off, shake off its leaves, and scatter its fruit. Let the animals and birds run away from it. But leave the stump with its roots in the earth. Wrap a band of iron around the stump. Let his mind change from a person's mind to an animal's mind for seven years. This will teach everyone that the Most High rules in the kingdom of mankind and gives it to whoever He will. He will set over it the humblest of men.'"

? Who is in control of all things?

A King in the Field

King Nebuchadnezzar waited for Daniel to interpret his dream, but Daniel was troubled by the dream and didn't speak for a while. When Daniel did speak, he had a heavy heart. "Your dream means good news for your enemies. That tree represents you. Your rule reaches the end of the earth. Like the tree, you are strong and great. But you will have your greatness taken from you. You will be chased out of your palace, and you will live with wild beasts in the fields. You will eat grass and act like an animal. You will be like this for seven years. Then, you will know that God is the ruler over the kingdom of mankind. God gives rule to whoever He desires. But the stump remains—that means you will receive your kingdom again, but only after you know that God in heaven rules. Please accept my advice. Stop sinning, start living a righteous life, and show mercy to the poor. Perhaps then your prosperity will continue."

? What does God rule over?

God Most High

Twelve months later, Nebuchadnezzar was walking through his palace and proudly praising himself. "Through my might and my power, Babylon has become great! It shows the world my honor and majesty!" While the words were still coming from his mouth, a voice came from heaven. It said that he had lost his kingdom until he knew that the Most High ruled the kingdom of mankind and gives the rule of it to whomever He desires. Nebuchadnezzar immediately began acting like an animal and was driven out of the palace into the fields. He ate grass like an ox, his hair grew long like an eagle's feathers, and his nails grew long like a bird's talons. This is what Daniel had told Nebuchadnezzar would happen.

After seven years, Nebuchadnezzar learned his lesson and returned to his palace. He said, "I looked up to heaven and my right mind returned to me. I blessed the Most High. I praised and honored Him who lives and rules forever. All on earth are nothing like Him. He carries out His will in heaven and on earth. Nobody can stop Him. Nobody can ask Him, 'What are you doing?'"

Nebuchadnezzar's officers were happy that he could rule his kingdom again. He had greater honor, but now he gave honor to God. He knew that God's works are true, God's ways are right, and God is able to humble the proud.

> **?** What lesson did Nebuchadnezzar learn after living like a beast for seven years?

Daniel's Dream

Several years after Nebuchadnezzar's rule, Belshazzar was the king of Babylon. During the first year of Belshazzar's reign, Daniel had a dream. When he woke up, he wrote it down. In the dream, it was nighttime, and the wind made large waves in the sea in four directions. Then four very large and very different beasts came out of the sea.

Three Beasts

The first beast looked like a lion with eagle's wings. When its wings were plucked off, it stood up on two feet like a person. It also had the mind of a person. The second beast looked like a bear. It was raised up on one side, and it held three ribs tightly in its teeth. It was told to eat a lot of flesh. The third beast looked like a leopard with four wings on its back. It also had four heads and was given power to rule.

What will Jesus rule over?

A Fourth Beast

The fourth beast was terrifying and very strong. It had great iron teeth. It used its teeth to eat and destroy things, then it would stomp on what it tore apart. It was very different from the first three beasts. The fourth beast also had ten horns. Daniel saw another horn appear on its head and tear up three horns. This horn had eyes like a person and a mouth that boasted great things.

? What did the first three beasts look like?

The Ancient of Days and the Son of Man

As Daniel looked at these four beasts coming out of the sea, he saw thrones set up on the earth. Then he saw the Ancient of Days, who is God the Father, sit on one of the thrones. His clothing was as white as snow and His hair was like pure wool. His throne was like a fiery flame. A flame of fire came out from before Him. Many served Him, and many more people stood before Him. The Ancient of Days was ready to judge, and books were open to help Him judge. The fourth beast was there, boasting of things it would do. But as Daniel watched, the beast was killed. Its body was destroyed and then burned. The other beasts lost their right to rule, but they were allowed to continue living for a while longer.

Next in his night visions, Daniel saw the Son of Man come with the clouds of heaven. He was presented before the Ancient of Days. The Son of Man was given dominion, glory, and a kingdom. People of all nations and languages were to serve Him. His rule was made to be forever, and His kingdom will never be destroyed.

? For how long will the Son of Man rule?

The Meaning of Daniel's Dream

Daniel was alarmed by all he saw, so he asked someone nearby what this all meant. The four beasts are four kings or kingdoms that will rise out of the earth. But in the end, the saints, who are the followers of the Most High God, will rule over the kingdom of God forever and ever. The fourth beast will go to war against the saints and will be winning until the Ancient of Days comes.

The fourth beast will be the fourth kingdom. This kingdom will be different from all other kingdoms. It will devour the whole earth, trample it down, and break it into pieces. The ten horns of this kingdom are ten future kings. After them, another very different horn will arise. This new horn will defeat three kings. He will speak against the Most High God and want to change the times and laws. He will be allowed to persecute the saints for three and a half years, but then the Ancient of Days will come and judge the new king. His rule will be taken away and destroyed.

The kingdoms, their rule, and their greatness will be given to the saints of the Most High God. His kingdom will be an eternal kingdom. Every person in every kingdom will serve and obey Him forever.

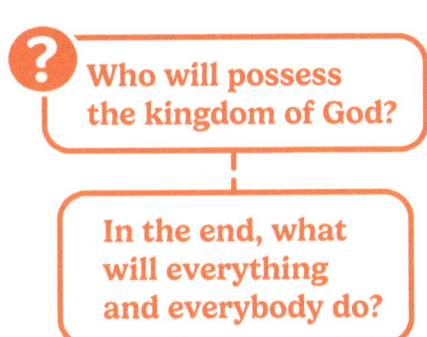

? Who will possess the kingdom of God?

In the end, what will everything and everybody do?

Bible Truth

55 **How is Christ the King?**
Christ rules over us, will come to judge the world, and will establish His kingdom on earth.

Psalm 2:6–8 • Acts 2:34–36
1 Corinthians 15:25

The Perfect Shepherd

How is Jesus the perfect Shepherd for His people?

Wicked Shepherds

While the people of Judah were removed from their land and living in Babylon, God gave the prophet Ezekiel a message for Israel's leaders. He told them, "You are like shepherds who feed yourselves instead of feeding the sheep. You don't comfort the people of Israel. You don't help the sick, the broken, or those who have wandered away. Instead, you rule them with force and cruelty. Because you are poor leaders, the people are scattered like sheep without a shepherd and have become food for wild animals. Because of this, other nations have taken advantage of them."

? Who were the leaders of Israel supposed to shepherd?

God Comforts His People

God said, "Hear my words. As I live, because my sheep are prey and have no shepherd, I will find My scattered sheep and bring them back. I will rescue them, feed them, and heal them. I will be a shepherd to My sheep, but I will judge and punish the wicked shepherds. You are like greedy cows and goats. You sin by eating the good pasture and then destroying the rest of the field. You drink the clear water and then make it muddy for the sheep.

"I will strengthen the weak. The well-fed and strong will be destroyed. You have forcefully pushed and separated the weak from you, but I will protect them. I will appoint my servant, David, as the one shepherd over them. I the Lord will be their God, and David will be a prince among them."

God's Covenant of Peace

God's covenant of peace would be one of safety and blessing. God will give Israel peace and freedom, deliver them from those who enslaved them, and bless them with an abundance of food. Israel will not be afraid of the nations. God said, "They will know that I, the Lord their God, am with them. They are My people. They are My flock of My pasture, and I am their God."

? How will God treat His sheep differently from the sinful shepherds of Israel?

Returning and Rebuilding

Cyrus Provides for the Jews to Return

God's message through Jeremiah came true. He spoke of Israel's repentance and being favored by God. God still had a plan for Israel, and He would accomplish it. God influenced King Cyrus to want to rebuild the temple in Jerusalem. Cyrus told God's people to go back to Jerusalem and begin rebuilding. Over forty-two thousand people and their cattle returned to Jerusalem. The king also returned thousands of items that had been stolen from the temple.

The people of Israel settled into their towns. Months later, the builders were ready to begin rebuilding. The first thing they rebuilt was the altar of God. With this, they could offer their sacrifices in the morning and evening as Moses instructed. They were also able to celebrate their special feast days again.

However, the foundation of the temple had not yet been laid. The people paid the workers and gathered food, drink, and olive oil. These were used to pay for trees from Lebanon, which they needed for rebuilding. Finally, the foundation of the temple was laid. The priests and Levites led a musical celebration of praise to God. Many older people who had seen the first temple wept and shouted for joy. The celebration was so loud that it could be heard from far away.

? What did building the altar of God allow the people to do?

Why does my relationship to God need to be restored?

FastFacts about

Ezra

Author: Ezra
Date: Approximately 450 BC
Theme: faithful worship and obedience
Meaning of *Ezra*: the Lord helps

Interesting Facts:
- The Persian Empire ruled after the Babylonian Empire.
- Ezra was part of the second group to return to Israel from Persia.

Opposition Stops the Progress

When Israel's enemies heard that the Israelites were building a temple, they made a plan to bother and frustrate them. They told the Israelite leaders, "Let us help you build. We have been worshiping your God for a long time." But the Israelites told them no. Since they were God's chosen people, they would build the temple, just as the king of Persia commanded. But the enemies continued to discourage Israel. They made Israel fearful. Even those being paid were afraid to work. When a new king began to rule Persia, Israel's enemies told the king, "The Israelites are rebuilding the rebellious city of Jerusalem. When they are done, they will not pay you their taxes, and your kingdom will suffer. Jerusalem was destroyed for being a rebellious city. If this city is built, you will not be able to rule it."

The king answered, "Yes, history tells us that Jerusalem had been rebellious. Tell them to stop." The men who received the king's letter went straight to Jerusalem and forced the Jews to immediately stop the construction.

Why did the king of Persia stop the rebuilding?

Encouragement and Completion

God sent two prophets, Haggai and Zechariah, to encourage Israel. With enthusiasm, the builders began to build again. An official from Persia heard about this and asked the builders who had given them permission to build. They answered him, "We are the servants of the God of heaven and earth."

The official in Jerusalem wrote a letter to King Darius of Persia. "The house of the great God is being rebuilt using all the quality materials that it had originally. The builders are servants of the God of heaven and earth. Because they disobeyed their God in heaven, Nebuchadnezzar took them away to Babylon. They request a search be made for the decree that King Cyrus gave. They say that the decree gives them permission to rebuild."

King Darius had his people search for that record. They found that King Cyrus did indeed command the rebuilding of God's temple. It was also recorded that he sent Israel back with everything needed to worship God. It even stated that money for rebuilding would come from Babylon's treasury. King Cyrus wrote, "Do not stop or interfere with the rebuilding. Whatever is needed to worship the God of heaven must be given to them. May their sacrifices please the God of heaven, and may they pray for the king and his sons. Anybody who changes this command will be punished, and his house will be torn down." King Darius understood that this decree from Cyrus must be honored, so he also gave money and supplies to help the temple and Jerusalem be rebuilt.

When the rebuilding was finished, all of Israel celebrated the dedication of this house with hundreds of animal sacrifices. They joyfully celebrated the Passover and the Feast of Unleavened Bread. Once again, God had done as He had said.

> **?** How did Darius respond to finding the decree made by Cyrus?

Zechariah
VISION OF THE HIGH PRIEST

Fast Facts about

Zechariah

Author: Zechariah

Date: Approximately 520 BC

Theme: God's future blessings on Israel

Meaning of *Zechariah*: The Lord remembers

Interesting Facts:
- Zechariah was a priest who was called to be a prophet.
- Zechariah prophesied to the Jews who had returned from Babylon.

Why do I need Christ's righteousness?

Satan, the Accuser

Zechariah, the same prophet who encouraged Israel to rebuild the temple, was shown a vision. In the vision, Joshua the high priest was standing before the Messenger of the Lord (Christ). Satan stood on Joshua's right side and was ready to accuse him. But the Lord did not rebuke Joshua. Instead, He said, "The Lord rebukes you, Satan! Isn't this man like a stick that was taken from the fire?" This was because Joshua had returned from exile* in Babylon like a stick pulled out of a fire.

Sins Removed; New Clothing Put On

Joshua's clothes were filthy. This was a symbol of the sins of Israel. The Messenger of the Lord commanded that his filthy clothes be removed. The Lord told Joshua, "I have taken away your sin from you. Now I will dress you in new, clean clothing." They clothed him and put a clean turban on Joshua's head. The Messenger of the Lord waited nearby.

? Who is the only one who can take away sin?

Obedience Brings Blessing

The Lord told Joshua, "Listen to what the Lord says. If you obey My words and do what I say, then you will be in charge of My house and have authority over the temple courts. You will also have the help of those who are standing here."

Peace and Security through the Branch

The Messenger of the Lord continued speaking. "Joshua, you and these men who sit with you are a sign concerning the future. I will bring the one who is called the Branch. In a single day, I will remove sin from this land. In that day, God's forgiveness and blessing will be found throughout all Israel. God's provision will be experienced by all of Israel. They will be able to rest securely and peacefully with their neighbors under their vines and fig trees."

Bible Truths

54 **How is Christ the Priest?**
Christ offered Himself as the sacrifice for our sin and intercedes with the Father for us.

Romans 3:25–26
Hebrews 2:17; 7:25–27

74 **Why can God accept me as righteous if I am a sinner?**
God can accept me as righteous because He has credited me with Christ's righteousness.

Romans 5:18–19
2 Corinthians 5:19, 21

Esther and the Plot to Kill the Jews

FastFacts about

Esther

Author: Unknown
Date: Approximately 475 BC
Theme: God's *providence*
Meaning of *Esther*: star

Interesting Facts:
- God is never mentioned by name, but His work is seen everywhere.
- The Jewish Feast of Purim was established while the Jews lived in Persia, outside of Israel.

key term
providence
God's providence is His guidance of all things to accomplish His purpose and plan

How do I know God is working?

A Jew Saves the King

King Ahasuerus of Persia invited many important people to a huge party that lasted six months. The guests enjoyed the best of everything.

At the end of this time, the king held a special week-long feast. On the last day of this feast, the drunken king gave an order to his wife, Queen Vashti, to come and show everyone how beautiful she was. But she refused to obey him. In his embarrassment and anger, he dismissed the queen. She was not allowed to see him again.

Who was Esther?

- Her Jewish name was Hadassah.
- She was from the tribe of Benjamin.
- She was adopted by her cousin Mordecai.
- The king of Persia chose her as his queen.
- She courageously risked her life to save the lives of every Jew in the kingdom by appearing in the king's presence without being invited.

After some time, the king's attendants recommended a way for the king to find a new queen. They would gather beautiful, young, unmarried women from all over the kingdom to the king's palace. Then he would decide which one pleased him the most, and she would be the new queen.

Mordecai was a Jew living close to the king's palace. He had raised his cousin Hadassah as his own daughter because her parents had died when she was young.

Hadassah's name in the Persian language was Esther. She was very beautiful, so she was called to be one of the young women who would go live in the king's palace. Of all the many beautiful women throughout the whole Persian kingdom, King Ahasuerus chose Esther to be his new queen. A large feast was prepared to celebrate this event. Esther did not tell the king that she was a Jew because Mordecai didn't want him to know.

One day, Mordecai heard two of the king's servants talking about killing the king. Mordecai told Queen Esther. When she told the king, the two men were put to death immediately. The plot to kill the king was written in the history book of the kingdom, and it mentioned that Mordecai was the one who stopped the plan.

? What did Mordecai hear?

A Plan to Kill the Jews

The king chose a man named Haman to be a leader above all other leaders. By the king's order, all people were to bow to Haman. However, Mordecai did not bow to Haman, which made Haman very angry. Because of this, Haman planned to have all Jews in the kingdom killed.

Haman told the king lies about the Jews. He also promised to pay the king a lot of money if he was given permission to kill all the Jews. The king allowed Haman to do this. Letters were written in every language in the kingdom and sent to everyone. The letters told people to kill all Jews of all ages on a certain day and take their belongings.

Throughout the kingdom, the Jews fasted and wept when they heard about their death sentence. Mordecai sent a messenger to Esther, telling her about the king's orders and asking her to keep the king from letting the Jews die. Esther answered, "You know that anyone who comes into the king's court without permission will be put to death, unless the king holds out his scepter to that person. Since I haven't seen the king for thirty days, I will most likely die."

But Mordecai said, "You are a Jew too. Even you aren't safe in the palace. Perhaps you are in this important position in the kingdom for such a time as this."

? Why did Haman want all Jews to die?

Why did God put Esther in the palace at this specific time?

Risking a Life to Save Lives

Esther answered, "Gather all Jews to fast for three days. Then I will enter the king's presence without being invited. If I die, I die."

Esther entered the throne room without the king's invitation. To her surprise, he held out the scepter to her and asked, "What is your request? I will give you up to half the kingdom, if you ask for it."

Esther answered, "I have prepared a feast for you, and I want you and Haman to come."

While at the feast, she invited them to come to another feast the next day. The king and Haman agreed.

On the way to his house, Haman passed Mordecai, and even seeing Mordecai made him angry. In his anger, he decided to hang Mordecai from seventy feet high the next day.

That same night, the king could not sleep. He ordered that the kingdom's history books be read to him. When the king heard about the time that Mordecai had saved his life, he realized that Mordecai had not yet been rewarded.

The next morning, Haman arrived early, eager to ask the king to have Mordecai killed. Before Haman could make his request, the king said he wanted to honor someone special and asked Haman how he could do that. Haman thought the king wanted to honor him, so he said that the man should be dressed as a king and taken on the king's royal horse throughout the city.

? Who did Haman think the king wanted to honor?

The Killer is Killed and the Jews Live

To Haman's horror, the king said, "I want you to immediately do all this for Mordecai the Jew." Haman had to obey, but he hated to do it.

That night, Esther prepared a second feast for Haman and the king. Finally, she explained her distress to the king. "My people and I are to be destroyed."

Enraged, the king asked, "Who dares to kill your people?" Esther answered that Haman made this wicked plan. The king commanded Haman to be hanged from the same place that had been prepared for hanging Mordecai.

The king honored Mordecai with royal clothes and Haman's ring. The king even gave Mordecai Haman's house and Haman's position. The king stopped Haman's plan to destroy the Jews and even gave the Jews permission to fight against anyone who tried to harm them. The Jews were safe, and there was great rejoicing in the kingdom.

> **?** How does the story of Esther end?

Nehemiah and the Rebuilding of the Walls

Prayer and the Return to Jerusalem

Nehemiah served the king of Persia as a cupbearer. Men came to him and told him that the walls and gates of Jerusalem were broken. Nehemiah wept and prayed for God's mercy.

As Nehemiah served, the king noticed his sadness and asked him what was wrong. Nehemiah explained, "My people's city is in ruins. I would like to go repair it." The king listened to Nehemiah's plans and granted him time to rebuild Jerusalem.

Nehemiah traveled to Jerusalem and secretly inspected the walls at night. Then he gathered the Jews together and revealed his plan to rebuild the wall. He said, "Jerusalem is in ruins. Let's get rid of the shame we have from that." The people got right to work. When Israel's enemies saw what they were doing, they mocked the Jews and accused them of rebellion. Despite this, Nehemiah said, "We serve God, and He will bless our work."

Why do we pray?

? What did Nehemiah want to do?

FastFacts about

Nehemiah

Author: Nehemiah
Date: Approximately 425 BC
Theme: the Lord's protection of His people; rebuilding Jerusalem's wall
Meaning of *Nehemiah*: the Lord comforts

Interesting Facts:
- The only Bible book to name Jerusalem's gates.
- Nehemiah led the third and final return to Israel from Babylon and Persia.

Work Continues through Opposition

Despite the enemy's mockery, God's people worked hard. Families were assigned different portions of the wall to rebuild.

Israel's enemies tried to discourage those who were working on the walls and gates. They said, "What are these weak Jews trying to do? They can't possibly use these burned up stones to rebuild a wall. A fox could jump on this wall and knock it down!"

When the wall was halfway built, the Jews' enemies plotted to stop the rebuilding by killing the workers. But God showed Nehemiah the enemies' plan. Nehemiah encouraged the people by saying, "Do not be afraid of them. Remember our great Lord. Be ready to fight for your families and for your homes!"

From that day on, each worker used one hand to work and one hand to hold his weapon. The people watched for the enemy day and night.

The Wall Is Finished

Israel's enemies planned to hurt Nehemiah. They told lies that he was rebuilding the wall only to make himself king. They also asked him to come out of the city so they could kill him. But Nehemiah understood their trick and carefully answered his enemies. He sought God's protection.

After just fifty-two days, the wall was finished and very strong. This caused the enemies of the Jews to be angry, but Israel rejoiced.

? What did Israel's enemies learn after Nehemiah and the Jews rebuilt the wall?

What makes me want to obey?

Confession and Recommitment

Reading, Confession, Idolatry, Covenant

After the wall had been completed, all the people stood and listened as Ezra, a priest and scribe, read the Book of the Law of Moses. At first, they cried with sadness for their sins, but they rejoiced when they were told of God's promises. As they learned how to obey God, they were filled with joy. They celebrated one of Israel's great feasts, and they gathered each day that week to hear the Book of the Law of God read to them.

Every reading was followed by hours of confession and worship. They joyfully remembered God's choice of Abraham. They praised God for His many miracles and victories, such as the pillar of fire, the Ten Commandments, the manna, and the water from the rock. They mourned because Israel disobeyed when they built and worshiped a golden calf. They were amazed that God didn't forsake them when they kept sinning. After all the reading was done, they made a serious written covenant with God.

The people dedicated themselves to honoring and obeying God. They listed all the obedient actions they vowed to do. They also chose and blessed ten leaders. Then they blessed everyone who willingly offered to live in Jerusalem.

The people celebrated and dedicated the wall of Jerusalem. Leaders and singers stood on the top of the wide wall. Their songs and rejoicing were heard from far away.

> **?** What took place after Israel listened to Ezra read the Law of Moses?

A Return to Keeping God's Laws

God had set Israel up to have their own nation once again. Foreigners were made to leave because of their idol worship. The house of God was restored to its purpose. The Sabbath day had been used as a workday, but Nehemiah warned them to keep the Sabbath holy. Nehemiah made sure the city gates were closed on the Sabbath. This way it truly was a day of obedience to God's law because traders and sellers would not even be allowed to camp near Jerusalem. Nehemiah also forbade the Israelites from marrying people from other nations because he didn't want Israel to fall into wickedness. He also made sure only the Levites served as priests and that they did their duties as God commanded.

> **?** How did the priests know what their duties were?

CHAPTER

16

Refuge in God Alone

Malachi's Message

How can I live for God?

Israel had received God's law but had not obeyed it. In Deuteronomy, the Lord promised continual blessings if Israel obeyed His law, but they continually refused to obey. They pretended to be righteous, but God saw their sinful choices and knew their hearts. Their lives and their worship of God were corrupt. He sent Malachi to point out those sins.

Questioning God's Love

God began His message through Malachi by declaring His love for Judah. But God knew their hearts and their ungratefulness. They asked God how He had loved them. God then reminded them that He chose to bless Jacob and not Esau. In His great love, God had blessed Israel and made them a great nation. But God had forever set Himself against Esau and his descendants.

Fast Facts about
Malachi

Author: Malachi
Date: Approximately 430 BC
Theme: Holiness of life and worship
Meaning of *Malachi*: My messenger

Interesting Facts:
- Prophesied to the Southern kingdom after they had returned from Babylon
- Ministered around the same time as Ezra and Nehemiah
- God used six questions to address Judah's sins.

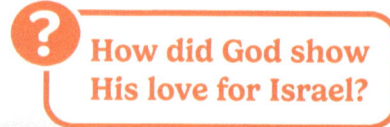

? How did God show His love for Israel?

Defiling God's Altar

God condemned Judah for giving Him unworthy offerings. Instead of offering the best of their flocks to the Lord, Judah had been offering unwanted sick or lame animals. The Lord even said, "If you offered these to your governor, would he be pleased with such a gift?" The Lord called these offerings polluted because they didn't honor Him at all. Judah didn't give God their best because they didn't love Him enough and didn't take their worship seriously. God called for someone to shut the doors of the temple and put a stop to these sacrifices.

> **?** What kind of sacrifices did Judah offer that God called polluted?

Curses upon the Priesthood

Next, God addressed the priests. Because priests made it possible for the people to worship God, their words should have been full of godly knowledge. Instead, the priests corrupted God's law. They turned many people away from the law because they turned away from it themselves. Now they would receive curses instead of blessings.

Divorce

God asked the men of Israel why they were unfaithful to their Israelite wives. They had left their first wives and married wives who worshiped false gods. This was the same sin that led Solomon away from the Lord. The priests pretended to repent for this great wrongdoing on behalf of the men, but they were surprised when God would not accept their offerings. God promised that a day of judgment was coming.

Questioning God's Justice

Judah wearied the Lord by teaching lies that God delights in everyone, even those who do evil. God never delights in evil, and He brings judgment against those who encourage it.

Malachi told the people about a messenger who would prepare the way for the Lord's arrival. The New Testament shows that this messenger was John the Baptist, who prepared the way for the coming ministry of Jesus. Malachi also spoke of Jesus as the Messenger of the Covenant who would come to His temple suddenly. He will judge the priests and purify them so they present righteous offerings to the Lord. None can stand in the day He comes. In that day, God's judgment will be swift. He will accept the believing righteous and judge the unbelieving sinners. God told the Israelites, "You aren't consumed because I, the Lord, do not change."

? Who is the Messenger of the Covenant?

Robbing God

Judah knew that it was foolish to rob God, but they robbed Him by not giving Him their best. The Lord questioned them for not giving Him tithes and offerings. Judah knew what was required of them, but they had refused to give what the Lord required. God challenged them to put His faithfulness to the test. He said, "Bring your tithes to me and test my faithfulness. I will open the windows of heaven and pour out so many blessings that you won't have enough room to receive them."

? How did the people of Judah rob God?

Speaking against God

Malachi next scolded the people of Israel for speaking against God. They claimed that God blessed the wicked instead of those faithful to His Word. They said, "What good is it to serve the Lord if He doesn't see our faithfulness?" They claimed that the proud were blessed and the wicked were exalted.

But God kept a book of remembrance with the names of those who feared Him and respected His name. God chose to remember the people written in this book. He said, "These will be mine, and I will make them my treasured possession. I will spare them as a good father spares his obedient son." God also declared that He will burn all the proud evildoers like how dry straw burns in an oven. Malachi said that the sun of righteousness will rise with healing in its wings over all those who fear God. This is a reference to Jesus the Messiah. He will rise like the sun, heal all who have trusted in Him, and destroy the wicked.

> **?** How does the Bible say God will deal with the wicked?

A Coming Day of Judgment

To finish his message, Malachi spoke about the coming judgment. He called the people to remember the law that God gave Moses. Israel was still supposed to follow the law. God told the people that at the judgment on the Day of the Lord, He would send Elijah to come and preach to the people. Even in the terrible destruction of the last days, there will be a great turning to God.

> **?** What is sure to happen during the destruction of the last days?

Christ as Prophet

What does the perfect Prophet look like?

Prophets were important people in the history of Israel. True prophets loved God and faithfully gave His messages to His people. However, there were also many false prophets who spoke lies and didn't love God. True prophets had a hard job for many reasons. They were disliked and rejected by many, including powerful kings and generals, because many people didn't like God's message. True prophets called out the people's sin and called them to repentance. Even though true prophets weren't perfect and still sinned, God used them to call His people to covenant faithfulness.

In the days of the Old Testament, many prophets were sent to Israel with messages from God. Two men stand out among these prophets for their faithfulness to God. The first was Moses. He was the first prophet in Israel, and he declared God's covenant to His people. Deuteronomy says that Moses was a great prophet because he knew God and spoke to Him face-to-face. He was so unique in his ministry that Scripture said the Messiah would prophesy like Moses. However, Moses struggled with his anger. His imperfect way of loving God and others kept him from entering the Promised Land.

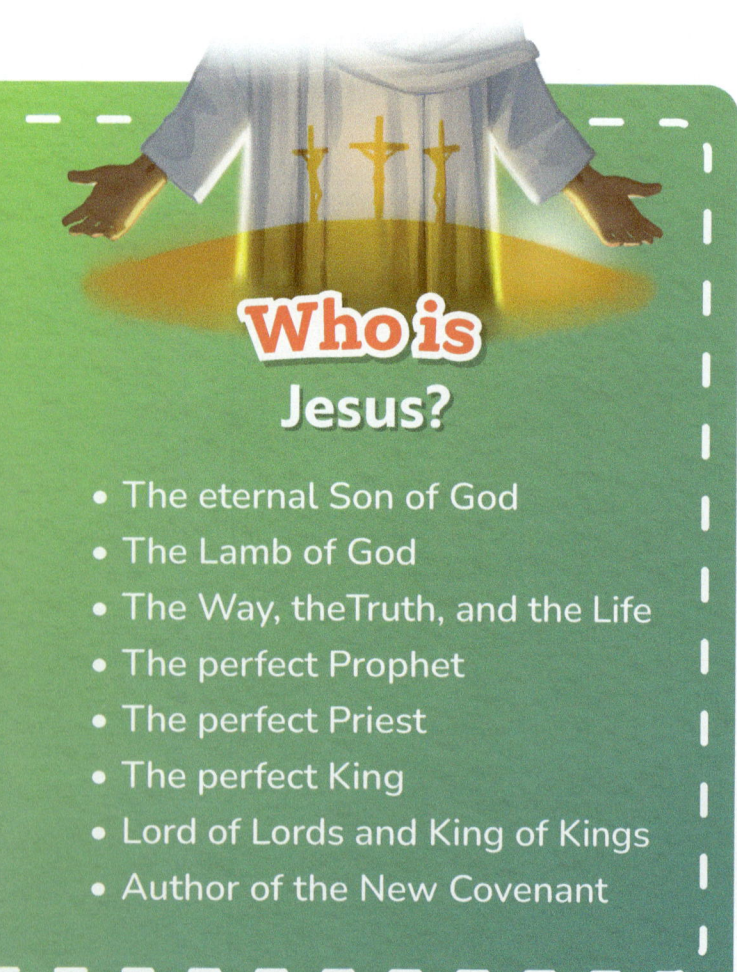

Who is Jesus?

- The eternal Son of God
- The Lamb of God
- The Way, the Truth, and the Life
- The perfect Prophet
- The perfect Priest
- The perfect King
- Lord of Lords and King of Kings
- Author of the New Covenant

? Who was the first prophet in Israel?

What did Moses give to Israel on behalf of God?

The second mighty prophet was Elijah. He called God's people to be faithful to God's covenant. God also used him to challenge wicked King Ahab and Queen Jezebel of Samaria. Elijah also faced hundreds of prophets of Baal and did many miracles. When he prayed that it wouldn't rain, God heard his prayer and held back the rain for three and a half years. But Elijah was not the promised Messiah. Elijah struggled with fear and doubt. After his great victory over the prophets of Baal, Jezebel threatened to kill Elijah, and he ran away in fear.

Jesus was a prophet like Moses because He spoke God's words to the people, but Jesus did this as God. He is the Word of God. Jesus didn't just speak the truth like Moses and Elijah did; He is the Truth. Jesus is the Author of the New Covenant, which God's people obey from the heart. Jesus is God, He spoke God's Word, and He perfectly fulfilled God's laws. Not one word of Jesus' messages was wrong or false. In times of temptation, Moses and Elijah both failed the Lord. Jesus also faced times of temptation, even from Satan himself, but Jesus didn't give in and He never sinned. He is the perfect Prophet.

? Who is the Author of the New Covenant?

"*I Am the Way, and the Truth, the Life.*"

Bible Truths

52 Why is Jesus called Christ?
He is called Christ because the Holy Spirit has anointed Him to fulfill the offices of Prophet, Priest, and King.

Acts 3:22 • Hebrews 5:5–6
Revelation 19:16

53 How is Christ the Prophet?
Christ reveals God to us and teaches us the will of God.

Luke 4:18–19 • John 1:18; 15:15
Hebrews 1:2

Christ as Priest

What does the perfect priest look like?

The priest's main job was to offer sacrifices and enter the presence of God to make it possible for men and women to have their sins forgiven. Though the Levitical priests offered sacrifices for sin, they were sinners themselves. Because of this, before a priest offered sacrifices, he first had to offer a sacrifice for his own sin. Even though the priest was faithful in offering sacrifices, he had no power to take away sins because he was a sinner too. The offering showed faithful obedience to the commands of God, but the offering itself could do nothing to take sin away.

A priest from the tribe of Levi would offer sacrifices for the sins of the people but could only do it for a while. In time, he would die, and another priest would have to take his place. Jesus is the great High Priest that lives forever, so His priesthood is forever. The Book of Hebrews says that Jesus lives forever to bring us to God and to intercede for those who believe. No other priest has the power to forever intercede for believers before God. Christ didn't have to offer a sacrifice for Himself, and His sacrifice happened only once and was enough to cover sins forever. Since His people are sinners who continue to sin, Jesus will intercede as a priest for them continually and perfectly.

? What was the priest's main job?

Jesus is the perfect Priest who provided Himself as the perfect sacrifice. Hebrews tells us that the priests had to offer animal sacrifices every year, but they couldn't actually take away sin. Because of this, those sacrifices never made it possible for people to come to God and stay in close fellowship with Him. Sacrifices were offered to remind the people that their sins had not been paid for. Those sacrifices were a clear sign that death and bloodshed were necessary for the forgiveness of sins.

The sacrifices of the Mosaic Covenant were temporary signs pointing to Christ's perfect sacrifice and eternal priesthood. Jesus, as the perfect Priest, also brings a better covenant. Christ is the perfect Priest of the New Covenant. Jesus offered Himself one time as a sacrifice for sin. There is now no longer any need for sacrifices because His perfect sacrifice paid the penalty of sin once for all.

Bible Truth

54 How is Christ the Priest?
Christ offered Himself as the sacrifice for our sin and intercedes with the Father for us.

Romans 3:25–26
Hebrews 2:17; 7:25–27

? What truth did the yearly sacrifices announce to the people?

What book of the Bible discusses Christ as the perfect Priest of the New Covenant?

Christ as King

What does the perfect King look like?

When God created Adam and Eve, He gave them rule over the entire creation. Adam and Eve were creation's king and queen, created in God's image and ruling under God's greater rule. But when Adam and Eve rebelled against God's rule, their fulfillment of the Creation Mandate was challenged. The first man and woman failed to perfectly fulfill the Creation Mandate and rule exactly as God had commanded them.

David was a man after God's own heart and a mighty king in Israel. God made a covenant with David. God promised David that He would one day send a perfect Son through David's family line. This Son would rule all the nations. Sadly, David sinned many times. Once, he had a man murdered to try to cover up other sins. But God's promise was not based on David's righteousness. His promise was based on His own faithfulness. He planned to send a Savior-King to redeem people and rule the earth with them.

David's son Solomon seemed to point to the fulfillment of that promise. Solomon was a great king, but like David and Adam before him, Solomon sinned terribly and was not the promised King sent to rule the nations.

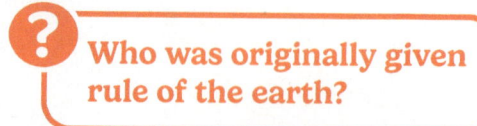
? Who was originally given rule of the earth?

Many sons of David ruled after Solomon. However, none of these kings were the Promised One who would rule the world. Isaiah wrote of the coming perfect King and referred to Him as "Mighty God." Isaiah wrote that the coming, perfect King will sit on the throne of David. His kingdom will never end, and He will rule all nations.

Only one person in all of history could perfectly fulfill the Creation Mandate and meet the requirements to perfectly fulfill the Abrahamic and Davidic Covenants—Jesus Christ. Jesus is not only the son of Adam and Eve, Abraham, and David; He is also the Son of God. The book of Revelation describes Christ as King and Lord of all. God allowed John to see what will happen before Christ claims His earthly throne. John saw a scroll in God the Father's hand. The scroll stood for ownership of the earth. No one was found worthy to open the scroll and break its seals. But Jesus, the Lion of the tribe of Judah and the Root of David, appeared and took the scroll. The perfect King Jesus will succeed where Adam, David, and Solomon failed.

Bible Truth

55 **How is Christ the King?**
Christ rules over us, will come to judge the world, and will establish His kingdom on earth.

Psalm 2:6–8 • Acts 2:34–36
1 Corinthians 15:25

What name proves that the great King is God?

Who will receive the rule of the world that Adam lost?

Glossary

A

atonement
reconciliation with God through a sacrifice for the sin that separates the sinner from God

C

captivity
being taken away and held prisoner, often becoming the conquering nation's slave

climax
the highest point in the plot of a story

covenant
an agreement between two or more people with certain requirements and promises

D

death
the separation of the body from the soul; also separation of the person from God

descendant
every person related to someone by birth; same as offspring and seed

E

exile
to be banished from or forcibly taken out of one's home country

F

foreshadow
to give a hint of something that is coming but has not yet been fully explained or revealed

G

grace

God's kindness to us that we don't deserve and can't earn

grieve

to make someone feel sad or upset

H

humility

thinking less about oneself and more about others; to recognize one's need for God

I

incense

something burned to make a strong smell

intercession

to plead on behalf of another person

L

loyal love

faithful, unfailing love; the love God has for His children

M

marriage

a lifelong covenant between one man and one woman

mercy

a holding back of deserved judgment

Messiah

Hebrew word that refers to Jesus Christ as the anointed Prophet, Priest, and King spoken of in the Old Testament

P

plunder

the spoils or loot of war which are the valuable things taken from a defeated enemy

pride
to think too highly of oneself and too little of others; to depend on oneself and to give no credit to God

prohibition
something that is forbidden; something that shouldn't be done

providence
God's guidance of all things to accomplish His purpose and plan

R

redemption
deliverance from captivity through payment of a price

repentance
the act of being sorry for, asking forgiveness for, and turning away from sin

rest
enjoying the presence of God without the disturbance of enemies

S

sacrifice
the offering of an animal burned on an altar as worship to God

seed
a person born in one's family line; can also refer to one specific person (as in Genesis 3:15) or to all of one's offspring

W

wisdom
the skillful use of knowledge to live successfully and rightly

worldly
the beliefs, values, thoughts, words, and actions controlled by Satan that characterize the life of the unsaved

Photo Credits

Key: (t) top; (c) center; (b) bottom; (l) left; (r) right; (i) inset; (bg) background; (fg) foreground

Front Matter
viiit maradon 333/Shutterstock.com; **viii**b Weil Mathias/Shutterstock.com

Chapter 1
8t maradon 333/Shutterstock.com; **8**b Weil Mathias/Shutterstock.com; **9**tl Stock High angle view/Shutterstock.com; **9**tc yaalan/Shutterstock.com; **9**tr Stephan Debelle/500px via Getty Images; **9** (dog) E LLL/Shutterstock.com; **9** (sheep) photomaster/Shutterstock.com; **9** (Butterflies) Vladfotograf/Shutterstock.com; **9** (horse) Viktoriia Bondarenko/Shutterstock.com; **9** (lion) aftabchoudhary217/Shutterstock.com; **9** (tortoise) Studio Empreinte/Shutterstock.com; **9**ibg Jacob_09/Shutterstock.com; **9** br WeerajitJames/Shutterstock.com; **10–11**bg MARK GARLICK/SCIENCE PHOTO LIBRARY via Getty Images; **10–11** Yiming Chen/Moment Open via Getty Images; **11** SpicyTruffel/Shutterstock.com

Chapter 2
25–26 Noah Ark by Ehab Yousif/Turbosquid/Shutterstock.com; **25**bl dkvektor/Shutterstock.com; **25**bc Michal Sanca/Shutterstock.com; **25**br Tunsale Ismaylova/Shutterstock.com; **28**l Joe Gough/Shutterstock.com; **28**r Oleg Begunenco/500px/500px plus via Getty Images; **29** Jason Edwards/The Image Bank via Getty Images

Chapter 3
37bg Sickchild1988/Shutterstock.com

Chapter 4
56t jeff1961/Imazins/ImaZinS via Getty Images; **56**br Prapat Aowsakorn/Shutterstock.com; **56**bl MiOli/Shutterstock.com

Chapter 5
72t Mark Newman/The Image Bank via Getty Images; **72**c lostbear/Shutterstock.com; **72**b Antagain/E+ via Getty Images; **72**blbg jopstock/Moment via Getty Images; **73**i Holger Kirk/Shutterstock.com; **73**b Pav-Pro Photography Ltd/Shutterstock.com; **77** isparklinglife/Shutterstock.com

Chapter 6
88 Zyabich family/Shutterstock.com

Chapter 7
107 Layue/Shutterstock.com; **110** Ratthaphong Ekariyasap/Shutterstock.com; **115** Roman Yanushevsky/Shutterstock.com

Chapter 8
126 Milton Rodriguez/Moment via Getty Images; **129** koya979/Shutterstock.com; **135** Hintau Aliaksei/Shutterstock.com

Chapter 9
154 P Maxwell Photography/Shutterstock.com

Chapter 11
179 Kirill Smimov/Shutterstock.com; **182** joshimerbin/Shutterstock.com

Chapter 12
186 Deep Desert Photography/Shutterstock.com; **188** Reload Design/Shutterstock.com; **188**i naskami/Shutterstock.com; **192**t Evgeny Subbotsky/Shutterstock.com; **192**i grafnata/Shutterstock.com

Chapter 13
212 Pixel-Shot/Shutterstock.com; **220** HAKINMHAN/Shutterstock.com

Chapter 14
224 sbayram/E+ via Getty Images; **228** jd8/Shutterstock.com; **230** Zev Radovan/Alamy Stock Photo

Chapter 16
264–65 Jordan Siemens/DigitalVision via Getty Images